ART MATTERS

ART MATTERS

HEMINGWAY, CRAFT, and the CREATION of the MODERN SHORT STORY

ROBERT PAUL LAMB

Louisiana State University Press

Baton Rouge

Published by Louisiana State University Press
Manufactured in the United States of America
Second printing, 2011

Designer: Laura Roubique Gleason
Typefaces: Minion Pro, Fournier MT
Printer: McNaughton & Gunn
Binder: Dekker Bookbinding

Library of Congress Cataloging-in-Publication Data

Lamb, Robert Paul, 1951–
  Art matters : Hemingway, craft, and the creation of the modern short story / Robert Paul
Lamb.
     p. cm.
  Includes bibliographical references and index.
  ISBN 978-0-8071-3550-1 (cloth : alk. paper) 1. Hemingway, Ernest, 1899–1961—Technique.
2. Short story. I. Title.
  PS3515.E37Z6885 2010
  813'.52—dc22
                                                                            2009020219

The paper in this book meets the guidelines for permanence and durability of the Committee
on Production Guidelines for Book Longevity of the Council on Library Resources. ∞

For the Sundance Kid

the better craftsman,
there at my side
from the start
of so many journeys.

Next time, seriously dude, Australia.

In your own art, bow your head over technique. Think of technique when you rise and when you go to bed. Forget purposes in the meanwhile; get to love technical processes; to glory in technical successes; get to see the world entirely through technical spectacles, to see it entirely in terms of what you can do. Then when you have anything to say, the language will be apt and copious.

—Robert Louis Stevenson, *Learning to Write*

Try to become a craftsman . . . A certain degree of craftsmanship is really indispensable. You can not always sit and wait for inspiration.

—Anton Chekhov, quoted in Bunin, *Memories and Portraits*

La peinture, comme tout art, comporte une technique, une manipulation d'ouvrier, mais la justesse d'un ton et l'heureuse combinaison des effets dépendent uniquement du choix de l'artiste.
[Painting, like every art, comprises a technique, a workmanlike handling, but the accuracy of tone and the fortunate combination of effects depend solely on the artist's decisions.]

—Paul Cézanne, quoted in Léo Larguier, *Le Dimanche avec
Paul Cézanne (Souvenirs),* translation mine

Look how it is at the start—all juice and kick to the writer and cant convey anything to the reader—you use up the juice and the kick goes but you learn how to do it and the stuff when you are no longer young is better than the young stuff—

—Ernest Hemingway to F. Scott Fitzgerald (1929),
Ernest Hemingway: Selected Letters

It is necessary from time to time to emphasize the fact that writing in general and imaginative writing in particular are the products of craftsmanship. In the middle ages a craft was called a mystery. It is a good word, for it is a mystery why we write and a mystery how great writers do it.

They do it by observing certain rules—or after having observed certain rules for a long time, by jumping off from them.

—Ford Madox Ford, "Techniques"

Art is nothing if it is not control. But we control only those of our acts whose outcome we foresee; and we foresee no result unless we have been over the ground before. It is *technique,* therefore, that gives direction to impulse and marks the difference between art and caprice.

—Arnold Isenberg, "The Technical Factor in Art"

It is the integrity of [Hemingway's] craft, a richness beyond legend, that will forever endure.

—Henry Louis Gates Jr., quoted in Thomas Putnam,
"Hemingway on War and Its Aftermath"

Contents

Preface

This book is the first comprehensive study of the short story art of the twentieth century's most influential fiction writer. It is aimed at several audiences: Hemingway scholars and enthusiasts, critics of twentieth-century literature, fiction writers, and people interested in the short story as a genre. Over the past four decades, a wealth of excellent cultural, thematic, and biographical scholarship has been written on Hemingway's stories. But explorations of his craft have been few and far between, and the most recent book-length study of his overall aesthetics, one not limited to the stories, came out in 1973. In attempting to redress this imbalance through a close analysis of his story art, I hope to illuminate an area, in both Hemingway studies and literary criticism, that has been neglected, incompletely analyzed, and, in some instances, badly misunderstood.

A second goal is to provide a set of analytic tools for exploring short stories. Academic studies of the genre have been plentiful but have also tended to focus on thematic and cultural concerns, or else on theories of narrative. Because scholarship on story craft is underdeveloped, I've found it necessary to coin conceptual terms in order to address aspects of Hemingway's short stories that have hitherto eluded literary criticism; this terminology should prove useful to future studies of the genre and other writers working within it. In some cases, the terms are new, and in others I've borrowed from a range of sources—theorists, critics, and practicing story writers. Such terms as *sequence displacement, implication omission, tonal openings, present absence, Conradian split, disjunctive bump, rounded closed endings, seeded closed endings, float-offs, normative center, illustrative stamp,* and *recapitulation with variation* are my own. Others—for instance, *impressionism* and *expressionism*—have been employed so loosely and variously—in literary criticism if not in art history—that I've been compelled to redefine them. Still others—*delayed decoding, the logic of the eye,* and even *focalizer*—derive from sources not widely known outside the circles of academic criticism. These conceptual tools describe and open up for analysis elements of the genre that readers will recognize in the fiction, elements to which they have already responded in their reading. I've tried to explain the terms clearly so that they will be useful rather than arcane and will keep our focus on Hemingway's art and not on my critical apparatus. Too much jargon for its own sake proliferates in English studies, serving as a gatepost to an increasingly limited, elitist, and out-of-touch discourse community. Fiction reading is, and should always be, a democratic affair. Criticism should be, too, extending the boundaries of understanding and appreciation rather than marking off who is damned and who is saved in some weird academic version of the Puritans' morphology of conversion. Therefore, I've attempted, above all, to be accessible, to write in such a way as to appeal to an intelligent general audience while at the same time not insulting the sensibilities of specialists.

A third and related goal is to reconfigure the place of short fiction in literary studies. Although the short story is one of the oldest and most popular of literary genres and, along with poetry, the genre most frequently employed for pedagogical purposes in literary surveys, nevertheless, in academia it has been something of a bastard stepchild. Short stories are used to demonstrate various approaches to literature and are mined for cultural content; rarely are they appreciated within the context of genre. Being short, a story is convenient. But, as with any literary genre, the art of the short story has changed over time, including such periods of accelerated evolution as the modern era, during which Hemingway was the major innovator. Not merely "more fiction," the story plays by its own set of rules, possesses its own conventions, and differs significantly from its younger siblings: the nouvelle, novella, and novel. In many ways, the short story is closer to lyric poetry than to other forms of fiction, a point made by such different writers as Frank O'Connor (Interview 165), Wallace Stevens (*Letters* 411–12), and Hemingway himself (qtd. in Mary Welsh Hemingway 352). As with poetry, story language is extremely compressed and rich, demanding detailed analysis. Thirty years ago, Jackson J. Benson complained that Hemingway's readability had caused critics to glide along the surface: "simplicity remains one of the main misconceptions about the stories, persisting among critics and general readers alike. This misconception has denied many of the stories the kind of close reading they deserve—a reading we automatically give to Joyce and too often just as automatically refuse Hemingway" ("Ernest Hemingway" 302). In this book, I will treat Hemingway's story art as one would poetry—or Joyce—through painstakingly close reading, and I will deny him nothing.

If close reading of Hemingway's story language is the method, and the development of an appropriate terminology for the short story is one result, a fourth aim is to demonstrate that studies of articulated technique—long out of favor in the academy—still matter. Similar to Henry James's figurative house of fiction, criticism, too, is an edifice of many windows in which critics sit at their own apertures surveying the scene. The history of literary criticism is the history of what windows critics have looked through and what vantage points the profession as a whole has preferred at any given point over time. It goes without saying, of course, that criticism is more than merely fad or fashion, that critical preferences, while emanating from the vicissitudes of individuality, are conditioned by and coalesce into the ever-expanding spheres of culture, ideology, and politics. Furthermore, critics, as do all who engage in public discourse, must (to borrow from Oliver Wendell Holmes Jr.) join in the action and passions of their times at peril of being judged not to have lived. Yet, that said, I have always been struck by the value of critical discourses not currently in vogue. All the windows of the house of criticism overlook vistas worth viewing and, to invoke James again, the critic's *donnée* should be as inviolate as that of the artist. Unfortunately, however, academic schools of criticism too often become quasi religions, evincing all of the intolerances to which such institutions chronically fall prey. At different times and places, some windows get boarded up while others are expanded; increasingly, most people are jockeying to look through the same window and remain either contemptuous of, or indifferent, to others. The field of general vision narrows, and literary texts are, as a whole, viewed less richly, less complexly, than they deserve to be. Many disappear from sight altogether.

Over the past quarter of a century in literary studies, one set of windows that has been closed to fiction criticism is that of technique, art, and craft. Paradoxically, these are the very windows through which practicing fiction writers look, have always looked. Equally perplexing, in related scholarly fields—poetry, music, the plastic arts, film—these matters remain crucially important. The poetry critic who cannot tell the difference between a sestina and a villanelle, or delineate the main elements of both, will not go far. But the fiction critic who knows nothing of the technical features of the short story, other than that it is shorter than the novel, will not suffer within the profession from this ignorance. In studies of fiction, critics, ever anxious that writers produce the material that they, the critics, can only analyze, have turned a blind eye toward these windows on craft that open out onto their subjects' scenes of authority and power, preferring to view authors merely as sites of cultural production who are mainly unaware—on the conscious level—of what it is they create.

Yet it is the assumption of this book that Hemingway and other authors actually have some idea what they are doing. After all, what professional doesn't? I am not saying that he was fully aware of every aspect of his creative process or of the entirety of cultural meaning inscribed in his texts, only that he had a good deal of *conscious* say about it. This claim may seem all too obvious, but it is something that many in my profession tend to forget and that many others choose not to remember. Although one of the main audiences for this book is creative writers, it should appeal every bit as much to those literary critics who do not perceive an impermeable boundary between form and content but who instead see the two as interdependent. As I show early on, a focus on the technical modes of impressionism and expressionism might be a better way of understanding fiction than by terming it realist, naturalist, or modernist. Furthermore, it is impossible, in understanding form, not to experience a greater grasp of cultural content. "In the act of writing," Flannery O'Connor observes, "one sees that the way a thing is made controls and is inseparable from the whole meaning of it" (129). As we will see, Hemingway's innovative dialogue techniques make possible his feminist critique in such stories as "Cat in the Rain" and "Hills Like White Elephants," and, as I have elsewhere shown, taking into account the formal properties of a story such as "Soldier's Home" is essential to negotiating the conflicting critical interpretations of the text (see "Love Song").

But I offer this caveat. Although I occasionally discuss Hemingway's life, his beliefs, and the cultural phenomena that helped form him and that inform his works, my aim is neither to interpret him nor to translate his fiction into abstract terms. One of our finest novelists, Robert Olen Butler, recently addressed this notion:

> It seems to me that a lot of literature classes go wrong because the teachers, unintentionally but often intentionally, give the impression that writers are rather like idiots savants: they really want to say abstract, theoretical, philosophical things, but somehow they can't quite make themselves do it. So they create these objects whose ultimate meaning and relevance and value come into being only after they have been subjected to the analysis of thoughtful literary critics, who translate that work into

theoretical, philosophical, ideational terms. And that is somehow the final usefulness, purpose, and meaning of the work. In how many literature classes have you heard it asked, "What does this work mean?" As if it had no meaning in the mere reading of it. Or, worse, "What is the author trying to say?" Trying. You've been in the presence of these attitudes, have you not? Well, this is nonsense, folks. Absolute nonsense. In the presence of such attitudes, your ability to read a work of literary art is actually being destroyed. (109)

I have tried to avoid the errors Butler cautions against, for more than anything I hope to enhance readers' appreciation of Hemingway's stories so that, upon rereading, they will engage them more richly, will see more in them, will possess a greater understanding of the immense art that makes them possible.

The opening of chapter 1 places the Hemingway story in the tradition of Edgar Allan Poe and Guy de Maupassant and looks at the nineteenth-century traditions he inherited: realist forms and a naturalist philosophy. The chapter then addresses two interrelated issues: his method of dispassionate presentation, which had become somewhat established since the days of Maupassant and Chekhov, and his rendering of authorial judgments through form. Chapter 2 treats three related elements of Hemingway's art that are connected to a story's "shortness": concision, suggestiveness, and omission. These techniques, which give the reader a greater role in constructing the story, were in vogue in the 1920s and in Hemingway's case were abetted by his journalism background and the mentoring of Ezra Pound. Chapter 3 redefines expressionism and impressionism as alternative modes for depicting consciousness. We explore these two modes in Crane, examine Cather and Hemingway as exemplary practitioners of expressionism and impressionism, respectively, and conclude with the influence of Hemingway's impressionism on F. Scott Fitzgerald and its links to T. S. Eliot's concept of the "objective correlative." The rigorous employment of impressionism is the sine qua non of Hemingway's short story art. Chapter 4 addresses Hemingway's employment of point-of-view and voice while also presenting an overview of his story-writing career from the early 1920s through the end of his significant work in the genre in 1939. The chapter provides a chronology of his development, linked to focalization, and analyzes his use of effaced third-person narration, fixed and variable internal focalization, first-person main and peripheral focalization, a kind of narration I term the *Conradian split,* and his expansion of the uses of external focalization, which, along with rigorous impressionism, is a defining element of his art. No issue in Hemingway studies is more misunderstood than the question of Gertrude Stein's influence. Chapter 5 analyzes Stein's aesthetics and what Hemingway learned from her, then explores his own theory and practice of repetition and juxtaposition. The chapter examines how he employed repetition and juxtaposition for the purposes of translating Cézanne's methods of landscape portraiture into fictional landscape depictions, creating mood and emphasis, and representing the processes of consciousness and the unconscious.

Moving from methods to formal elements of stories, chapter 6 is devoted to openings and endings, establishing a taxonomy of the genre's, and Hemingway's, strategies for beginning and concluding texts—a spectrum consisting of traditional openings, openings without exposition, openings with displaced exposition, tonal openings, open endings, seeded closed endings, rounded closed endings, and float-offs. To different degrees, Hemingway's endings emphasize or mitigate what I term the *disjunctive bump* inherent in the end of a story. Chapter 7 contrasts two new terms I've coined, the *normative center,* an important part of the novel's aesthetics, and the *illustrative stamp,* which serves a similarly significant function in the short story. The chapter concludes by distinguishing the illustrative stamp from the epiphany, explains what Joyce meant by the latter term, and analyzes why Hemingway eschewed it in his stories. Chapter 8 contrasts Hemingway's theory and practice of dialogue with that of Henry James, showing how Hemingway's innovations created an unprecedented role for fictional dialogue, which hitherto had been used solely for purposes of illustration. The chapter explores his dialogue techniques of indirection, juxtaposition, omission, repetition, the objective correlative, and what I term *referential ambiguity,* through which he enabled dialogue to represent the highly complex unconscious motivations of all kinds of characters, not just the conscious motivations of highly developed characters. Chapter 9 dismisses the significance of plot per se to the short story, focuses on how characterization functions in a genre in which there is little space to develop character, and finishes with an anatomy of the settings and types of characters Hemingway uses in the fifty-three stories under consideration. The book concludes with a brief assessment of Hemingway's importance—to both writers and readers.

Title Abbreviations

BY HEMINGWAY

Art	"The Art of the Short Story"
BL	*By-Line: Ernest Hemingway: Selected Articles and Dispatches of Four Decades* (ed. William White)
CR	*Ernest Hemingway, Cub Reporter:* Kansas City Star *Stories* (ed. Matthew J. Bruccoli)
CSS	*The Complete Short Stories of Ernest Hemingway: The Finca Vigía Edition*
DT	*Ernest Hemingway, Dateline: Toronto: The Complete* Toronto Star *Dispatches, 1920–1924* (ed. William White)
DIA	*Death in the Afternoon*
FTA	*A Farewell to Arms*
FWBT	*For Whom the Bells Tolls*
GHA	*Green Hills of Africa*
Interview	Interview by George Plimpton
iot	*in our time*
IOT	*In Our Time*
MF	*A Moveable Feast*
NAS	*The Nick Adams Stories* (ed. Philip Young)
Poems	*Complete Poems* (ed. Nicholas Gerogiannis)
SAR	*The Sun Also Rises*

SL   *Ernest Hemingway: Selected Letters, 1917–1961* (Carlos Baker)

SS   *The Short Stories of Ernest Hemingway*

OTHER

ACSS   *Anton Chekhov's Short Stories* (ed. Ralph E. Matlaw)

ACAW   "Authors and Critics Appraise the Works," *New York Times,* 3
          July 1961

HLS   *Ernest Hemingway: A Life Story* (Carlos Baker)

HR   *Hemingway's Reading, 1910–1940: An Inventory* (ed. Michael S.
          Reynolds)

LSS   *Letters on the Short Story, the Drama, and Other Literary Top-
          ics by Anton Chekhov* (ed. Louis S. Friedland)

ND   *Narrative Discourse* (Gérard Genette)

NDR   *Narrative Discourse Revisited* (Gérard Genette)

ART MATTERS

INTRODUCTION

The Hemingway "Problem" and the Matter of Art

Hemingway is the one who had the most to do with my craft—not simply for his books, but for his astounding knowledge of the aspect of craftsmanship in the science of writing.
> —Gabriel García Márquez, "Gabriel García Márquez
> Meets Ernest Hemingway"

Lawrence, De Maupassant, Chekhov, and Hemingway were also a great influence on me when I first began to write short stories, very different as they all are. But, then, who is there, what modern writer of short stories has not been influenced by those four? They created the modern short story.
> —Nadine Gordimer, *Conversations with Nadine Gordimer*

[Hemingway's prose is an] achievement superior to anything in poetry—I include Pound, I include Eliot, and I include Auden. You cannot align it with the verse of Frost. You cannot align it with anything experimental, even syllabically with Whitman. This is the work of a poet who has arrived at originality at great cost. And finally, it comes into an ease that is the ease present in *Troilus and Cressida* or any one of the great plays.
> —Derek Walcott, quoted in Eric McHenry, "BU Scholars
> Grace Hemingway Centennial"

The ultimate goal of this book is to justify Hemingway's centrality in the canon by focusing on his aesthetics. This may seem a curious objective, since his place in literary history hardly seems threatened: Hemingway scholarship proliferates, critics of modern fiction continue to hold him in high regard, and no author of the past century has been more esteemed by other writers. Nevertheless, there remains a strong current of antipathy among academic critics toward him and his work, sometimes resulting in downright dismissal, especially among generalists and non-twentieth-century scholars. In academia, the thoughtless put-down of Hemingway is often, if not *de rigueur*, at least an acceptable substitute for reasoned discourse.

By way of example, some years ago Lawrence Buell, a major scholar of nineteenth-century literature, suggested, as a self-evident afterthought in the pages of a prestigious journal, *American Literature,* that the "demotion of Hemingway" would be a fine way to begin improving the canon and ridding it of sexism (114). Offered with the insouciance of the old joke— "What do you call three hundred lawyers at the bottom of the ocean? . . . A good start."—this attitude is not uncommon. Over the years I've run across many English professors who, upon discovering that I write on Hemingway, have casually assumed that I must therefore be a mesomorph. On such occasions, I've recalled William Faulkner's response to Hemingway's detractors, that "the man who wrote some of the pieces of *Men Without Women* and *The Sun Also Rises* and some of the African stuff (and some— most—of all the rest of it too for that matter) does not need defending" ("Faulkner to Waugh" 6). But neither Buell's casual insinuation that a central author in the canon be busted without a court martial nor Faulkner's defiant retort to critics (which followed upon a similarly vigorous defense of Hemingway by novelist Evelyn Waugh) bothers to argue its point. In both cases, the writer simply issues an edict that he assumes will be amply manifest to his own specific audience. In this book, I show why Faulkner felt the way he did about Hemingway, and why Buell's comment is as inappropriate to Hemingway as it would be to, say, such academic darlings as Henry James, Virginia Woolf, or Faulkner himself.

On 3 July 1961, the day after Ernest Hemingway took his life, the *New York Times* devoted a section of its coverage to brief appraisals of his work. For once, the famous Hemingway mystique took a back seat to art as authors working in a variety of literary genres offered their tributes. Robert Frost observed, "His style dominated our story-telling long and short." Faulkner called him "one of the bravest and best, the strictest in principles, the severest of craftsmen, undeviating in his dedication to his craft." To James Thurber, he was "unquestionably one of the greatest writers of the century"; Tennessee Williams flatly stated that "twentieth-century literature began with Proust's 'The Remembrance of Things Past' and with Hemingway's 'The Sun Also Rises'"; and Cyril Connolly termed him "a Titan of the age," placing him with "Joyce, Eliot and Yeats among the real founders of what is called the modern movement in writing." Others focused upon his art's impact. John O'Hara could not "think of any other in history who directly influenced so many writers." C. P. Snow praised him as "a great original artist whose influence has spread all over the world. No novelist in the world has produced such a direct effect on other people's writing." And V. S. Pritchett observed, "His influence on the short story was enormous, wherever you go, whether in India, the Middle East or elsewhere, you find that young writers have read his short stories and are trying to imitate him" (ACAW 6).

Pritchett's comment about Hemingway's influence, even on non-Anglophone authors, was echoed in a 29 July 1961 special memorial issue of the *Saturday Review,* in which writers from around the globe assessed the debt their own national literatures owed him. Novelist Carlo Levi wrote that Hemingway's art "had a fundamental influence in determining the character and mode of thought of our time" and that his nation "counts among her greatest writers two not born in Italy, but Italian through love: Stendhal and Hemingway" (19). Russian author Ilya Ehrenburg placed Hemingway second only to Chekhov as a master of the short story, "loved not only by our writers, but also by our readers." As an example, he related how in the mid-1950s a long line of Russians waited for about thirty hours in the cold of a Moscow winter for the chance to purchase a new two-volume edition of his works (20). From Japan, translator Edward Seidensticker noted that "Hemingway's influence on the matter of recent Japanese writing is beyond question" and that "Japan is among his most loyal realms" (22). The exiled Spanish political philosopher Salvador de Madariaga especially appreciated what today would be called the multiculturalism of Hemingway's work, which "revealed to his country and to the world many Iberian aspects until then badly misunderstood," and also "revealed to the Iberians that lesser-known aspect of American life: a capacity for direct approach to the life of others without distance, prejudice, or reprobation, which may well turn out to be the chief asset of the United States in this period of inevitable American leadership." Then he turned from politics to art: "Hemingway's manner of writing, his direct, simple, yet forceful prose, his straightforward approach to life even at its most awkward, his boldness in tackling even the unpleasant . . . have exerted an undoubted influence on the new generation of Spanish novelists. Spain no longer looks down on powerful America as a nation of meat packers without history. She has learned to respect and admire the nation that gave Ernest Hemingway to the world" (18). Back in America, Archibald MacLeish summed up the consensus in a tribute for *Life* magazine: "The style remains as surely as the fame. It has been praised, imitated and derided for 30 years, but it endures: the one intrinsic style our century has produced" (70).

The critics, for once, agreed with the authors, and this included three of the brightest stars in the academic firmament. To Lionel Trilling of Columbia University, Hemingway's "place in American literature" was "secure and pre-eminent." He added that "no one in the whole range of literature of the modern world . . . has a better claim than he to be acknowledged as a master." Alfred Kazin observed: "Probably no other American writer of our time has set such a stamp on modern literature. Hemingway was one of our true poets. He gave a whole new dimension to English prose by making it almost as exact as poetry, by making every word sound, by reaching for those places of the imagination where the word and the object are one." And Van Wyck Brooks, the chancellor of the American Academy of Arts and Letters, noted, "he was unquestionably a great writer, a great artist in prose, the inventor of a style that has influenced other writers more than any other in our time" (ACAW 6).

Few speak ill of the dead, especially in public, but these opinions merely echoed what major authors had been saying publicly and privately for years, from the day in 1924 when Ezra Pound told Ford Madox Ford that young Hemingway was "the finest prose stylist in the world" (qtd. in *HLS* 123), to James Joyce's claim in 1936 that "giants of his sort are truly modest; there is much more behind Hemingway's form than people know" (qtd. in Ellmann 695), to a private letter John Steinbeck wrote to a close friend upon hearing of Hemingway's demise: "He has had the most profound effect on writing—more than anyone I can think of" (qtd. in Plimpton and Crowther 206). As with the *New York Times* tributes, these opinions were often expressed by authors whose own work little resembled Hemingway's. For instance, in 1942 Wallace Stevens noted, "Most people don't think of Hemingway as a poet, but obviously he is a poet and . . . the most significant of living poets, so far as the subject of EXTRAORDINARY ACTUALITY is concerned" (*Letters* 411–12). And in 1958 Truman Capote observed, "For the past thirty years Hemingway, stylistically speaking, has influenced more writers on a world scale than anyone else" (296).

Nor have the views of subsequent generations diverged from those of Hemingway's contemporaries, except for focusing more on personal rather than general influence. Responding to Irving Howe's crude attempts to categorize him as a "black" author indebted to Richard Wright, Ralph Ellison protested: "One can, as artist, choose one's 'ancestors.' Wright was, in this sense, a 'relative'; Hemingway an 'ancestor'" (140). Hemingway was also the literary forebear of Joan Didion, who claimed him as her single greatest influence, recalling, "When I was fifteen or sixteen I would type out his stories to learn how the sentences worked . . . I mean they're perfect sentences. Very direct sentences, smooth rivers, clear water over granite, no sinkholes" (343). Ellison, too, learned to write by copying Hemingway's stories in longhand, "in an effort to study their rhythms, so as not just to know them but to possess them" (qtd. in O'Meally 755).

To be sure, the enthusiastic responses of authors to Hemingway, then and since, is not limited to his art. In his reply to Howe, Ellison addressed other reasons why Hemingway mattered to him more than Wright:

> Not because he was white, or more "accepted." But because he appreciated the things of this earth which I love . . . weather, guns, dogs, horses, love *and* hate and impossible circumstances which to the courageous and dedicated could be turned into benefits and victories. Because he wrote with such precision about the processes and techniques of daily living that I could keep myself and my brother alive during the 1937 Recession by following his descriptions of wing-shooting; because he knew the difference between politics and art and something of their true relationship for the writer. Because all that he wrote—and this is very important—was imbued with a spirit beyond the tragic with which I could feel at home, for it was very close to the feeling of the blues, which are, perhaps, as close as Americans can come to expressing the spirit of tragedy . . . Because Hemingway loved the American language and the joy of writing, making the flight of birds, the loping of lions across an African plain, the mysteries of drink and moonlight, the unique styles of diverse peoples and individuals come alive on the page. Because he was in many ways the true father-as-artist of so many of us who came to writing during the late thirties. (Ellison 140–41)

Such personal feelings are echoed by authors who came of age both before and after Ellison. In his *New York Times* tribute, Faulkner noted, "To the few who knew him well he was almost as good a man as the books he wrote" (ACAW 6). Nine years later, John Updike summed up these feelings eloquently: "I suspect few readers younger than myself could believe . . . how we *did* love Hemingway and, after pity feels merely impudent, love him still" (489).

The opinions of authors on Hemingway, then, have followed two separate but not incompatible lines: their debt as writers to his craft (or their recognition of that craft and its worldwide influence) and their personal responses as readers. Sometimes, as with Stevens and Frost, there is no indebtedness, only recognition. Other times, as with Ellison, Didion, Gabriel

García Márquez, and Derek Walcott, there is both debt and readerly appreciation. Often, the influence of his craft is acknowledged despite an ambivalent personal response to the fiction. For instance, Nadine Gordimer criticized his African stories for their obliviousness to Africans and his entire opus for the absence of African Americans. At the same time, however, she admitted "there were certain skills I learned from him and am grateful for" and that from his stories "I learned to listen, within myself, for what went unsaid by my characters; what can be, must be conveyed in other ways, and not by body language alone but also in the breathing spaces of syntax: the necessity to create silences which the reader can interpret from these signs" ("Hemingway's Expatriates" 86–87).

The main point is that however authors may feel about Hemingway's fiction, they have always recognized him as a towering figure whose art matters enormously, for the one indisputable fact is that Hemingway's techniques have profoundly influenced generations of writers across all boundaries of nationality, gender, race, ideology, sexual orientation, class, religion, and artistic temperament. In this regard, one need only mention Hemingway's impact on authors as different as—and this is but the tip of the iceberg, although it includes thirteen Nobel Prize laureates (denoted by an asterisk) and others, like Welty and Updike, equally deserving of that honor—Raymond Chandler, Ilya Ehrenburg, Dorothy Parker, James Thurber, Isaac Babel, John Dos Passos, F. Scott Fitzgerald, *William Faulkner, Sean O'Faolain, Nathalie Sarraute, *John Steinbeck, *Halldór Laxness, Evelyn Waugh, Graham Greene, *John-Paul Sartre, Simone de Beauvoir, Elio Vittorini, Eudora Welty, Cesare Pavese, Chester Himes, *Albert Camus, Bernard Malamud, Ralph Ellison, *Saul Bellow, Robert Ruark, Walker Percy, *Camilo José Cela, *Heinrich Böll, Maria Aurèlia Capmany, J. D. Salinger, José Luis Castillo-Puche, Manuel Zapata Olivella, Charles Bukowski, Jack Kerouac, Norman Mailer, *Nadine Gordimer, Flannery O'Connor, Gore Vidal, Elmore Leonard, *Gabriel García Márquez, Guillermo Cabrera Infante, John Munonye, Edna O'Brien, *Derek Walcott, John Updike, Ernest Gaines, Joan Didion, Cormac McCarthy, *Kenzaburo Oe, Ellen Gilchrist, E. Annie Proulx, Robert Stone, Hunter Thompson, Raymond Carver, Bobbie Ann Mason, Russell Banks, *Jean-Marie Gustav Le Clézio, Richard Ford, Robert Olen Butler, Tim O'Brien, Ann Beattie, Patricia Henley, Terry Tempest Williams, Douglas Coupland, Chuck Palahniuk, Bret Easton Ellis, and Junot Díaz.

The critical responses to Hemingway, however, have become increasingly complex since the monolithic approval of Trilling, Kazin, and Brooks in 1961. As Susan F. Beegel pointed out in 1996, the overwhelming majority of academic critics in the 1960s, when Hemingway was canonized, were white male Protestants. Their "criticism was profoundly value-centered, focusing on heroism and existentialism, and on attitudes toward love and religion" ("Conclusion" 275). She posits, "When potential readers reject Hemingway as indifferent to minorities and hostile to women, they are often responding not to Hemingway's fiction, but to the indifference and hostility of some of his early critics, and a negative image of the author those influential first admirers unintentionally projected" (277). In the 1970s, both feminists and the Vietnam generation moved into Hemingway studies, the former finding his work a gold mine for gender studies, the latter seeing their own sense of alienation reflected in his writings. The critical ground had shifted from heroism and philosophy to gender and politics. In this period, too, a large mass of unpublished material became available, leading to a surge in textual studies and what Beegel refers to as the "Hemingway industry"—with books devoted to organizing the now vast amount of criticism on Hemingway, the founding of *Hemingway Notes,* and the posthumous publication of new Hemingway books.

The 1980s saw the removal of Hemingway's manuscripts to the new John F. Kennedy Library, the formation of the Hemingway Society, and the evolution of *Hemingway Notes* into the *Hemingway Review,* which soon emerged as one of the largest and most respected single-author journals in the academy. Beegel observes that although Hemingway's "prose, based on his belief in the ability of concrete language to construct an objective reality," proved "extremely resistant to" poststructuralism, many feminist scholars entered the field, especially after the publication of a problematically edited version of his *The Garden of Eden* in 1986 (282–83, 286–91). Feminist scholarship was initially critical of Hemingway, but this changed relatively quickly, as seen in the shift from the views of Judith Fetterly to those of such major scholars as Linda Wagner-Martin, Nina Baym, and Wendy Martin.[1] By 1996, Beegel estimates, women critics accounted for 29 percent of published Hemingway scholarship (275, 277, 287, 290–91, 293).

In the past two decades, Hemingway scholarship has been further enhanced by ecocritical, multicultural, psychoanalytical, and increasingly sophisticated gender studies and masculinity studies approaches, as evident in such works as Mark Spilka's *Hemingway's Quarrel with Androgyny* (1990), Toni Morrison's *Playing in the Dark: Whiteness and the Literary*

Imagination (1992), J. Gerald Kennedy's *Imagining Paris: Exile, Writing, and American Identity* (1993), Nancy R. Comley and Robert Scholes's *Hemingway's Genders: Rereading the Hemingway Text* (1994), Rose Marie Burwell's *Hemingway: The Postwar Years and the Posthumous Novels* (1996), Robert E. Fleming's collection *Hemingway and the Natural World* (1999), Debra A. Moddelmog's *Reading Desire: In Pursuit of Ernest Hemingway* (1999), Carl P. Eby's *Hemingway's Fetishism: Psychoanalysis and the Mirror of Manhood* (1999), Lawrence R. Broer and Gloria Holland's collection *Hemingway and Women: Female Critics and the Female Voice* (2002), many of the essays in Robert E. Gajdusek's posthumous collection *Hemingway in His Own Country* (2002), Thomas Strychacz's *Hemingway's Theaters of Masculinity* (2003), and the Hemingway chapter in Glen A. Love's landmark *Practical Ecocriticism: Literature, Biology, and the Environment* (2003).[2]

But despite this flowering and diversification of Hemingway criticism, the current of hostility toward him remains. As Carl P. Eby comments, although "it has become increasingly clear that Hemingway's reign as the hairy-chested icon of American masculinity is coming to an end . . . this message hasn't yet filtered down to the general reading public . . . Neither has the message filtered down to many academic English departments, where opinions like those expressed by Judith Fetterly in *The Resisting Reader* (1978) (i.e., that Hemingway was merely a male-chauvinist-pig) are as often as not still in vogue" (3). Thus Hemingway remains, for many, a sexist, and the Hemingway critic, like myself, a mesomorph.

In addition to the "boy's club" nature of early Hemingway criticism, there are other historical reasons for the continued hostility, much of it having to do with Hemingway's public image. Hemingway's literary career coincided with, and fed off of, the rise to dominance of the mass media in the United States. During this period, which began in the late nineteenth century, the United States was transformed from a culture of character into a culture of personality in which how one was seen became a more important indicator of the self than what one actually did. While many other modernist authors either tried but failed to achieve celebrity or else relished their obscurity as a badge of artistic worth, Hemingway, aided by his editor Maxwell Perkins and the Scribner's publishing machine, rushed headfirst into the public limelight. He was well equipped for the part. Handsome, charismatic, and possessed of an imposing physical presence, he was an outdoorsman who fished, hunted, and had been wounded in the Great War. He would come to seem ubiquitous, associated in the public mind with such international events as the World Wars and the Spanish Civil War, and with locations as varied as the upper American Midwest, Spain, France, Italy, Africa, Idaho, the Florida Keys, and Cuba. He perfectly fit the construction of gender in the midcentury, embodying a strong but sensitive, slightly "bad boy" masculinity that charmed women and appealed to men. He was kept constantly before the public eye by photographs in slick magazines that never tired of reporting on his comings and goings or quoting his opinions on everything. Like Babe Ruth and his boyhood hero Theodore Roosevelt, he was a star—the literary world's biggest.

Hemingway's rise to public celebrity was simultaneous with that of two other larger-than-life stars from the cinema: Clark Gable, whom he physically resembled, and Gary Cooper, a friend who played the protagonist in the highly successful romantic film versions of *A Farewell to Arms* (1932) and *For Whom the Bell Tolls* (1943). These were just two of thirty-nine films, television movies, and stage plays (twenty-seven during his lifetime) that were based, often loosely, on Hemingway's works. The films' male leads were played by such icons as Cooper, Humphrey Bogart, Burt Lancaster, Gregory Peck, John Garfield, Tyrone Power, Rock Hudson, and Spencer Tracy. Just as Hemingway was often conflated with his fictional protagonists—even today many people assume he was a soldier rather than an ambulance driver and war correspondent—so too did many conflate their image of Hemingway with those of the movie stars who played these characters upon the screen. He was modest, romantic, and idealistic like Cooper, a tough guy with a heart of gold like Bogart and Garfield, handsome and charismatic like Peck and Hudson, and even, toward the end, philosophical and wise like Tracy. These were, of course, merely images, fashioned by publicists and self-fashioned (Hemingway himself bears some blame for the conflation), but he rode them into a celebrity that no other author, then or since, has come close to matching, one surpassed in the history of American letters only by Mark Twain.

Americans love to build things up, almost as much as they enjoy tearing down what they have built, and Hemingway was no exception. As notions of masculinity changed, Hemingway's brand of manhood became increasingly passé. Worse, it became associated with forms of macho aggressiveness, insensitivity, and violence. The Hemingway who believed in older codes of romantic love became the sexist Hemingway whose women were either goddesses or bitches; the Hemingway who wrote so unflinchingly of the horrors of war became the warmongering Hemingway; and the Hemingway who hunted, fished, and loved the bullfights became the poster boy of the National Rifle Association and the worst nightmare of the eco-conscious. Removed from his historical context, he turned grotesque in the eyes of many academic intellectuals who had come of age during the feminist movement, Vietnam, and the green movement. This new image was amply buttressed by misreadings of his works. Critics rarely conflate Edith Wharton with Undine Sprague, Faulkner with Thomas Sutpen, or Vladimir Nabokov with Humbert Humbert. But Hemingway became the oppressive male figures of "Cat in the Rain" and "Hills Like White Elephants," the callous hunter of "The Short Happy Life of Francis Macomber," and the self-absorbed Harry of "The Snows of Kilimanjaro." Brett Ashley of *The Sun Also Rises* became a hedonistic ur-bitch instead of what she actually was—the most sexually liberated woman character in 1920s fiction. Catherine Barkley, the real hero and moral center of *A Farewell to Arms,* and the victimized Maria of *For Whom the Bell Tolls* were dismissed as merely insipid male fantasy figures. To many non-Hemingway critics, the author of these texts was but a caricature who represented much of what was most pernicious in the unrevised canon: the physically imposing, bullying, bearded, cigar-smoking, misogynist, racist, sexist, homophobic, antisemitic, white man who hunts, fights, fishes, and fornicates—and, what is worse, writes endlessly about it. Is it any wonder, then, that when Lawrence Buell suggested Hemingway be dismissed from the canon, he didn't think it necessary to argue the point?

Hemingway will always have his detractors, but increasingly balanced perspectives are prevailing. As many self-appointed canon busters must surely by now realize, it's hard to extirpate a writer whose work inspires so many readers around the world and who plays such a large role in the development of other authors. It's also hard to reconcile ideological predispositions to dismiss the fiction with the experience of actually reading and responding to that fiction.[3] And it's difficult for a conflation of Hemingway with his characters to stand the test of time when major canonical authors—from Faulkner and Ellison to García Márquez and Morrison—continue to rise so eloquently to his defense. Asserting an important principle for all literary critics to heed, Morrison cautions against judging "the quality of a work based on the attitudes of an author or whatever representations are made of some group" and specifically states that it "would be irresponsible and unjustified to invest Hemingway with the thoughts of his characters." This does not mean, of course, that Morrison advocates giving Hemingway, or any author, a free pass. Hers is merely a call for fair, informed, and intelligent criticism. After all, she makes the above statements while exploring how the Africanist presence influences the form and content of one of Hemingway's novels. But in that critique she is quick to point out that "there is no evidence I know of to persuade me that Hemingway shared [the racist views of one of his characters]. In point of fact there is strong evidence to suggest the opposite" (90, 85, 86).

Although I consider Hemingway to have been an admirable if flawed man and his works to be culturally rich and continually inspiring, this book does not focus on these issues. Instead, I take for granted the importance of Hemingway's art—in the belief that all of those Nobel Prize winners cannot be mistaken—and will explore his short story craft. That is to say, this book focuses on a neglected genre and an author whom many critics dislike by employing a passé form of criticism.

Behind any book on a single author lies a tale, usually untold, of how the critic first became acquainted with that writer, and I would like to close this introduction by narrating such a story. I was not a conscientious student in high school, more interested in playing football and my guitar than I was in the poorly taught classics assigned by—as I came to realize in retrospect—uninspired pedagogues who could reasonably pass for the errata of creation. Although I remember being coerced into reading Shakespeare, Milton, and *The Brothers Karamazov*, I honestly don't recall whether I was ever assigned anything by Hemingway. The summer after graduation—realizing that I would never make it to the National Football League, waiting to find out whether I'd be going off to college or Vietnam, and curious as to whether my dislike for literature was the product of poor teaching or the fault of literature itself—I made my first unforced visit to a bookstore and purchased a copy of *The Sun Also Rises*. I was attracted by the yellow and gray cover of the old Scribner edition and, on the back, the impressive photograph of a buff Hemingway at his typewriter—here was a writer who looked as though he could play some football. The blurb on the back cover called the book "a truly gripping story, told in a lean, hard narrative prose" (which seemed to distinguish it from the last book imposed upon me, Ford Madox Ford's *The Good Soldier*, taught by an instructor who doubled as the school gardener and chaplain, and who ominously referred to his young charges as little flowers just opening their buds). The accompanying brief bio stated that Hemingway had been a wartime ambulance driver, infantryman, and war correspondent. In a word, there seemed a chance he might possibly be cool.

The 400-family apartment project in the south Kingsbridge section of the Bronx where I lived was built on a hill overlooking the Harlem River. Near the base of this monstrous edifice, in the back and facing the river, was a small cavelike depression, and to get to it you had to mount a steep hill covered with broken bottles, then climb a formidable tree and hoist yourself into this modern semi-oubliette, which I did, carrying my book and a lunch bag in a sack depending from my belt. For the first time in my life, I read a book literally from cover to cover in one sitting, and the next day I returned with a copy of *In Our Time,* then *A Farewell to Arms,* then *For Whom the Bell Tolls,* and then a hardcover copy of *The Short Stories* I had discovered in my mother's bookcase, and so on until I had read everything. I soon had another new experience—I reread a book, and then another, and another. Although he has never been credited for it by scholars, among Hemingway's many remarkable achievements was that he converted Dave and Lena Lamb's only child into a bibliophile.

In college, I read other books and somehow forgot about Hemingway, and years later in graduate school at Harvard, he seemed démodé among my fellow students, if not among the professors, many of whom had served in the Second World War. I began to think of Hemingway as a second-rate writer—too simple, too easy to read, certainly not in a class with James, Stein, Joyce, and Proust. Nor did the criticism help—the old stuff about the Hemingway code seemed too repetitively chest-thumping, and the new stuff about androgyny and sexuality seemed to miss the point. Then one day I picked up my copy of *A Farewell to Arms* and started to reread it, and it all came back—the prose as perfect as pebbles distinctly seen in a clear stream, the exquisite portraiture, the gripping scenes that leaped off the pages, the dialogue that seemed more real than in real life, and, most of all, that unique voice—worldly, idealistic, ironic, sensitive, tragic, and, in its own strange way, so wonderfully, painfully, movingly human. The rush was there, but it was different. Before, I had been amazed to discover that someone had written fiction that engaged me; now I was startled to find that Hemingway could hold his own with anyone, even in the mind of a jaded graduate student. For first and foremost, Hemingway was an artist, indispensable to any meaningful understanding of twentieth-century literary history, and I could now hear echoes of his art in the fiction I had read by subsequent writers, just as I could see connections with authors who had gone before.

It has been many years since I first discovered Hemingway and quite a few since I rediscovered him. My scholarly work has for some time taken me away from him and away from questions of technique and craft. But to these—a first love that has endured and a critical area that is neglected but shouldn't be—I now return.

1

Historical Genre, Dispassionate Presentation, and Authorial Judgment

THE LEGACY OF MAUPASSANT AND CHEKHOV

The less you feel a thing, *the more capable you are of expressing it as it is . . .*
Exhalations of the soul, lyricism, descriptions—I want all that to be in the
style. Elsewhere, it is a prostitution of art and of feeling itself.
    —Flaubert to Louise Colet (1852), *The Letters of Gustave Flaubert*

Car l'artiste ne note pas ses émotions comme l'oiseau module ses sons: il
compose.
[For the artist does not jot down his emotions as the bird modulates its
sounds: he composes.]
    —Cézanne, quoted in Léo Larguier, *Le Dimanche avec*
        Paul Cézanne (Souvenirs), translation mine

I was watching, freezing myself deliberately inside, stopping the excitement
as you close a valve, going into that impersonal state you shoot from.
    —Ernest Hemingway, *Green Hills of Africa*

By the time Ernest Hemingway commenced his career as a professional
author, the short story had been developing for nearly a century, emerging from a variety of traditional short narrative forms—fable, myth, par-
able, tale, yarn, sketch, and anecdote. Such major innovators as Aleksandr
Pushkin, Nathaniel Hawthorne, Nikolai Gogol, Edgar Allan Poe, Mikhail
Lermontov, Ivan Turgenev, Leo Tolstoy, Nikolai Leskov, Alphonse Daudet,
Guy de Maupassant, Anton Chekhov, Stephen Crane, and James Joyce had
already made their influence felt. Other important writers had dissemi-
nated that influence, as well as their own, in their original short fiction, including Henry James, Sarah Orne Jewett, Kate Chopin, Mary Wilkins Freeman, George Moore, Joseph Conrad, Charles W. Chesnutt, Edith Wharton,
Rudyard Kipling, Ivan Bunin, Jack London, Sherwood Anderson, James
Stephens, Ring Lardner, D. H. Lawrence, and Katherine Mansfield. More
difficult to locate within this mainstream tradition, such experimental authors as Gertrude Stein, Lu Hsun, and Franz Kafka had come upon the

stage. And still others were starting upon significant careers in the genre: Katherine Anne Porter, Bruno Schultz, Dorothy Parker, Isaac Babel, Jean Toomer, Liam O'Flaherty, F. Scott Fitzgerald, William Faulkner, Elizabeth Bowen, Andrey Platonov, Sean O'Faolain, and Frank O'Connor.

Hemingway, an avid if self-taught student of literature, was well read in the short fiction of many of these authors, and he learned a great deal from them, especially Turgenev, Maupassant, Chekhov, Crane, Anderson, Stein, and Joyce. With the exception of his innovations in dialogue—the subject of our eighth chapter—he was hardly the first to employ most of the techniques discussed in this book. But he drew upon the innovations of others—not just story writers but also novelists, playwrights, poets, and even painters, sculptors, and musicians—in highly original ways. In doing so, he forged one of the few original styles of his time, produced some of the finest stories of the twentieth century, and changed the genre forever.

In an important essay on nineteenth-century narrative aesthetics, G. R. Thompson delineates "two major divergent lines of formal development of short 'fiction' in America from the earlier nineteenth to the later twentieth centuries—namely, the Poesque and the Hawthornesque." As opposed to Hawthorne's self-reflexive authorial presence—a tradition connected to such later metafictional, postmodern authors as Vladimir Nabokov, Jorge Luis Borges, John Barth, Philip Roth, Cynthia Ozick, and Paul Auster—Poe tried to establish an art of short fiction that centered on "a dramatic 'effect' via an overall organic unity conforming to a Freytag Triangle of carefully constructed sequence—an Aristotelian exposition, complication, crisis, climax, denouement—in which every word contributes to the 'preconceived' effect." Thompson rightly locates Hemingway's stories within this tradition: "Poe's concept of dramatized, presentational fiction anticipates Henry James's famous dictum of 'showing' rather than 'telling' and the general author-effacing mode of the earlier Ernest Hemingway" (171, 179, 172).

In Hemingway's youth, Poe, as well as most American authors, was absent from school curricula, but he was well represented in the Oak Park public library (*HR* 16). Poe's stories were frequently anthologized and popular in the general culture. By the 1920s—due to his employment of symbolism and ambiguity, his representations of the unconscious, and his focus on the psyche in conflict—he had emerged as one of the major ancestors of modernism. In 1945, after reading *The Portable Edgar Allan Poe,* Hemingway wrote to Malcolm Cowley: "I looked forward to reading Poe.

Thought that would be good to do this winter. Then found I'd read it all before ever went to Italy and remembered it so clearly that I couldn't re-read. Had forgotten them all but they were all there—intact" (*SL* 605).

Indeed, Hemingway had absorbed Poe so thoroughly that even many of his pronouncements on the art of the short story seem eerily to echo his predecessor with regard to plot, the goal of the single effect, and unity of impact. Here is Poe in the oft-cited opening of "The Philosophy of Composition" (1846) discussing how he achieves a single effect in his stories:

> It is only with the *dénouement* constantly in view that we can give a plot its indispensable air of consequence, or causation, by making the incidents, and especially the tone at all points, tend to the development of the intention . . . I prefer commencing with the consideration of an *effect* . . . [After having chosen a novel and] vivid effect, I consider whether it can best be wrought by incident or tone—whether by ordinary incidents and peculiar tone, or the converse, or by peculiarity both of incident and tone—afterward looking about me (or rather within) for such combinations of event, or tone, as shall best aid me in the construction of the effect. (13–14)

Elsewhere, Poe elaborates on this integration of design by defining the term *plot* as *"that in which no part can be displaced without ruin to the whole* (original emphasis). It may be described as a building so dependently constructed, that to change the position of a single brick is to overthrow the entire fabric" (Review 148). And here is Hemingway to his publisher in 1925, taking, as usual, fewer words: "[my] stories are written so tight and so hard that the alteration of a word can throw an entire story out of key" (*SL* 154). There is no Hawthornian repose in Hemingway's best and most typical stories, nothing of his chiaroscuro tones, little authorial playfulness. Hemingway's stories work to a maximum effect, they employ a minimum number of words selected with great care, and, in third-person narratives, the narrator and author are virtually absent.

Although Poe's influence on storytelling is immeasurable and broadly diffused throughout the subsequent development of the genre, the more direct model for young Hemingway was another story writer in the Poesque tradition, albeit the Gallic branch of the tree—Guy de Maupassant. From Maupassant, Hemingway learned understatement, brevity, careful word choice (Flaubert's "le mot juste"), the effaced narrator, and the ironic reversal that drives home the story's effect. Hemingway's youthful exposure to

Maupassant was confined to the much-anthologized translations of lesser stories that depended upon an unexpected twist in the ending. In 1941, he recalled in a letter to Maxwell Perkins: "I'll never forget how sick I was of 'A Piece of String' and 'The Necklace' of de Maupassant. But I suppose they couldn't put his good ones in the school books" (*SL* 527). Once in Paris in the early 1920s, however, he began devouring Maupassant stories in the original French; he personally owned six volumes (*HR* 157). In 1925, just after the start of his greatest creative period as a story writer, he referred to Maupassant as "a professional writer," always a term of praise for Hemingway (*SL* 179); in 1933 he took pride in favorably comparing his "The Light of the World" with Maupassant's "La Maison Tellier," both stories about prostitutes (*SL* 393); and near the end of his life, when asked which "literary forbears" he had most learned from, Maupassant—along with Chekhov, Turgenev, and a qualified "the good Kipling"—was one of four story writers who immediately leaped to mind (Interview 227). The second name he mentioned, right after Mark Twain, was Flaubert—Maupassant's mentor—four of whose books Hemingway had carefully read upon arriving in Paris (*HR* 124–25).

I mention these influences in order to create a space within which to discuss the Hemingway story, as opposed to the story in general. The aesthetic principles we will explore are those that pertain to Hemingway's type of short stories, which critics have alternatively labeled "realist," "naturalist," and "modernist" (some have even delved into "postmodern Hemingway"). The characteristic Hemingway story can be classified as realist in form. It treats either an episode or series of causally linked episodes, usually chronologically; it aims at achieving the two main dictates set down by the leading American advocate of realism, William Dean Howells, that characters follow a probability of motive and that the text possess verisimilitude; and the author/narrator is effaced in third-person, and even in first-person, narratives.

The naturalist story does not formally differ from the realist story, but philosophically it is much less sanguine about a character's ability to affect his or her fate. Not coincidentally, many classic American naturalists—Stephen Crane, Theodore Dreiser, Jack London, Upton Sinclair—either began their writing careers as reporters or were intimate with journalism. As reporters, they were exposed to the world of have-nots, the marginal existences of the poor, the working class, prostitutes, drunkards, and other victims of the large-scale forces that were ushering in modernization and overwhelming so many Americans. The naturalists developed their peculiar brand of involvement and detachment, sympathy and distance, directness and irony, while investigating the lives of those crushed or left behind as America evolved into a modern nation-state and the American sense of self shifted from a culture based on production and character to one based on consumption and personality. Nor is it an accident that the naturalists were all, in some way, fatalistic. They saw little room for agency or moral choice in the lives they wrote about, lives not far removed from the animal world. Hemingway, too, started in journalism. Working as a reporter in the Midwest and later in Europe, he saw firsthand the worlds of crime, poverty, transience, and war. As with the naturalists' work, a tremendous sense of loss and nostalgia pervades his fiction. He focuses on characters who have been, in some way, physically or spiritually wounded. Like Poe before him—but less abstractly and with more obvious reference to historical events—in his stories he, too, is a poet of the haunted mind.

A rich vein of naturalist philosophy runs through American modernism, although modernism differs from naturalism in its focus on consciousness and the unconscious, its concern with epistemology, and its continual experiments with form and narration. When one thinks of the classics of high modernist American fiction—e.g., Stein's *Three Lives,* Toomer's *Cane,* Cather's *The Professor's House,* Dos Passos's *USA* trilogy, and Faulkner's *Absalom, Absalom!*—the naturalist element is clear. It's equally discernible in such Hemingway novels as *The Sun Also Rises, A Farewell to Arms, To Have and Have Not,* and *The Old Man and the Sea,* and it runs through his short fiction.

If one were to seek a credo embedded in the dramatic action of naturalist fiction, two Stephen Crane stories Hemingway cited in 1935 as "necessary" for all writers to read (*BL* 218) would amply serve: "The Blue Hotel" and "The Open Boat." In "The Blue Hotel," just after the Swede has beaten up Johnny Scully but before he finds his way through a snowstorm to the saloon where he will be murdered, there is this passage:

> He might have been in a deserted village. We picture the world as thick with conquering and elate humanity, but here, with the bugles of the tempest pealing, it was hard to imagine a peopled earth. One viewed the existence of man then as a marvel, and conceded a glamour of wonder to these lice which were caused to cling to a whirling, fire-smote, ice-locked, disease-stricken, space-lost bulb. The conceit of man was ex-

plained by this storm to be the very engine of life. One was a coxcomb not to die in it. However, the Swede found a saloon. (822)

Several passages from "The Open Boat" offer naturalist credos, including one near the end, when the correspondent in the boat views the wind-tower and wonders if anyone ever ascended it and looked out to sea:

> This tower was a giant, standing with its back to the plight of ants. It represented in a degree, to the correspondent, the serenity of nature amid the struggles of the individual—nature in the wind, and nature in the vision of men. She did not seem cruel to him then, nor beneficent, nor treacherous, nor wise. But she was indifferent, flatly indifferent. (905)

These passages articulate the heart of Crane's naturalism: the indifference of nature, the insignificance of human beings, the detached fatalism of the narrative voice that sees life as a bad jest, the randomness and hence amorality of fate, even the role of chance compressed into the word *however* at the end of the first passage, a word that will lead the Swede to the location of his unforeseen death.

Here now is Hemingway's protagonist, Frederic Henry—his surname an homage to Crane's Henry Fleming from *The Red Badge of Courage*—meditating as he waits outside the operating room where a doctor is trying to save Catherine Barkley's life after their son is stillborn:

> Once in camp I put a log on top of the fire and it was full of ants. As it commenced to burn, the ants swarmed out and went first toward the centre where the fire was; then turned back and ran toward the end. When there were enough on the end they fell off into the fire. Some got out, their bodies burnt and flattened, and went off not knowing where they were going. But most of them went toward the fire and then back toward the end and swarmed on the cool end and finally fell off into the fire. I remember thinking at the time that it was the end of the world and a splendid chance to be a messiah and lift the log off the fire and throw it out where the ants could get off onto the ground. But I did not do anything but throw a tin cup of water on the log, so that I would have the cup empty to put whiskey in before I added water to it. I think the cup of water on the burning log only steamed the ants.
>
> So now I sat out in the hall and waited to hear how Catherine was. (*FTA* 327–28)

In this passage, Frederic is Crane's wind-tower and the ants are real ants. Nature, in the form of Frederic, is as indifferent to the suffering of the ants as it was to the men in Crane's boat or to the Swede. Fate is random and is also, as Crane's correspondent puts it, flatly indifferent.

Émile Zola's "formula" for naturalism—that fate results from heredity plus environment plus chance—looms over the world of the naturalist story. Given the small canvas on which Hemingway works, we do not see such metaphorical or philosophical passages as the ones above—with the possible exception of the "nada-ization" of the Lord's Prayer at the end of "A Clean, Well-Lighted Place"—nor do we usually see heredity, environment, and chance all in one story, but at least one such element is typically present. To cite some stories where "heredity"—roughly defined as inherited dispositions and biological needs—is the controlling force, one could point to the similarities between Nick Adams and his father, likenesses that closely represent those of Ernest and Clarence Hemingway. One could also look at the manipulative hedonistic desires of the man in "Hills Like White Elephants" and the major in "A Simple Enquiry," the more brutal sexual desire of Jim Gilmore in "Up in Michigan," the chemical addiction of William Campbell in "A Pursuit Race," the human avarice depicted in "After the Storm," and the homicidal rage portrayed in "A Natural History of the Dead."

"Environment," as Zola understood it, included social conditioning—what literary critics now refer to as the "social construction of the subject" (or self)—as well as "environment" in the sense of the deterministic conditions, both social and physical, in which humans negotiate their lives. This naturalist element pervades Hemingway's stories. The main human environments in which his characters struggle for survival are war and family. Both crucially influence Nick Adams in his maturation from childhood to fatherhood. Closely mirroring the dynamics of war are the environments of the boxing ring and horse track—both compromised by corruption, as in "The Killers," "Fifty Grand," and "My Old Man"—and the bullring, a place possessed of the possibility of transcendence but threatened by a spiritually numbing commercialism, as in "The Undefeated" and several of the vignettes of *in our time*. The hunt also holds out the possibility of transcendence, but in such a story as "The Short Happy Life of Francis Macomber" it, too, has been devalued by commercialism and polluted by social dynamics. The most deterministic environments in Hemingway's stories are those glimpsed through transience—characters enter strange worlds whose codes they cannot comprehend, worlds formed at the margins of society where the inhabitants have been doomed by limited opportunity, poverty, or politics. Examples include the prostitutes, lumberjacks, and Indians in "The Light of the World," the inhabitants of "Indian Camp," the Mexican farm workers of "The Gambler, the Nun, and the Radio," the gunmen and fated boxer of "The Killers," the dehumanized peasant of "An Alpine Idyll," and the Italian villagers in "Che Ti Dice la Patria?"

We see "chance," the third partner in the naturalist equation, mainly in stories with an unexpected turn; in Hemingway this reversal is not significant per se but reveals either character or some larger theme of the story. Chance, or randomness, brings the death of the major's wife in "In Another Country," the death of Francis Macomber, the fatal goring of Paco in "The Capital of the World," the gangrene that infects Harry's scratched leg in "The Snows of Kilimanjaro," and the "malady" of "One Reader Writes." In Hemingway's fiction, we see the self-reliant, Emersonian, American ego run head first into the brick wall of naturalist determinism. Sometimes it is shattered, most of the time it is badly wounded, and occasionally it achieves some small measure of psychic victory—Manuel, badly gored but refusing to allow Zurito to cut off his *coleta* (pigtail), may be destroyed, yet he remains, as the story's title puts it, "undefeated." Such is what passes for optimism in Hemingway's world.

If the Hemingway story is, as I believe it to be, realist with regard to form, verisimilitude, and authorial effacement, and naturalist in philosophy, it nevertheless often departs from those earlier forms in its modernist narrative techniques, drawing liberally on the innovations of earlier story writers. Some, such as Joyce, were modernists; others, such as Chekhov, are difficult to place generically; still others, such as Crane, anticipated many modernist strategies.[1]

In this book, I delineate the technical features of Hemingway's short story art. In doing so, the modernist aesthetics of his texts become apparent, as do some of the ways in which modernism itself was indebted to earlier authors who initially employed these techniques. Such a dissection has its obvious value; it gets beneath the surface to show how texts actually work. But it is also tends to make stories into clinical specimens, treating parts of them rather than looking at each story as a whole. Hemingway, I should hasten to note, would probably have detested what I am doing here. As penance, in a future book I intend to examine a number of stories thoroughly as autonomous texts, putting back together what here I so callously take apart. The short story is a living thing; even in its final form it continues to grow, change, and reveal hidden aspects of itself to new generations of readers. But, as with human bodies, a certain knowledge of basic anatomy illuminates.

For many readers, the most characteristic feature of a Hemingway story is the author's dispassionate prose; his language is always less emotional than the events narrated seem to demand. Paradoxically, this understated and often stoic language becomes the vehicle by which a strong emotional response is elicited from the reader. The modern short story developed in the cultural/aesthetic contexts of nineteenth-century realism, a historical genre that—as we see in the Flaubert epigraph with which this chapter began—rejected sentimental prose. This rejection, however, was often accompanied by realism's acceptance of sentimental values. In other words, both realism and the modern short story embraced dispassionate presentation as a narrative strategy while employing it in the service of the very sentimentalism they so often disparaged: the validation of feeling over thought, filiation over isolation, the social over the individual. If the short story presents us with, as Frank O'Connor puts it, "an intense awareness of human loneliness" (*Lonely* 19), then by its very nature it makes an implicit plea for human connection. But it does so with dry eyes. Even writers as different as Guy de Maupassant and Anton Chekhov—arguably the two immediate ancestors of the twentieth-century short story—embraced dispassionate presentation as indispensable to the emerging genre.

In the mid-nineteenth century, many authors, not just sentimental novelists such as Harriet Beecher Stowe and Susan Warner, indulged to varying degrees in emotional rhetoric. Such passages did no harm to the novels because they accorded with the reading conventions of the era. In the case of *Uncle Tom's Cabin*, Stowe's aesthetic form derived from millennialist Christian typology, so the author's personal appeals were central to the novel's rhetorical effectiveness. In the hands of such stylists as Melville and Dostoevsky, occasional emotionally laden prose lifted the reader from the particulars of the novel into the realm of metaphysical speculation. Even in the less stylistically skilled hands of a naturalist such as Theodore Dreiser, emotional excess along with pseudo-scientific explanations could be borne by the novel because they were dispersed over so many pages. His novels succeeded despite such passages. But the emerging modern short story could not afford to be demonstrative. Because its emotional content is so compressed and amplified by brevity, authors had to develop vigilance in disguising their own feelings.

Maupassant, who learned from Flaubert to be everywhere felt but nowhere seen, cultivated a deliberately unliterary prose—cold, precise, impersonal, unflinching—in order to treat the primordial human passions that comprised his fictional material. He understood that emotion is essential to short stories; it must be conveyed and evoked but never by language that is itself emotional. As Elizabeth Bowen observes, Maupassant "transcribed passions in the only terms possible—dispassionate understatement" and "his sort of erotic nearness to what he wrote of [gave] him a cautious language that never exceeds art" ("Faber" 39). Maupassant's method, Bowen continues, found favor with the writers of the Irish Renaissance, such as Liam O'Flaherty, and of postwar America, such as Hemingway. To this I would add postrevolutionary Russia and cite Isaac Babel as an example. Hemingway himself felt that a "civil war is the best war for a writer" and that personal experiences of pain and suffering have literary value. Maupassant endured France's humiliating defeat in the Franco-Prussian War, and Chekhov learned about suffering as a physician on Sakhalin Island. As Hemingway observed: "Dostoevsky was made by being sent to Siberia. Writers are forged in injustice as a sword is forged" (*GHA* 71).

"Extraverted coldness in art," Bowen speculates, "objectivity, may be the fruit of a life that is, or has been lately, physically exciting or uncertain, life that is quick, rough or lived at high nervous tension, in which either sexual or political passion makes society unsafe. Precipitate feeling makes for hard form in art." In a world where "events assault the imagination," there exists mystery, wonder, and strong emotion—what she calls "amazement." But although in poetry such amazement is "involuntary and to a degree fathomed," such is not the case with the short story:

In the short story, semi-poetic, amazement is not only not fathomed but not stated; but has to be made evident. The writer must so strip fact of neutralizing elements [i.e., emotions] as to return to it, and prolong for it, its first power: what was in life a half-second of apprehension must be perpetuated. The extraverted short story—bare of analysis, sparse in emotional statement—is the formula for, never the transcript of, that amazement with which poetry deals. The particular must be given general significance. Narration is bound to be exact and impassive. ("Faber" 40–41)

Such narration, as Hemingway stated, is the only way to convey "the real thing, the sequence of motion and fact which made the emotion" (*DIA* 2).

On the other end of the stylistic spectrum from Maupassant stands Chekhov—sensitive, introverted, gently ironic—a writer interested in the subtlest nuances of mood and subjective states of consciousness, the sorts of feelings that Maupassant either ignored or scorned. But both Chekhov and Maupassant described themselves as "objective writers," and the former was every bit as careful to remain dispassionate in his presentation as the latter. "You should only sit down to write when you feel as cold as ice," Chekhov once told the young storyteller Ivan Bunin (qtd. in Bunin 36). For him, this was partly a matter of modesty. Writers have no answers; they only pose questions. In a letter to his publisher, Chekhov said that it is not the purpose of writers to solve problems; their "function is only to describe by whom, how, and under what conditions the questions . . . were discussed. The artist must be only an impartial witness of his characters and what they said, not their judge." An emotional presentation, it goes without saying, implies both prejudgment and partiality. The time has come, he added, for writers "to admit that you can't figure out anything in this world" (*ACSS* 270). Writers need to be cautious because they are no less narrow and limited in their understanding than other people. Thus their judgments may be unjust, even ridiculous. Citing the case of Ham, Noah's son, who "noticed only that his father was a drunkard, and completely lost sight of the fact that he was a genius, that he built an arc and saved the world," Chekhov implored a fellow writer not to make the same mistake: "I do not venture to ask you to love [your characters], but I venture to remind you of the justice which for an objective writer is more precious than the air he breathes" (*LSS* 78).

Ultimately, however, Chekhov embraced dispassionate presentation for the same reason Maupassant did—effectiveness. The narrator is a witness, the reader a jury of one. A witness who is emotional is less credible than one who is not; like Rosa Coldfield in Faulkner's *Absalom, Absalom!,* such a witness appears to have a stake in persuading the reader to share her own emotion, and the reader naturally grows as suspicious as does Quentin Compson. An emotional presentation diverts the reader's attention from the scene, undermining the fictional dream, and onto the source of the narration—the writer. Here, in another letter of advice to a writer, is Chekhov at his most practical: "When you describe the miserable and unfortunate, and want to make the reader feel pity, try to be somewhat colder—

that seems to give a kind of background to another's grief, against which it stands out more clearly. Whereas in your story the characters cry and you sigh. Yes, be more cold" (*ACSS* 273). Such advice, from a humanitarian doctor who was anything but cold, speaks volumes about the necessity of dispassionate presentation.

In today's criticism, sociological inquiry and cultural critique crowd out aesthetic appreciation in the belief that all aesthetics are socially constructed and ideologically determined. Thus, when critics address Hemingway's dispassionate presentation, they typically, and often facilely, link it to gender anxieties. Simply stated, their claim is that Hemingway is afraid to show emotion because that would undermine his sense of his own masculinity; so, his rhetorical strategies involve understatement, detachment, and a stoic sparseness of feeling. But whatever the value of Hemingway as a case of gendered cultural pathology, the fact is that twentieth-century writers of the short story—men and women, in both theory and practice—have tended to concur with Chekhov on this point. As Flannery O'Connor puts it, "The fiction writer has to realize that he can't create compassion with compassion, or emotion with emotion, or thought with thought" (92).

That said, let's return to the idea I perhaps too easily discounted: that Hemingway's dispassionate style is related to gender anxieties. There may indeed be some relation, but it is not direct, nor is it limited to either Hemingway or gender. The great Irish story writer, Sean O'Faolain, begins his book on the genre with a consideration of what he terms supremely important—"literary personality" or "voice" (that same voice that, according to Philip Roth's fictional story writer, E. I. Lonoff, "begins at around the back of the knees and reaches well above the head"; 72). According to O'Faolain, what distinguishes a short story from longer fiction is "the fact that the writer has deliberately selected some special incident or character . . . because it is [quoting Maupassant] 'in good concordance with all the tendencies of his thought'":

The short story is an emphatically personal exposition. What one searches for and what one enjoys in a short story is a special distillation of personality, a unique sensibility which has recognised and selected at once a subject that, above all other subjects, is of value to the writer's temperament and to his alone—his counterpart, his perfect opportunity to project himself. The reader acknowledges this to be so when he speaks of a "good Hemingway," or "a good Coppard"; or when he says—"That story is pure Chekov," or admits ownership in a distinctive point of view by saying, "That is a Maupassant situation."

. . . It is this very characteristic of the short-story which has [led to] the technique of "suggestion" rather than "statement," a technique which is really an invisible cloak to cover the author, sensitive about intruding himself, fully conscious of the personal nature of his work, and just because he is so near at hand, for that very reason sensitive about being discovered prowling among his characters.

. . . It is not the subject that a man writes; it is himself. I cannot say it too often. (30, 53, 179)

Because it deserves emphasis, here is Maupassant on the same subject:

Our vision and knowledge of the world and our ideas of life are acquired by the aid of our senses, and we can but transfer them partially to all the characters whose secret and unknown nature we propose to reveal. Thus it is always ourselves that we disclose in the body [of our characters]; for we are compelled to put the problem in this personal form: "If *I* were a king, a murderer, a prostitute, a nun, or a market-woman, what should *I* do, what should *I* think, how should *I* act?" We can vary our characters only by altering the age, the sex, the social position, and all the circumstances of life, of that ego which Nature has in fact enclosed in an insurmountable barrier of organs of sense. Skill consists in not betraying this ego to the reader, under the various masks which we employ to cover it. (673–74)

Hemingway's friend, F. Scott Fitzgerald, summed it up nicely when he observed: "we learn our trade" and "tell our two or three stories—each time in a new disguise—maybe ten times, maybe a hundred, as long as people will listen . . . It is rather like Ed Wynn's famous anecdote about the painter of boats who was begged to paint some ancestors for a client. The bargain was arranged, but with the painter's final warning that the ancestors would all turn out to look like boats" ("False" 132). Without dispassionate presentation, suggestiveness, and other techniques for masking the author and the author's emotions in the writing of the inherently deeply personal short story, the reader would readily view the writer's subjectivity, a "terrible thing" according to Chekhov, because "it reveals the author's hands and feet" (*LSS* 69).

If Hemingway had reason to hide his gender anxieties—about his adequacy as a husband and partner (consider "Cat in the Rain," "Out of Season," "Cross-Country Snow," "Hills Like White Elephants," "A Canary for One," "The Snows of Kilimanjaro"), his adequacy as a heterosexual man ("A Simple Enquiry," "God Rest You Merry, Gentlemen," "The Sea Change," "The Short Happy Life of Francis Macomber," and, of course, such novels as *The Sun Also Rises* and *The Garden of Eden*), and his even more pervasive, less specific, existential anxieties ("Indian Camp," "Big Two-Hearted River," "In Another Country," "The Killers," "Now I Lay Me," "After the Storm," "A Clean, Well-Lighted Place," "A Way You'll Never Be")—the larger point is that all writers, and especially story writers, return repeatedly to their own obsessions. They disguise themselves for self-protection and to protect their stories from being undercut by the very emotions that led to their having been written in the first place.

Related to the question of dispassionate presentation is the matter of authorial judgment. If language must remain unemotional, then surely overt judgments, too, present a threat to the modern story's aesthetic effectiveness. Hemingway understood this in the same way as Chekhov: a writer has no special corner on the truth and is as prone to error as anyone else. Hemingway observes: "As a man things are as they should or shouldn't be. As a man you know who is right and who is wrong. You have to make decisions and enforce them. As a writer you should not judge. You should understand" (*BL* 219). The practical exigencies of life compel us to evaluate others and act upon those assessments, but true art, as Hemingway saw it, must be more sensitive to human complexity in its representations. Prone as he was to misjudging others and to being unkind in acting upon those judgments, he tried to guard his fiction from his own imperfect temperament and to a remarkable extent, given his passions, succeeded.

Yet if overt judgment must be kept at bay in the short story, nevertheless, judgment of some sort must occur, if only because fiction represents life in the actual rather than in the ideal. How, then, does judgment take place in the Hemingway story? Most of the time, it occurs in the reader's mind as characters reveal themselves through their thoughts, words, and actions, and as they judge each other. Take, for instance, Dr. Wilcox in "God Rest You Merry, Gentlemen." In his actions toward the young man who, out of religious obsession and fear of his own "unclean" sexual desires, mutilates himself, he reveals himself to be insensitive and incompetent. In his speech to the Jewish Dr. Fischer, Wilcox reveals his religious intolerance and sanctimoniousness. The naïve young narrator doesn't know what to make of all of this, so the judgment of Dr. Wilcox is not coming from him, but readers can draw their own conclusions. Not surprisingly, two things that Hemingway most hated in people were professional incompetence and smug religiosity, and in the figure of Dr. Wilcox he condemns both. At the same time, Dr. Fischer reveals competence, compassion, and wit, evoking a positive assessment from the reader (see Lamb, "Hemingway's Critique").

In a similar way, Hemingway depicts his own mother's pat religious assumptions and passive-aggressiveness in such stories as "The Doctor and the Doctor's Wife," "Soldier's Home," and the flashbacks of "Now I Lay Me." Other people he either disliked or was troubled by include bullies, promoters, socialites, and homosexuals; not coincidentally, his stories are peopled by characters—sometimes flat, sometimes more developed—who represent them. Take, for examples, the Fascist who uses his authority to rob the narrator in "Che Ti Dice la Patria?"; the bullfight promoter Retana who chisels the desperate bullfighter Manuel in "The Undefeated"; the socialite who accidentally shoots her husband in "The Short Happy Life of Francis Macomber"; or the major who sexually harasses his orderly in "A Simple Enquiry." In each case, Hemingway portrays in these characters his own judgments, but always within the dramatic action of the story. (I should note that whenever his authorial judgment imposed itself upon a narrative, it led to a bad story, as in the thin and unengaging "Mr. and Mrs. Elliot," a silly sketch in which he uses two lesbian characters for the purpose of mocking two poets he resented, Chard Smith and T. S. Eliot.)

Judgment need not, of course, be negative; juxtaposed with the unappealing characters are those such as Dr. Fischer who display the sorts of qualities that Hemingway admired. One thinks, first of all, of competent professionals: the hunter Wilson of "Macomber," Dr. Adams of "Indian Camp," the Italian major of "In Another Country," the matador Villalta of "Chapter XII" of In Our Time, the picador Zurito of "The Undefeated." Then there are those who combine worldly wisdom with sympathy for others—not the kind but clueless nun of "The Gambler, the Nun, and the Radio" nor the experienced but corrupted father of "My Old Man," but the older waiter of "A Clean, Well-Lighted Place," Zurito, the padrone of "Cat in the Rain," the fathers of "A Day's Wait" and "Fathers and Sons," Captain Paravicini in "A Way You'll Never Be." Finally, there are those who are mentally tough, who can "take it," the prototype being Christ on the cross in "Today Is Friday."

Lest I appear to be saying that Hemingway distributes his authorial judgments across a simple system of binary oppositions represented by "good" and "bad" characters, I should note that few of his characters are purely one or the other. To the extent that it is possible to portray complex characters in a short story (see our ninth chapter)—and it is very difficult—Hemingway did so.

Authorial judgment, always indirect, can take place in a Hemingway story in something as small as the selection of a single word; it can also be something as large as the deep structure of the text. In the former case, Hemingway is a Flaubertian realist, in the latter, a modernist. A few months before telling his publisher that "the alteration of a word" could throw "an entire story" of his "out of key" (*SL* 154), he finished "The Undefeated." Manuel Garcia, an aging bullfighter just out of the hospital after a bad goring, is unwilling to retire from his vocation. Desperate for a fight, he is forced by Retana, an unsympathetic promoter, to perform for insulting wages as a substitute matador in a nocturnal, in which the bulls are especially difficult and the crowds are rowdy and unknowledgeable. The nocturnal's picadors, whom the matador depends upon to weaken the bull before the kill, are inept, and so Manuel persuades his friend, Zurito, a highly competent picador, to participate. Zurito agrees on one condition—that if Manuel doesn't do well he will cut his *coleta,* the matador's pigtail, and retire. Zurito is the moral center of the story, so his doubts about his friend's ability carry weight. Manuel's performance starts off well, but Hemingway is too much the realist (and perhaps the naturalist) to make this into a Disney tale. Although he earns the praise of Zurito and another bullfighter, Manuel's skills are not appreciated by the amateur crowd or by the newspaper's second-string critic. Then, everything goes wrong. In the end, Manuel is unable to drive his sword into the bull, he is knocked over, and his sword is bent. Manuel pursues the bull, and Hemingway writes, "As he ran, his jacket flopped where it had been ripped under his armpit" (*SS* 261).

Hemingway has gone to great lengths to make the reader care about Manuel. The matador's passion and determination are impressive, and, as an aging professional athlete in the twilight of his career, he is a sympathetic figure. His own kid brother had been killed nine years earlier by a bull whose stuffed head hangs on the wall of Retana's office. Retana, whom Hemingway describes three times on the first page as a "little man," has cheated Manuel, and everything is stacked against him in this fight—the callous promoter, the difficult bull, the incompetent handlers, the unsympathetic newspaper critic, and the ignorant crowd that later pelts him with cushions and a bottle just before he is gored. Even the story's title, which should not be read as ironic, shows Hemingway's sympathies. But sympathy and judgment are two different things. As Zurito suspects, Manuel has indeed lost his stuff—when one of Retana's men, early on, calls Manuel a "great bull-fighter," a worried Zurito replies, "No, he's not" (SS 259). So Hemingway renders his judgment with a single word, *flopped,* which not only carries symbolic resonance (Manuel, too, is "flopping") but also makes the matador look undignified. Placing the rip under the armpit also hints at the way Manuel is stinking up the bullfight. Not to put too fine a point on it, but another sentence, say—"As he charged, his torn jacket waved in the wind behind him"—would have functioned equally well in describing the action, but it would have undermined the judgment Hemingway offers, or rather, it would have presented a different judgment.

Turning from the smallest unit of a story—the single word—to something as large as structure, we find that Hemingway frequently makes his judgment implicit through form. This is easiest to observe in his shortest narratives. Take, for example, "chapter 8" of *in our time* ("Chapter VII" of *IOT*). In it, a soldier in a trench during a bombardment "lay very flat and sweated and prayed" fervently to Jesus, promising that if Jesus spares his life, "I'll tell every one in the world that you are the only thing that matters" ("only one that matters" in *IOT*). The shelling moves further away, and the next night "he did not tell the girl he went upstairs with at the Villa Rossa about Jesus. And he never told anybody" (*iot* 16). Robert Scholes observes that this sketch is constructed by a series of oppositions, principally Jesus versus the prostitute and the trench versus the brothel, each term of which carries a great deal of cultural allusiveness. Scholes also connects the two main actions; while in the trench, the soldier lies flat, sweats, and calls to Jesus, and we may assume that, although Hemingway omits it from the narrative, the next night with the prostitute he also lies flat and sweats (to which I add, he might be once again be calling to Jesus). In going from the trench to upstairs at the brothel, he moves from his lowest physical position in the story to his highest, but on the moral level he moves from his highest position to his lowest, from praying to God to having sex with a prostitute (*Textual* 26–38).

Although Scholes does not address the matter of judgment per se, I maintain that this contrasting double movement along the axes of physicality and morality is how Hemingway offers his judgment. It is akin to the movement in Howells's *The Rise of Silas Lapham,* a novel in which a businessman's decline in status and fortune is linked to his moral rise, or better still, Abraham Cahan's *The Rise of David Levinsky,* in which a businessman's rise in fortune is accompanied by a moral decline. This well-known fictional theme hardly needs to be signaled in its title. For instance, Edith Wharton's *The House of Mirth,* in which the protagonist's social position declines as she grows from an amoral naturalist character into a moral realist character, could have just as well been entitled *The Rise of Lily Bart.* Within the space of a mere vignette, Hemingway makes the same point, and his judgments are as manifest as those of Howells, Cahan, and Wharton; to state it directly in Hemingway's case, spirituality during wartime danger does not last in the face of mundane desires.

A more complex example of structure implying judgment occurs in the second *in our time* vignette, in which six bulls are killed in six sentences: (note that the word "out" at the end of the first sentence was deleted when republished as "Chapter IX" of *In Our Time*):

> The first matador got the horn through his sword hand and the crowd hooted him out. The second matador slipped and the bull caught him through the belly and he hung on to the horn with one hand and held the other tight against the place, and the bull rammed him wham against the wall and the horn came out, and he lay in the sand, and then got up like crazy drunk and tried to slug the men carrying him away and yelled for his sword but he fainted. The kid came out and had to kill five bulls because you can't have more than three matadors, and the last bull he was so tired he couldn't get the sword in. He couldn't hardly lift his arm. He tried five times and the crowd was quiet because it was a good bull and it looked like him or the bull and then he finally made it. He sat down in the sand and puked and they held a cape over him while the crowd hollered and threw things down into the bull ring. (*iot* 10)

This vignette is subtly structured around the action, both real and metaphorical, of "throwing up." The crowd hoots the first matador "out" of the ring, figuratively throwing him up out of the belly of the arena. When the second matador is gored, catching the horn "through the belly," the horn is eventually "thrown up" out of his stomach. After the third matador finally kills the last of the five remaining bulls, he literally throws up, and the crowd responds by throwing things down into the bullring, figuratively throwing up. But since the young matador is not responsible, in the author's judgment, for the distasteful bullfighting exhibition, the cape protects him from the crowd's figurative vomit while further preserving his dignity by hiding his own literal act of throwing up. This is an example of what Flannery O'Connor means when she says that, "for the fiction writer, judgment begins in the details he sees and how he sees them" (92).

Nevertheless, the incident is sickening: for the author, the reader, the matadors, and the spectators. Therefore, when Hemingway has the young matador "puke," he expresses (through that character's action) the revulsion everyone feels, identifies the operative metaphor in the story, and brings the narrative to an appropriate climax. He also brings to a climax a sub-sequence of actions that employs drunkenness as a metaphor for the chaos that has broken out in this bullring. The second matador, after his injury, lies in the sand, gets up "like crazy drunk," tries to slug the men helping him, yells, and passes out. These actions, taken out of the context of the story, perfectly describe someone who is drunk. Hemingway disliked similes—he once punningly referred to them as being "like defective ammunition" (*SL* 809)[2]—but here he offers a clue to the sequence in the simile "like crazy drunk." The omitted action of this sub-sequence—as every college student knows—is "puking," and it should have taken place somewhere between yelling and passing out. But this literal action is relocated at the end of the third matador sub-sequence—a technique I term *sequence displacement*—in order to increase the emotional intensity of the story's climax.

That emotion is also conveyed through the word chosen to describe the action (which takes us back to "flopped" in "The Undefeated"). Hemingway could have used the verb *to vomit,* but *to puke,* a monosyllabic verb that, with its hard *p* and common vernacular usage is less euphemistic, more closely approximates the "sound" of the act of throwing up with the "sense" of the word chosen to express it. The vignette contains 162 one-syllable words, seventeen two-syllable words, and five three-syllable words (three of which are unavoidable uses of the word *matador*). Since it is written in the simple past tense, the form of *to vomit* used would have been *vomited,* a three-syllable word that not only sounds less effective than the singly stressed *puked* but whose three syllables also call attention, in this monosyllabic story, to their own dactylic blandness. By choosing *puked* and displacing it from the second matador sub-sequence to the end of the third matador sub-sequence, it becomes the conduit through which the author expresses his feelings about what has transpired in the story and renders his judgment on these events. This vignette is a perfect example in miniature, then, of Hemingway's use of dispassionate presentation and his method of indirect authorial judgment.

2
Minimizing Words and Maximizing Meaning

SUGGESTIVENESS, CONCISION, AND OMISSION

Guess I got in the habit [of counting words] writing dispatches. Used to send them from some places where they cost a dollar and a quarter a word and you had to make them awful interesting at that price or get fired. Then I kept it up when started writing stories etc.
—Hemingway to Charles Scribner (1940), *Ernest Hemingway: Selected Letters*

It wasn't by accident that the Gettysburg address was so short. The laws of prose writing are as immutable as those of flight, of mathematics, of physics.
—Hemingway to Maxwell Perkins (1945), *Ernest Hemingway: Selected Letters*

Hemingway certainly helped to bury the notion . . . that the more you pile on the adjectives the closer you get to describing the thing.
—Tom Stoppard, "Reflections on Ernest Hemingway"

The short story's lack of space leads to prose that relies heavily on suggestiveness and implication, allowing the reader a greater role in bringing the narrative to life. Sean O'Faolain observes: "Telling by means of suggestion or implication is one of the most important of all the modern short-story's shorthand conventions. It means that a short-story writer does not directly tell us things so much as let us guess or know them by implying them. The technical advantage is obvious. It takes a long time to tell anything directly or explicitly . . . and it does not arrest our imagination or hold our attention so firmly as when we get a subtle hint" (150–51). To better understand O'Faolain's point, let us turn to the most suggestive of story writers. In counseling his older brother, an aspiring writer, Chekhov told him "to seize upon the little particulars, grouping them in such a way that, in reading, when you shut your eyes, you get a picture." He then penned the classic commentary on the technique of suggestiveness: "For instance, you will get the full effect of a moonlight night if you write that on the mill-dam a little glowing star-point flashed from the neck of a broken bottle, and the round, black shadow of a dog, or a wolf, emerged and ran, etc." (*LSS* 70–71). This passage—which Chekhov thought enough of to later incorporate into the final act of *The Seagull* (*Plays* 798)—gives us not only a moonlit night but also a suggestively resonant landscape of broken bottles and animals running loose.

One need only rewrite the passage in more direct prose to substantiate Chekhov's point: "The full moon shone down from the sky, illuminating everything in sight. On the mill dam lay the neck of a broken bottle, the glass reflecting in the light. Then a dog or a wolf appeared, casting a shadow as it ran across the scene, etc." What one first notices is that Chekhov's passage is shorter (29 words as opposed to 45) because the language is more compressed. A passage relying on prosaic explanation usually employs more words than a similar passage of suggestive prose. The Chekhov passage is also more convincing—the reader is less conscious of the writer's presence because the images appear and appeal without interruption. The scene is more verisimilar because our minds have taken part in creating it, and, vain creatures athirst for narrative, we overlook the obvious fact that the author has successfully enabled us to participate. By contrast, the passage told through direct statement bypasses our senses and makes its appeal to our abstract recollection. Our intellect, forced into passive acceptance, naturally grows suspicious and locates the source of the information—the author—and our absorption in the text is compromised.

This sort of Chekhovian suggestiveness can be found almost at random in Hemingway's stories. Consider, for example, the opening sentence of "The Light of the World": "When he saw us come in the door the bartender looked up and then reached over and put the glass covers on the two free-lunch bowls" (*SS* 384). In a mere thirty-one syllables, we have a vigilant and distrustful bartender, two suspicious-looking and perhaps hungry protagonists, a hint of a down-and-out world, and a certain sense of apprehension that we are in a community lacking in civility. Imagine how many words it would have taken most nineteenth-century writers to conjure up all of this.

Ultimately, suggestiveness is so important to the story because without it the reader is kept at bay. Frank O'Connor speaks of "making the reader a part of the story" (Interview 181). Using the theater as an analogy, he says, "If I use the right phrase and the reader hears the phrase in his head, he sees the individual. It's like writing for the theater, you see. A bad playwright will 'pull' an actor because he'll tell him what to do, but a really good playwright will give you a part that you can do what you like with. It's transferring to the reader the responsibility for acting those scenes" (Interview 169). Readers *want* to become engrossed in stories; as Herman Melville observes, they are looking "not only for more entertainment, but, at bottom, even for more reality, than real life itself can show" (*Confidence-Man* 259–60). Good readers—the sort that Vladimir Nabokov pictured as possessing "imagination, memory . . . and some artistic sense" (3)—demand suggestiveness from a story, the technique that allows them a role in creating the narrative.

But it is not just a matter of reader involvement. A story must speak in compressed prose because it has more work to do and less time to do it. Flannery O'Connor states: "A good short story should not have less meaning than a novel, nor should its action be less complete. Nothing essential to the main experience can be left out of a short story" (93). Nor can "an inadequate dramatic action" be made complete by adding to it "a statement of meaning" (75). She concludes: "The peculiar problem of the short-story writer is how to make the action he describes reveal as much of the mystery of existence as possible. He has only a short space to do it in and he can't do it by statement. He has to do it by showing, not by saying, and by showing the concrete—so that his problem is really how to make the concrete work double time for him" (98).

Like Flannery O'Connor—who suspected "that any idiot" with some talent could be taught to "write a competent story" (86)—Henry James also believed the short story was "an easy thing . . . to do a little with," but that the risks of compression for a true artist were "immense, for nothing is less intelligible than bad foreshortening, which, if it fails to mean everything intended, means less than nothing" ("Story-Teller" 285). The difficulties of compression made James ambivalent about the genre. On the one hand, he thought that "the innumerable repeated chemical reductions and condensations . . . tend to make . . . the very short story . . . like the hard, shining sonnet, one of the most indestructible, forms of composition in general use" (preface to "The Author of Beltraffio" 1244–45). But the effort to write one was exasperating, and James was about as comfortable in the genre as an eagle in a birdcage. He remembered "the process" of writing "The Middle Years" as "one of the most expensive of its sort in which I had ever engaged" and recalled that in his "struggle to keep compression rich" he felt as though he were "some warden of the insane engaged at a critical moment in making fast a victim's straightjacket" ("Beltraffio" 1238–39).

Independent of the generic exigencies of the short story, a shift toward greater concision and simplicity in American fiction had been occurring since the Civil War, a movement that Edmund Wilson once referred to as the "chastening of American prose style": "The plethora of words is reduced; the pace becomes firmer and quicker; the language becomes more what was later called 'efficient,' more what was still later called 'functional'" (638). In the fullest study of this evolution, Richard Bridgman delineates the differences between nineteenth- and twentieth-century fictional prose, using the works of Hawthorne and Hemingway as exemplary of each:

> Long words are eliminated or infrequently used, and then as deliberate contrasts. The sentences themselves are shorter. What was hinged and stapled by semicolons in the earlier prose is broken up into a series of declarative sentences in the later. Fewer details are provided, and those offered are precise and concrete. References to a cultural and historical past are stripped away, and the haze of emotive words is dispelled. Primary colors are accented. The immediate material world claims all the reader's attention. The result is a sharp, hard focus. (12)

Concision and simplicity were abetted, in Hemingway's case, by two key influences: journalism and poetry. Biographer Charles Fenton recounts that as a cub reporter for the *Kansas City Star,* Hemingway was handed a one-page style sheet with 110 rules, which began: "Use short sentences. Use short first paragraphs. Use vigorous English." Rule 21 especially made its mark: "Avoid the use of adjectives, especially such extravagant ones as *splendid, gorgeous, grand, magnificent,* etc." (qtd. in Fenton 31, 33).[1] (Many of these were rules that an earlier reporter-turned-writer had mastered, and Mark Twain stated rule 21 with Hemingwayesque brevity—"As to the Adjective: when in doubt, strike it out" [*Pudd'nhead* 52]). "Those were the best rules I ever learned for the business of writing," Hemingway would later recall. "I've never forgotten them. No man with any talent, who feels and writes truly about the thing he is trying to say, can fail to write well if he abides by them" (qtd. in Fenton, 34). As Fenton sums it up, Hemingway's vocational habits were being formed during this impressionable period of his life: "Language and words could never from this point on be lightly regarded. The effort would always be toward authenticity, precision, immediacy" (32).

If Hemingway took to heart the rules of journalism preached by the *Star*'s assistant city editor, Pete Wellington, those rules were complemented

by the principles he learned from a more renowned mentor, the poet Ezra
Pound. As Linda Wagner-Martin observes, the revolution in modern poetry preceded by more than a decade the emergence of modern fiction.
Because "so many writers worked in more than one genre, they were interested in developments everywhere, and the transfer of principles and
devices from one mode to another was much easier than it might have
been in a period more conscious of the boundaries of genre" (*Modern* 26,
28). Pound tutored many of the young authors who would change the face
of literature in the 1920s, and no one, not even James Joyce or Gertrude
Stein, had a greater personal or professional impact on Hemingway's development. With the great generosity he customarily showed to fellow writers,
Pound took the fledgling author under his wing and educated him. Hemingway eagerly devoured all that Pound recommended, including the poetry and essays of T. S. Eliot and all of Joyce; the nineteenth-century novelists Flaubert, Stendhal, and James; and such authors as Homer, Ovid,
Chaucer, Dante, Villon, and Donne. He had a natural affinity for some of
these writers, such as Stendhal and Joyce, but for others, especially James
and Eliot, he did not. Pound forced Hemingway to learn the lessons of
these masters, lessons that would directly influence his own fiction. Although he personally detested and ridiculed Eliot, he owned twelve of Eliot's books, and he had the invaluable experience of having Pound, who
had just recently edited *The Waste Land*, pruning it by about a third, take
him through the poem (Reynolds, *Paris* 29–30; *HR* 20–22, 120–21).

Pound also blue-penciled several of Hemingway's manuscripts, showing him how less can be more. Many of Pound's imagist principles of this
period had to do with cutting, eliminating, omitting, and compressing,
and the second of his three imagist tenets was "To use absolutely no word
that does not contribute to the presentation" (qtd. in Gelpi 176). Pound
would later describe Hemingway's fiction as "imagist" ("Small" 700) and
possessed of "the sensitivity of real writing" that showed the "touch of the
chisel" (qtd. in Carpenter 425). But this is exactly what his poet-mentor
had taught him to do, as Hemingway acknowledged when he said that he
had learned more about "how to write and how not to write" from Pound
than he had from anyone else (qtd. in Stock 311).[2]

Omission is the most radical form of concision and as old as narrative
itself. But because Hemingway possessed a theory of omission, directly
stated it on several occasions, and employed it for various purposes, liter-

ary criticism has linked him to omission as though he were its originator and even, it sometimes seems, its exclusive practitioner. We therefore need to locate omission in a larger context and to delineate exactly what Hemingway meant by the term and how he practiced it.

In its widest sense, omission is part of the selection process that all authors must undertake in creating a narrative from the "fabula," or basic story material. The fabula consists of everything that would have occurred in real life were the story true. In the fabula, events happen in chronological order, and their frequency and duration are as they would be in real life (e.g., an event that occurred once would occur once, two hours would last twice as long as one hour). All characters in the fabula are equally significant since, in real life, there are no minor characters. In other words, the fabula, or basic story stuff, is chaotic and unstructured—it is life exactly as it is, perfectly verisimilar, before someone imposes order on it. From this basic material—whether emanating from real life or from the author's imagination—the author plots a narrative through a process of selection and arrangement. In the plot, as opposed to the fabula, events can be presented out of chronological order. Similarly, something that happened once can be narrated several times, and something that happened many times can be narrated once (e.g., "every Sunday, they would walk down by the pier"). Also, an event that took five minutes can go on for many pages, while years can be dismissed in such a phrase as, "twenty years later, she was playing with her grandchild," with two decades summed up in three words. The fabula has no point of view—it is everything from every possible perspective and told in every possible voice. But plot brings point of view, the selection of voice(s), the elimination of nonessential material, and a spectrum of significance among the characters, with many characters omitted altogether. There are three sets of roughly synonymous binaries that critics use to label what I am here calling *fabula* and *plot*: *fabula/ sjužet, histoire/discours,* and *story/plot.* I am arbitrarily choosing *fabula/ plot* to represent this binary. In the creation of a narrative, then, as the plot is constructed from the fabula, some things are selected for inclusion and some things are left out.

In the short story, omission assumes an even greater role because it is one of several techniques employed to create a complete narrative within a small space. Hemingway first articulated his theory of omission in *Death in the Afternoon* (1932). After stating that "Prose is architecture, not interior decoration, and the Baroque is over" (191)—his own version of Pound's second imagist tenet—he then discussed how the acquired knowledge of a writer's life experience is the hard earned fuel of fiction, concluding:

> If a writer of prose knows enough about what he is writing about he may omit things that he knows and the reader, if the writer is writing truly enough, will have a feeling of those things as strongly as though the writer had stated them. The dignity of movement of an ice-berg is due to only one-eighth of it being above water. A writer who omits things because he does not know them only makes hollow places in his writing. A writer who appreciates the seriousness of writing so little that he is anxious to make people see he is formally educated, cultured or well-bred is merely a popinjay. (*DIA* 192)

Hemingway iterated this iceberg theory in a 1958 interview with George Plimpton: "I always try to write on the principle of the iceberg. There is seven-eighths of it underwater for every part that shows. Anything you know you can eliminate and it only strengthens your iceberg. It is the part that doesn't show. If a writer omits something because he does not know it then there is a hole in the story" (Interview 235). His third and fourth statements on omission came in what was intended to be a preface for a student's edition of his short stories, the publication of which was later dropped (Art 3), and in a passage from his posthumous memoir, *A Moveable Feast* (75).

The three most oft-cited examples of Hemingway's use of omission are the suicide of Peduzzi in "Out of Season," the absence of any reference to the war in "Big Two-Hearted River," and the absence of the word "abortion" in "Hills Like White Elephants." These are all, however, red herrings that have little to do with the real function of omission in his fiction. Hemingway specifically pointed out the omission of the war from "Big Two-Hearted River" in a 1953 letter, noting, "It is a story about a boy who has come back from the war. The war is never mentioned though as far as I can remember" (*SL* 798). A few years later, he stated more assertively that Nick comes home "beat to the wide" from the war and that "the war, all mention of the war, anything about the war, is omitted" (Art 3). Concerning Peduzzi, the Italian fishing guide in "Out of Season," Hemingway claimed that he "had omitted the real end of [the story] which was that the old man hanged himself" and repeated his by now well-known theory of omission, that "the omitted part would strengthen the story and make people feel something more than they understood" (*MF* 75).

I don't deny that direct mentions of the war, the suicide, and the abortion are absent from these stories—in fact, he deliberately removed the war from "Big Two-Hearted River" when he deleted the original ending (see *NAS* 237). But these are hardly prime examples of Hemingway's use of omission. For example, we have only Hemingway's word that the real-life character upon whom Peduzzi was based took his own life, a claim the author made not only many decades later in *A Moveable Feast* but also in a Christmas Eve 1925 letter to Scott Fitzgerald (*SL* 180–81). Yet Paul Smith makes an airtight case that the real Peduzzi's alleged suicide could *not* have taken place before Hemingway wrote the story (*New* 4–5). In addition, the pathos of Peduzzi in "Out of Season" is amply clear, as is his alcoholism; there is no clue in the text that he will commit suicide, and this extratextual knowledge in no way affects the story. In other words, if it was indeed omitted, the effect of that omission was not to make readers "feel something more than they understood." Regarding "Big Two-Hearted River," in the context of *In Our Time*, the reader would already know that Nick was wounded in the war (in "Chapter VI") and would later have certainly known this in the larger context of the Nick Adams stories, where Nick's part in the war is featured. Eliminating any mention of the war increases the story's ambiguity when it is read out of context, leaves open the question of why Nick is so unhinged (see Lamb, "Fishing"), and provides rich fodder for critics, but it doesn't make readers feel more than they can understand so much as it causes them to reach conclusions they cannot textually support. As for "Hills Like White Elephants," although the couple does not mention the word "abortion," what adult reader wouldn't know that this is what they are arguing about? Although having them not mention it directly contributes to the verisimilitude of the story's dialogue, here the effect is to have readers feel what they do indeed understand.

Hemingway's statements on omission are no different from those of other story writers. For example, in 1922 Katherine Mansfield wrote in her journal: "[Chekhov] made a mistake in thinking that if he had had more time he would have written more fully, described the rain, and the midwife and the doctor having tea. The truth is one can get only *so much* into a story; there is always a sacrifice. One has to leave out what one knows and longs to use" (287). Note her emphasis on "what one knows," so strikingly similar to Hemingway's insistence on leaving out only what you know. In fact, a few years after Hemingway first articulated his iceberg theory, the same point was made in a posthumously published book by Rudyard Kipling, who used a different metaphor: "a tale from which pieces have been raked out is like a fire that has been poked. One does not know that the operation has been performed, but everyone feels the effect. Note, though, that the excised stuff must have been honestly written for inclusion. I found that when, to save the trouble, I 'wrote short' *ab initio* much salt went out of the work" (224). Kipling did his omitting after he had written a longer draft, while Hemingway tended to perform this process in his head from the start, but they are both saying the same thing—the raked fire and the iceberg are equivalent metaphors.

A theory of omission, then, is not peculiar to Hemingway (and in our next chapter we'll see how close his theory is to Willa Cather's); moreover, the above examples are hardly illustrative of it. Often, critics go astray by taking their cue from Hemingway himself. For instance, in the preface to the unpublished student's edition of his stories, Hemingway singled out five stories in which he had employed omission. In addition to "Big Two-Hearted River," he cited "The Sea Change," "Fifty Grand," "The Killers," and "A Clean, Well-Lighted Place." "The Sea Change" resembles "Hills Like White Elephants" in being related mainly through the dialogue of a couple in which the "problem" between them is not directly identified. It is easily deduced, however, that she has just revealed she left him for another woman and he has asked her to return to him. Just as the abortion in "Hills" is referred to by a surrogate word, an "operation," here the man refers to the woman's lesbianism as a "vice" and, later, a "perversion." Hemingway said of the story: "Everything is left out. I had seen the couple in the Bar Basque in St.-Jean-de-Luz and I knew the story too too well . . . So I left the story out. But it is all there. It is not visible but it is there" (Art 3). Aside from employing suggestive dialogue rather than direct statements about the woman's sexual orientation, beginning the story in the middle of their argument rather than giving the whole conversation, and not mentioning *lesbian*, the only elements omitted from this story are details and contexts from the real-life couple and other couples that Hemingway drew upon in constructing the narrative. Although, as with *abortion*, the omission of *lesbian* might result from the characters' own sensibilities (i.e., their feelings of social propriety render the word unspeakable), this does not justify an actual theory of omission.

In "Fifty Grand," a story about a prizefighter, Hemingway—on the advice of Fitzgerald—omitted the opening three pages, part of which duplicated an exchange between the real-life participants on whom the story was based (Art 3–4). "This information," Hemingway observed, "is what you call the background of a story. You throw it all away and invent from what you know" (Art 6). But this, again, is merely a matter of revision, cutting, and selection—not some special technique of omission. "The Killers" also drew upon a real-life situation. Hemingway claimed that he changed the boxer's name from Andre Anderson to Ole Andreson, and, "That story probably had more left out of it than anything I ever wrote. More even than when I left the war out of 'Big Two-Hearted River.' I left out all Chicago" (Art 11). Except for not specifying why the gunmen from Chicago have come to Summit, a town eleven miles away, to kill Andreson—which is germane to the fabula but not to the plot—and not providing a history of Chicago, which would have made the story into a Dreiser novel, it is hard to see how omission plays a more significant role here than in any other story. In "A Clean, Well-Lighted Place," Hemingway again claimed that he "left out everything. That is about as far as you can go" (Art 11). Although this story doesn't seem based on real-life characters, what's left out are details. We know the story is set in a Spanish-speaking country, but not necessarily where, and we know a little about the three main characters, but not much. The narrative is not cluttered with exposition, which is typical for Hemingway, and here the lack of detail serves to make the story more universal and to underline general existential anxieties suffered by the old man and understood by the older waiter. Surely there must be more to the theory and practice of omission than this.

In short, then, the examples Hemingway provides of omission are merely stories in which he did not specifically identify the topic being discussed by his characters ("Hills Like White Elephants" and "The Sea Change"), did not openly address something in their past ("Big Two-Hearted River"), excluded or changed material from the fabula ("Fifty Grand" and "The Killers"), or gave minimal exposition ("A Clean, Well-Lighted Place"). By contrast, he claimed that in "The Undefeated" he left nothing out, adding: "The stories where you leave it all in do not re-read like the ones where you leave it out. They understand easier, but when you have read them once or twice you can't re-read them" (Art 11). The differences between "The Undefeated" and these other stories are that it is longer and contains more exposition. Because of the greater exposition, it is closer to being a realist story, rather than a modern story in which the reader must fill in the blanks and can interpret the text in a variety of ways. This latter, modernist method of narration is typical of the Hemingway story, but again, it hardly justifies a theory of omission in its own right.

The most comprehensive study of Hemingway's art of omission is Susan F. Beegel's *Hemingway's Craft of Omission,* which provides fascinating insights into how Hemingway transmuted the material of his experience into art. Hemingway's process of revision, she observes, "was principally a business of omission, of discovering the story in the stream of consciousness, and eliminating the personal material leading to and sometimes from it" (11). At the end of her study, Beegel sums up the five categories of material "left out." First, there is material from Hemingway's personal experience that may have given rise to the story in the first place. I would expand this category slightly beyond its biographical focus to include all material from the real or imagined fabula that doesn't find its way into the text. The omitted material from this category is most discernible in cases where Hemingway based a story on a real-life event he had either heard of or experienced, as in "After the Storm." The second category consists of experiences affecting the author during the time of composition that somehow influence the story but are never mentioned, since they are not part of the fabula. For example, Beegel insightfully notes how "Hemingway's conflicting admiration of and disillusionment with F. Scott Fitzgerald may have influenced the . . . themes of professional integrity and corruption" in "Fifty Grand" (90). Neither of these kinds of omission, however, is peculiar to Hemingway. For example, in *The Portrait of a Lady,* Henry James does not address his personal concerns with what it means to be an American (he had recently moved permanently to Europe), but this theme pervades the text.

The third category of omitted knowledge, which we will explore in our next chapter, concerns feelings. As Beegel observes, Hemingway's early fiction tended to focus on objects and actions, allowing the reader to respond to these without the author directly stating his characters' or his own emotional responses. Pound's mentoring and Eliot's poetry reinforced this tendency. Hemingway's fiction presents the objective data—this is the "tip of the iceberg"—but it leaves unstated the characters' and the author's responses to that data. "The underwater part of the iceberg is the emotion, deeply felt by reader and writer alike, but represented in the text solely by its 'tip'—[what Eliot termed] the objective correlative" (91).

The final two categories of omission Beegel cites are, first, moments that emerge from Hemingway's use of irony, and, second, the links between omission and his thematic concerns with "nothingness." Irony, by definition, employs omission, since it is "dependent on the reader's recognition that the experience expressed in the text is at odds with other, omitted experience" (91). I'll illustrate with two examples. At the end of "Indian Camp" when young Nick Adams feels that he will never die, the reader knows otherwise. In "In Another Country," the narrator is told that the Italian major had not married his young wife, who has died suddenly from pneumonia, until he knew that he would be invalided out of the war. The narrator does not point out the irony, nor does he link it to similar wartime ironies or use it to generalize about life; in fact, he says nothing about it. But the reader draws on his or her own experience and feels something more than, perhaps, he or she understands. The omissions arising from irony, however, are no different in Hemingway than in other ironic authors. As for the "thematic" category of omission—what Beegel terms the "significant omission at the heart of the universe" and "what Harold Bloom has called 'the Real Absence' in Hemingway's" fiction: "When everything is left out, nothing remains, and like 'A Clean, Well-Lighted Place,' Hemingway's archetypal story of 'nada,' much of his writing is ultimately about nothing" or about nothingness (Beegel 91–92). But this, too, has nothing to do with omission as a technique—it's a thematic concern.

What, then, can we say about omission in the Hemingway story? I believe he employs three types of omission: a minor form having to do with his general tendency toward concision, a form in which some piece of knowledge important to the story is mentioned or implied but barely treated, and a major form that derives from his method of objectivity, which I will shortly define as impressionism.

There are four kinds of minor omission. First, he usually eliminates or severely condenses formal exposition. More than just beginning in medias res rather than ab ovo, he often presents no exposition at the beginning or anywhere in the story. Second, he often implies exposition through indirect reference rather than statement, allowing the reader to fill in the blanks. For example, in "Cross-Country Snow," after Nick and George ski down a slope with Nick skiing in one manner and George then skiing "in telemark position, kneeling; one leg forward and bent, the other trailing," Nick tells George, "I can't telemark with my leg" (SS 184). Because Hemingway doesn't explain this, the reader must assume either that Nick has hurt his leg or else that he doesn't have enough strength in it to telemark. Hemingway will not intrude to explain, or even to define *telemark* more fully, and often when presenting a sequence of technical actions by characters who are expert in something, he will merely let them speak and act as they do without caring whether readers understand either their lingo or the nature of their actions. Third, Hemingway omits implied words and phrases, anything that readers can surmise for themselves. In "Cat in the Rain," at the end of the first paragraph a waiter is "looking out at the empty square." The next paragraph begins, "The American wife stood at the window looking out" (*SS* 167). It is implied by juxtaposition and the repetition of "looking out" that she is gazing at that same "empty square," so he can omit this information. Nor does he connect that sentence to the next sentence in which a cat is crouching under a table, but the reader understands that this is what the woman is staring at.[3] I term this sort of omission an *implication omission;* what is omitted is implied and clear, and the reader both feels *and* understands it. The fourth kind of minor omission is the elimination of connecting actions. Hemingway moves the reader quickly through a sequence to get to where he wants to go by omitting actions within the sequence, as in this snippet from "The End of Something":

> Marjorie stepped out of the boat and Nick pulled the boat high up the beach.
>   "What's the matter, Nick?" Marjorie asked.
>   "I don't know," Nick said, getting wood for a fire.
>   They made a fire with driftwood. Marjorie went to the boat and brought a blanket. (*SS* 109)

In a few words we go from the boat to sitting before the fire, and even have time for a brief exchange. All of these examples of minor omission have to do with, as I've said, concision—in Hemingway, a spartan form of removing from the narrative all words and information that are not absolutely necessary.

The second type of omission has to do with important knowledge that is implied but not explained—and sometimes not even clearly implied. Abortion is not mentioned in "Hills Like White Elephants," but it is clear that this is what the characters are discussing. What Dr. Fischer in "God Rest You Merry, Gentlemen" got in trouble for on the coast may have been his performing abortions, but in this case it is not clear (Lamb, "Critique" 29). And then there's the war in "Big Two-Hearted River" and the suicide in "Out of Season," both of which are omitted and cannot be inferred by the reader.

Aside from these sorts of omissions, however, a third major form of omission exists in Hemingway's stories, one that, I believe, he is really referring to in his various theoretical statements. It is Beegel's third category—the subjective emotional responses of characters and of the narrator, whether first person or third person, to the actions and events of the narrative. To see exactly what Hemingway meant by *omission*—as opposed to selection, concision, and minimal exposition—we must now turn to how he portrayed the consciousnesses of his characters. Something huge is indeed omitted in Hemingway's stories, and the omitted parts do give the reader a more powerful feeling of those things than if the author had stated them.

3

Depicting Consciousness in Modern Fiction

EXPRESSIONISM AND IMPRESSIONISM FROM CRANE TO

CATHER AND HEMINGWAY

Watch what happens today. If we get into a fish see exactly what it is that everyone does. If you get a kick out of it while he is jumping remember back until you see exactly what the action was that gave you the emotion. Whether it was the rising of the line from the water and the way it tightened like a fiddle string until drops started from it, or the way he smashed and threw water when he jumped. Remember what the noises were and what was said. Find what gave you the emotion; what the action was that gave you the excitement. Then write it down making it clear so the reader will see it too and have the same feeling that you had.

—Hemingway, *By-Line*

What Hemingway went for was that direct pictorial contact between eye and object, between object and reader. To get it he cut out a whole forest of verbosity. He got back to clean fundamental growth. He trimmed off explanation, discussion, even comment; he hacked off all metaphorical floweriness; he pruned off the dead, sacred clichés; until finally, through the sparse trained words, there was a view.

—H. E. Bates, *The Modern Short Story*

All literary historical genres possess an epistemological dimension: How can the self know the world? Related to this question is another: Where does "reality" reside? Generally speaking, American narrative from the mid-nineteenth through the mid-twentieth century swung between two main foci: what might be called a *world-out-there* and a *world-in-here*. That is to say, throughout this period we see a pendulumlike movement between fiction that locates reality in the "objective" external world and fiction that locates it in the "subjective" internal landscape of the mind. For romance writers, the truest reality lay in the middle, in what Hawthorne termed a "neutral territory, somewhere between the real world and fairy-land, where the Actual and the Imaginary may meet, and each imbue itself with the nature of the other" (*The Scarlet Letter* 35). For Hawthorne, the "actual" was the objective world and the "imaginary" was the subjective mind—reality was produced in tandem, and the romance was the transgeneric fictional form in which this combination could best be represented. For the romance writer, verisimilitude had to take into account both realities—that of the world-out-there and of the world-in-here. Thus, if one looks at a tree in the moonlight and sees a monster, then the "truth" is that what one sees is both a tree *and* a monster; the subjective truth is not subordinated to the objective. Realists, on the other hand, located reality purely in the external world and believed that the way to know it was to strip away subjective associations and view it as it was; in their formulation, the "imaginary" was an impediment to viewing the "actual" and how it functioned. In Twain's *Life on the Mississippi,* the passenger looks at the river (a synecdoche for the world) and sees "nothing but all manner of pretty pictures in it," but the pilot, who knows how to read the river/world, can view the pretty pictures and see in them the underlying reality they represent (94–96). The realists did not ignore the existence of the world-in-here, but they only thought it "real" to the extent that it mirrored, or accurately grasped, the observable external world. For them, a tree was a tree, no matter what one projected onto it. The naturalists also believed that reality was located in the external world, and in biological forces within individuals, but, as opposed to the realists, they felt that humans were merely a part of that world—they did not acknowledge a human/extrahuman binary—and they did not believe that humans had the ability to read the world, let alone act meaningfully in it. Crane's Henry Fleming may think, by the end of *The Red Badge of Courage,* that he understands both the external world and his own mind, but the text makes it amply and ironically clear that he grasps very little.

By the time we get to modernism, there has been another major swing of the pendulum. The external world is incoherent, fragmented, and yields no meaning; only the human mind can provide order. This order, to invoke Wallace Stevens, may be nothing more than a necessary fiction, but it is all we have. Ultimately, for such modernists as Stevens, reality resides in the mind: "Divinity must live within herself: / Passions of rain, or moods in falling snow; / Grievings in loneliness, or unsubdued / Elations when the forest blooms; gusty / Emotions on wet roads on autumn nights; / All pleasures and all pains, remembering / The bough of summer and the winter branch" ("Sunday Morning," *Poems* 67). The artist creates meaning and order from the chaos of the external world: "I placed a jar in Tennessee, /

And round it was, upon a hill. / It made the slovenly wilderness / Surround that hill." The man-made jar that produces order takes "dominion everywhere" ("The Anecdote of the Jar," *Poems* 76).[1] Given the modernists' belief that the external world is fragmented and holds no inherent meaning, and that order and reality are produced by the mind and the form it imposes on that world, it is no coincidence that central to modernist fiction is its focus on consciousness and the unconscious.

The above is a fairly standard critical take on the general perspectives of romancers, realists, naturalists, and modernists toward the relation of self and world. But it tells us nothing about how these epistemological assumptions are actualized in their fiction. Here, however, a focus on technique redeems us, for all historical genres must represent consciousness, and the methods by which they represent it are of far greater concern to writers (and should mean something to critics) than whether one is labeled a romancer or a modernist.

In real life, the human consciousness apprehends the external world through perception and sensation, which are *parallel and not serial* processes. We do not perceive something in the external world and then have our emotional response to it, nor do we experience the feeling and then perceive what in the external world is making us feel that way. Rather, in the apprehension of any event by the consciousness, one internal pathway of the mind *records perceptions* of "what is going on out there" while another internal pathway *experiences sensations* of "what is being felt in here" (Humphrey 45–55), after which the mind synthesizes the two processes. The latter process—sensation—consists of what neuroscientists call *qualia,* or the individual's experiences of a property. For instance, if I look at a tomato in my hand, one quale might be my experience of the color red, another might be the scent of the tomato, another might be the feel of the tomato skin's texture, and so forth. All such experiences involve complexes of qualia, since a quale rarely exists in isolation.[2]

A quale is something much more complicated and subtle than any language available to describe it. We can say that facing a red wall causes a diffuse feeling of excitement or that looking at a green wall produces a feeling of calm, but we really have no way to communicate our sensation of "redness" or "greenness." Perceptions, on the other hand, can be represented in language with some specificity. I can say of that hypothetical tomato that it is large, red, and roughly round, that it smells ripe, feels soft, and tastes sweet—and someone else will have a fairly good sense of my perceptions of the tomato. But if I try to describe my sensations of "redness" or "round-ness" or "softness" or "sweetness"—my qualia of the tomato—language proves inadequate. Although perception may seem objective and sensation subjective, there can, in fact, be no "objective" experience of the external world by the consciousness. Both perception and sensation, the mind's instantaneous perception of what is going on out there and its equally instantaneous sensation of what is being felt in here, are ultimately subjective and peculiar to that mind, however much other minds might have similar perceptions and sensations in response to the same stimulus. Perception is more communicable because it involves a subject apprehending a material object outside of itself, whereas in sensation the subject is dealing with an ineffable experience within itself.

Diagram 1 indicates how consciousness experiences the external world. In this diagram, the objective data of the external world impress themselves upon (or are apprehended by) the five senses of the consciousness and produce immediate perceptions and sensations along different pathways in that consciousness.

Diagram 1

In representing consciousness experiencing the external world, fiction may attempt to depict perception, sensation, and what, in Diagram 1, I term *retrospective understanding,* which is the awareness the mind develops as it processes its perceptions and sensations. Most fiction depicts all three: a character's perceptions of external phenomena, the sensations these phenomena produce within the character, and what that character makes of his or her perceptions and sensations in retrospect. Even fiction that aims for a sense of immediacy by eliminating retrospective understanding tends to depict both perceptions and sensations. But Hemingway purposely limits himself to depicting perception, allowing readers to infer sensation, while Willa Cather focuses on sensation and expects readers to infer perception.

Hemingway and his contemporaries, of course, did not have the benefit of our recent discoveries in neuroscience and cognitive studies. For them, a diagram of how consciousness experiences the external world would appear simpler (see Diagram 2). In this rough schema, the objective data of the external world impress themselves upon (or are apprehended by) the five senses of consciousness and produce in that consciousness a subjective response. Although Hemingway would certainly have understood that perception, like sensation, takes place within the mind, he did not in his fiction distinguish between the objective data of the external world and the perceptions of it in the consciousness. He was more concerned with differentiating between "what is happening out there" (world) and "what is happening in here" (mind). For Hemingway and other writers of his day, the subjective response and the objective data that produce it are two sides of the same process. Since I am here delineating the perspective that informs Hemingway's art, I redefine impressionism and expressionism as technical methods for depicting consciousness in that type of fiction in which, as James Nagel puts it, "direct sensory experience is rendered without [the narrator's] expository intrusion into the flow" (*Crane* 21). This is the sort of fiction that Ford Madox Ford claims "renders" rather than "describes" ("Techniques" 31), and it is what Hemingway meant when he said that a writer "does not describe. He invents or *makes*" (Interview 237).

Diagram 2

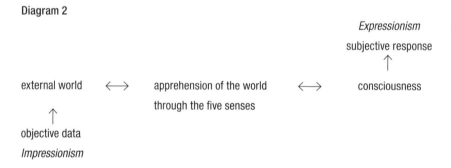

Fiction that focuses primarily on the subjective response in trying to depict consciousness is what I hereafter refer to as *expressionist,* and fiction that focuses on the external data is what I term *impressionist.* Before proceeding, however, I should present two caveats and an explanation. First, the sort of fiction I am discussing here is that which tries to represent consciousness at the moment of its instantaneous awareness, that attempts to produce a feeling of immediacy by placing the reader in *the moment as it*

is being experienced. All other kinds of depiction are retrospective; they portray consciousness after it has sorted out and processed the impressions and sensations it receives. Second, most fiction that aims for immediacy addresses the whole spectrum, presenting the impressions the mind receives (perceptions) as well as its emotional responses (sensations). Moreover, after it has presented both the objective data and the subjective response to that data, it then presents what that consciousness makes of it all in retrospect. Traditionally, all three of these processes have been termed *impressionism*, as in this classic 1935 definition by Ford: "It was perhaps [Stephen] Crane of all that school or gang—and not excepting Maupassant—who most observed that canon of Impressionism: 'You must render: never report.' You must never, that is to say, write: 'He saw a man aim a gat at him'; you must put it: 'He saw a steel ring directed at him.' Later you must get in that, in his subconsciousness, he recognized that the steel ring was the polished muzzle of a revolver . . . That is Impressionism! ("Techniques" 31–32). For Ford, then, impressionism includes both the data of the external world that impress themselves on the consciousness and that consciousness's retrospective understanding of what those impressions mean.

Subsequent literary critics have concurred. For example, James Nagel posits that impressionism covers a spectrum: we have the impressions, whether focusing on the data (perceptions) or the receiving consciousness (sensations), and we have the retrospective understanding. All are subsumed under the rubric *impressionism*: "Depending upon emphasis, an Impressionistic writer can modulate his fiction between the 'objective' stance of presenting sensations at the instant of reception, and before cognitive processes have begun to interpret and formulate them into patterns of meaning, and the 'subjective' stance of recording the internalization of sensory experience, what a given mind understands having received and analyzed the data" (*Crane* 22). In this definition, perception is mistaken for sensation, the "subjective" is conflated with the "retrospective," and we are left with the question—"What isn't impressionism?" For reasons we shall soon see, however, I believe that each of these processes requires its own term—that what is now seen as impressionism needs to be separated into impressionism, expressionism, and retrospective understanding—which are three very different modes of depicting consciousness.

In redefining impressionism as well as expressionism, I ought to note their historical foundations in the world of visual art, from which they

both originally derived. Impressionism was a style of painting that flourished in France beginning in the 1870s. Although complex, its most distinguishing feature was the effort to represent through surfaces a particular
transitory moment rather than a more formally and retrospectively composed picture intended to reveal depths. Expressionism, which began in
Germany in the 1910s, was partially a revolt against impressionism. Rather
than mimetically reproducing the impressions of the scene, expressionists
sought to portray the emotions these impressions evoked in the artist. Although expressionists depicted the external world, the objects of that world
were not accurate representations so much as they were externalized depictions of subjective states. Expressionists typically used exaggeration, dis-
tortion, dislocation, and fantasy to disrupt the surface of impressionism
and wrench from the scene the truth of the artist's inner experience. Expressionist art rejected any form of realism and sought to render, according to Ulrich Weisstein, "soul states and the violent emotions welling up
from the innermost recesses of the subconscious" (23). If impressionism in
painting focused almost solely on the world-out-there, expressionism was
mainly a depiction of the world-in-here.

Both of these movements heavily influenced literature, and there are
clear affinities between, say, impressionism in art and imagism in poetry,
or expressionism in art and the expressionistic techniques of such literary
works as Eugene O'Neill's *The Emperor Jones* and T. S. Eliot's *The Waste
Land*. The early twentieth-century German critics who initially addressed
the question of these artistic modes in fiction viewed naturalism, impressionism, and expressionism as a logical sequence. For them, as Julia Van
Gunsteren observes, naturalism "was dominated by the outer world" and
impressionism by "the meeting of the outer world and the inner ego," but
expressionism is ruled "wholly by the inner ego" (49). The subsequent practice of subsuming under impressionism all perceptions and sensations at
the moment they are being experienced (and in some cases also mistakenly including retrospective understanding), regardless of whether the fiction focuses on the external world or on the subjective response, began
with these critics. Expressionism was therefore applied not to fiction that
focuses on the subjective response but reserved for fiction that is hyperre-
alist and surrealist, best exemplified in the works of such writers as Franz
Kafka and Bruno Schultz.

I do not, however, wish to accept this current terminological muddle
and settle for a definition of impressionism which does not distinguish be-

tween fiction that focuses purely on the impressions of the external world recorded by the mind and fiction that focuses solely on the subjective response. As for retrospective understanding, this has nothing whatsoever to do with impressionism, which *always* depicts the moment as it is being experienced. Nor do I wish to substitute such terms as *objective* and *subjective* because these vague words fail to distinguish between the subjective response to impressions and the more radically subjective modes of surrealism that seem divorced from mimetic fiction.

Critics typically refer to Stephen Crane as a naturalist or an impressionist, depending on whether they address his literary themes and philosophical beliefs, on the one hand, or his mode of presentation, on the other. But Crane was both an impressionist *and* an expressionist (as I have redefined these terms). Looking at passages from *The Red Badge of Courage,* we can see how he alternated between these modes. Here is the scene in which Henry Fleming stumbles across the corpse of his comrade:

[P1]   Near the threshold he stopped, horror-stricken at the sight of a thing.

[P2]   He was being looked at by a dead man who was seated with his back against a columnlike tree. The corpse was dressed in a uniform that once had been blue, but was now faded to a melancholy shade of green. The eyes, staring at the youth, had changed to the dull hue to be seen on the side of a dead fish. The mouth was open. Its red had changed to an appalling yellow. Over the gray skin of the face ran little ants. One was trundling some sort of a bundle along the upper lip.

[P3]   The youth gave a shriek as he confronted the thing. He was for moments turned to stone before it. He remained staring into the liquid-looking eyes. The dead man and the living man exchanged a long look. Then the youth cautiously put one hand behind him and brought it against a tree. Leaning upon this he retreated, step by step, with his face still toward the thing. He feared that if he turned his back the body might spring up and stealthily pursue him.

[P4]   The branches, pushing against him, threatened to throw him over upon it. His unguided feet, too, caught aggravatingly in brambles; and with it all he received a subtle suggestion to touch the corpse. As he thought of his hand upon it he shuddered profoundly.

[P5]   At last he burst the bonds which had fastened him to the spot and fled, unheeding the underbrush. He was pursued by a sight of the black ants swarming greedily upon the gray face and venturing horribly near to the eyes. (126–27)

Except for the phrase "being looked at by a dead man" and the adjectives *melancholy* and *appalling,* which present Henry's subjective sense of the scene, the second paragraph is completely impressionist. Crane presents only the external data and refrains from depicting either the youth's or his own subjective responses. In lieu of such depiction, the reader supplies the emotional response based upon his or her own experience (in Crane's day, this experience would come from memories of actual corpses or photographs; nowadays, it would be supplemented by film, television, and news media). We are clearly in Henry's consciousness—for instance, "some sort of bundle" would be more specific if this were omniscient narration. But we only get the impressions recorded by Henry's mind, not what he makes of this data (retrospection) or how he feels about it (expressionism). The first two sentences of the entire passage do provide glimpses of the upcoming subjective response: Crane states that the youth is "horror-stricken," and the phrase "He was being looked at" depicts the youth's feelings. After the impressionist second paragraph, the third paragraph combines statements about the objective data ("gave a shriek," "remained staring," "put one hand behind him and brought it against a tree," the youth's retreat from the corpse), but it also adds Crane's representations of what the youth is feeling ("turned to stone," "exchanged a long look," the youth's fears that the corpse might "stealthily pursue him"). This continues into the fourth paragraph, which combines physical sensations of the brambles touching the youth with the youth's own inner promptings to touch the corpse. In the final paragraph we are fully immersed in the youth's consciousness, and the objective and subjective have merged; he is pursued by the memory of what he has seen.

In contrast to the impressionist second paragraph above, here is one of many passages in which Crane employs pure expressionism to depict Henry's subjective state:

His fingers twined nervously about his rifle. He wished that he was an engine of annihilating power. He felt that he and his companions were being taunted and derided from sincere convictions that they were poor and puny. His knowledge of his inability to take vengeance for it made his rage into a dark and stormy specter, that possessed him and made him dream of abominable cruelties. The tormentors were flies sucking insolently at his blood, and he thought that he would have given his life for a revenge of seeing their faces in pitiful plights. (173)

Aside from the first sentence, which shows Henry engaged in a specific activity, this passage expresses his inner psychological state by means of abstract language and metaphor. As is typical in expressionist depiction, the passage lacks specificity and referentiality because it is virtually impossible to describe pure feeling in language. The sort of language that does describe emotion with some precision (e.g., psychological analysis) distances itself from those feelings being described, and Crane wishes to plunge the reader into the torment transpiring in Henry's mind.

In *The Red Badge of Courage,* Crane's combination of impressionism and expressionism works to immerse the reader in the flow of Henry's experience. He impressionistically presents Henry's perceptions, and we respond with our own emotions (which we use to infer Henry's emotions), or Crane expressionistically depicts what is going on in Henry's mind, the vagueness of which is somewhat ameliorated by the impressionist details of the prose surrounding it. What we rarely get are the sorts of markers used in histories to describe battles, for such orderings are always retrospective, especially for those directly engaged in combat. These markers would act to distance us from Henry's experience of confusion amid the chaos of battle. Aside from those moments of calm in which Henry reflects on what has happened, Crane doesn't try to organize his paragraphs or even his sentences in expository order, giving us only the impressions as they are received by Henry:

A furious order caused commotion in the artillery. An officer on a bounding horse made maniacal motions with his arms. The teams went swinging up from the rear, the guns were whirled about, and the battery scampered away. The cannon with their noses poked slantingly at the ground grunted and grumbled like stout men, brave but with objections to hurry (121).

This method of presenting impressions in the order they are received by the experiencing consciousness is a trademark of Crane's impressionism, which tremendously influenced, among others, his friend Joseph Conrad, who is more closely associated with the technique, as in the famous passage in *Heart of Darkness* (1899) in which Marlowe comes to realize that his boat is under attack by natives shooting arrows (45). Ian Watt refers to this technique as "delayed decoding," which "combines the forward temporal progression of the mind, as it receives messages from the outside world, with the much slower reflexive process of making out their meaning" (175).[3]

Another of the many authors whom Crane influenced was Willa Cather. Although born in 1873, twenty-six years before Hemingway, the two had much in common. Both commenced their writing careers as journalists, strove for concision, and brought to their fiction a significant theory of omission. Cather, who claimed to have spoken at length with Crane when he came to Nebraska in 1895, later wrote of him: "I doubt whether he ever spent a laborious half-hour in doing his duty by detail—in enumerating, like an honest auctioneer. If he saw one thing in a landscape that thrilled him, he put it on paper, but he never tried to make a faithful report of everything else within his field of vision" ("Introduction" xi).[4] This comment speaks directly to Crane's concision in selecting a few effective details and indirectly to his omission of other details (although it leaves aside his mode of presentation).[5]

Cather had not started out writing concisely, but from the mid-1910s on she was working toward a new aesthetic that would become pronounced in her fiction of the following decade, when she would hit the peak of her career. In 1920, she wrote: "Art, it seems to me, should simplify. That, indeed, is very nearly the whole of the higher artistic process; finding what conventions of form and what detail one can do without and yet preserve the spirit of the whole—so that all that one has suppressed and cut away is there to the reader's consciousness as much as if it were in type on the page" ("Art of Fiction" 939). In her 1922 essay, "The Novel Démeublé" ("The Unfurnished Novel"), she elaborates on this theory. After complaining that fiction has "had too much of the interior decorator" since the days of Balzac, she claims to see "hopeful signs that some of the younger writers are trying to break away from mere verisimilitude" and to "present their scene by suggestion rather than by enumeration. The higher processes of art are all processes of simplification." So far, Cather has been speaking about concision and the winnowing down of the many details that realist fiction employs for the purpose of verisimilitude. But then she moves toward something that anticipates Hemingway's later iceberg theory: "Whatever is felt upon the page without being specifically named there—that, one might say, is created. It is the inexplicable presence of the thing not named . . . that gives high quality" (835–37). She finishes with a flourish: "How wonderful it would be if we could throw all the furniture out of the window; and along with it, all the meaningless reiterations concerning physical sensations, all the tiresome old patterns, and leave the room as bare as the stage of a Greek theatre . . . ; leave the scene bare for the play of emotions, great and little . . . The elder Dumas enunciated a great principle when he said that to make a drama, a man needed one passion, and four walls" (837).

Cather and Hemingway are the yin and yang of American modernist minimalism. In depicting consciousness, they seek the same goal and both employ an aesthetics of omission and concision, but what one omits, the other features. Here is Cather's first-person narrator in *My Ántonia* describing the coming of spring:

> There were none of the signs of spring for which I used to watch in Virginia, no budding woods or blooming gardens. There was only—spring itself; the throb of it, the light restlessness, the vital essence of it everywhere; in the sky, in the swift clouds, in the pale sunshine, and in the warm, high wind—rising suddenly, sinking suddenly, impulsive and playful like a big puppy that pawed you and then lay down to be petted. If I had been tossed down blindfold on that red prairie, I should have known that it was spring. (790)

This is pure expressionism. Rather than any specific data from the external world that would conjure up spring in the mind of the reader—what Cather meant by "all the meaningless reiterations concerning physical sensations" (she means "perceptions")—we get the lyrical subjective response to that data from the mind of the first-person narrator. The "signs of spring" are all vaguely drawn—budding woods, blooming gardens, clouds, sunshine, wind—but what is specific is Cather's representation of her narrator's sensations of spring. The reader must infer from the character's subjective response the external data producing it—"all that one has suppressed and cut away is there to the reader's consciousness as much as if it were in type on the page." This process is modernist in that it makes the reader participate in producing the text, and it is minimalist and expressionist in that it only presents one side of the coin, the subjective response. A typical realist text would have given both the objective data and the subjective response, leaving readers with no role in making the fiction come to life.

Like Cather—who wanted to "throw all the furniture out of the window" and strip the stage "bare for the play of emotions"—Hemingway, too, sought to defenestrate furniture. But his targets were statements about emotions. For him, the "play of emotions" depended on retaining selected physical details that would evoke these feelings in the reader. In *Death in the Afternoon* he recalled his early years in Paris, when he was fashioning his craft:

> I was trying to write then and I found the greatest difficulty, aside from knowing truly what you really felt, rather than what you were supposed to feel, and had been taught to feel, was to put down what really happened in action; what the actual things were which produced the emotion that you experienced. In writing for a newspaper you told what happened and, with one trick and another, you communicated the emotion aided by the element of timeliness which gives a certain emotion to any account of something that has happened on that day; but the real thing, the sequence of motion and fact which made the emotion and which would be as valid in a year or in ten years or, with luck and if you stated it purely enough, always, was beyond me and I was working very hard to try to get it. (2)

A few pages later, he gives a specific example of what he means by "the sequence of motion and fact" (the external data) that causes the "emotion" (the subjective response). He recounts a *novillada* (an apprentice bullfight) in Madrid, in which Domingo Hernandorena—a rusty matador who "could not control the nervousness of his feet"—made a "technical error" that caused him to be injured by a bull, his leg torn open from hip to knee (*DIA* 17–19). Hemingway describes the real-life event fully, presenting the action and his commentary on the action, as well as the crowd's unsympathetic response to Hernandorena, during and after his wounding, and the reasons for their attitude.

In *Death in the Afternoon,* the story of this incompetent matador exemplifies poor bullfighting technique. But it causes Hemingway to wonder about technique of another kind: were he to use this event as the fabula for a work of fiction, how would he evoke the complex emotions arising from this matador's performance:

> For myself, not being a bullfighter, . . . the problem was one of depiction and waking in the night I tried to remember what it was that seemed just out of my remembering and that was the thing that I had really seen and, finally, remembering all around it, I got it. When he stood up, his

face white and dirty and the silk of his breeches opened from waist to knee, it was the dirtiness of the rented breeches, the dirtiness of his slit underwear and the clean, clean, unbearably clean whiteness of the thigh bone that I had seen, and it was that which was important. (*DIA* 20)

From the many images surrounding Hernandorena's incompetent bull-fighting—his nervousness and twitching feet, his bungled attempt to lure the bull to him by getting down on his knees, the crowd's disdain during the fight and their lack of sympathy afterward—Hemingway found the objective detail that would evoke the emotions of the event without his directly stating these emotions.

Hemingway did, in fact, create a brief story based on such an incompetent bullfight in "chapter 13" of *in our time* ("Chapter XI" of *IOT*):

The crowd shouted all the time and threw pieces of bread down into the ring, then cushions and leather wine bottles, keeping up whistling and yelling. Finally the bull was too tired from so much bad sticking and folded his knees and lay down and one of the *cuadrilla* leaned out over his neck and killed him with the *puntillo*. The crowd came over the barrera and around the torero and two men grabbed him and held him and some one cut off his pigtail and was waving it and a kid grabbed it and ran away with it. Afterwards I saw him at the café. He was very short with a brown face and quite drunk and he said after all it has happened before like that. I am not really a good bull fighter. (*iot* 23)

The emotions of this vignette should be disgust for the unruly crowd and the incompetent bullfighter who knows he doesn't belong in the ring. The only pity is for the bull, who is prematurely killed, almost out of the author's sympathetic desire to remove him from this disgraceful exhibition of bad bullfighting. Nowhere in this impressionist vignette are these emotions stated; only the carefully selected sequence of motions and facts are given. But the reader infers the emotions of the crowd, the bullfighter, the *puntillero,* the author, and perhaps even the bull.

Like Crane, Hemingway often employs delayed decoding; the sensory perceptions are presented as they appear in the experiencing consciousness, simulating how the mind records them before it starts processing them. The composition of such passages seems informal and spontaneous, although of course Hemingway is deliberately crafting them. In "An Alpine Idyll," the narrator and his friend John have been skiing in the mountains and are now in the valley heading toward an inn. The opening sentences emphasize the effect of the sun through a series of repetitions in different contexts:

> [1] It was hot coming down into the valley even in the early morning. [2] The sun melted the snow from the skis we were carrying and dried the wood. [3] It was spring in the valley but the sun was very hot. (*SS* 343)

Note how Hemingway disperses expository information across these three sentences and how different it would have been with a tighter organization, one produced by the mind retrospectively, for instance: "Early one spring morning, we were coming down into the valley. The sun was very hot and it melted the snow from the skis we were carrying, drying the wood." The rewritten passage is more strictly composed and even more concise (thirty words in two sentences versus Hemingway's forty in three sentences). It gathers up the time, season, and location markers of the original passage into an opening sentence, and then observes the sun and its effect on the skis.

But reordering the information loses the immediacy. The narrative voice of the rewritten passage is more distant because retrospective; such a formal organization indicates that the narrator has had time to compose his thoughts about the experience. The Hemingway passage, by contrast, begins with the narrator noting the heat as they walk, adding as a seemingly spontaneous afterthought that it is early morning, which indirectly emphasizes just how hot it is. Then the passage presents two related concrete details that further emphasize the heat (melting the snow and drying the wood), it further emphasizes the unusual heat (it is not only early morning but also spring), and it concludes with the direct statement the whole passage has prepared us for—"the sun was very hot." The point of this opening is to make us *feel* the heat, and Hemingway does this in two ways. First, he devotes a sentence to "hot," then a sentence to "sun," then a sentence combining "hot" and "sun," and he places these sentences in the context of "early morning," "valley," and "spring." Second, the narrator lets the reader compose the passage in his or her own mind by organizing the impressions he reports as he experiences them, so that when he finally says "the sun was very hot," we have already felt this before thinking it.

A few paragraphs later, in a passage summarizing their month of skiing, after noting that the snow was only good in the early morning and in the evening (two more indirect allusions to the hot sun), he observes:

"The rest of the time it was spoiled by the sun. We were both tired of the sun. You could not get away from the sun." This would seem to be an expressionist passage in that it lacks impressionist details (in fact, it contains only one—the sun) and it appears to focus on the narrator's subjective response. Yet the three repetitions of *sun* keep us riveted on the external by adding to the semic code of the sun (it spoils skiing, it tires us, you can't escape it), while the subjective emotions expressed are as vague as were the objective data in the expressionist passage from Cather's *My Ántonia*. In addition, the repetitions of *sun* throughout the passage begin mimetically to oppress the reader in the same way that the actual sun is oppressing the characters. The rest of the paragraph continues to build up this effect of the sun's oppressiveness and how it is spoiling everything: the only escape is in shadows or a hut, but then your sweat freezes; you can't sit outside "without dark glasses"; "the sun had been very tiring"; you can't "rest in it"; it's "too late in the spring" to be skiing; he's "tired of skiing"; they've "stayed too long"; the drinking water melting off the hut's tin roof tastes bad; skiing tastes bad; and successive "I was glad to be done" with this clauses. The prose continues to make the reader tired of the sun, both its specific repetitions in various contexts and its pervasiveness throughout the text. The characters finally escape the actual sun, but it reemerges in dialogue as the innkeeper asks how their skiing went and the narrator replies, "A little too much sun." The innkeeper sums it up: "Yes. There's too much sun this time of year" (SS 343–44).

After ordering beers, they sit at a table, and Hemingway uses this moment of repose to present another Crane-like series of immediate perceptions:

> The sun came through the open window and shone through the beer bottles on the table. The bottles were half full. There was a little froth on the beer in the bottles, not much because it was very cold. It collared up when you poured it into the tall glasses. I looked out of the open window at the white road. The trees beside the road were dusty. Beyond was a green field and a stream. There were trees along the stream and a mill with a water wheel. Through the open side of the mill I saw a long log and a saw in it rising and falling. No one seemed to be tending it. There were four crows walking in the green field. One crow sat in a tree watching. Outside on the porch the cook got off his chair and passed into the hall that led back into the kitchen. Inside, the sunlight shone through the

empty glasses on the table. John was leaning forward with his head on his arms. (*SS* 345)

Although we see Crane's method of presenting impressions as they impinge on the narrator's consciousness before being processed, another powerful artistic influence is present here: the post-Impressionism and proto-Cubism of Paul Cézanne. Edward F. Fry observes that Cézanne moved beyond the Renaissance technique of creating the illusion of three-dimensional space from a one-point perspective. He undid that illusion by flattening his paintings, "integrating surface and depth" by the "running together of planes otherwise separated in space" (14). That is what one eye sees when it looks at a scene.

In this respect, the above Hemingway passage is the equivalent of a Cézanne painting. The perceived objects of the tableau are dispersed across a decentered canvas, and the narrator's eye directs the reader's/observer's attention from the scene's foreground to its depth and back again, covering the entire visual field. But these planes of space are flattened, so that the elements of the scene appearing within the frame of the window are rendered in the manner of a Cézanne landscape. From the white road to the crow in the tree, position markers are either absent or else indicate contiguity (e.g., "aside" or "along") but not levels of depth. The only exception is "beyond," when we move from the trees and road to the field and stream. But in this tableau, "beyond" points to height rather than depth. (Compare it with our next Hemingway passage, in which depth markers are prominent and restore the illusion of a three-dimensional perspective.)

Fry notes that Cézanne also went "beyond the break with tradition represented by the impressionists' optical realism, to a realism of the psychological process of perception itself." He would "organize his subject according to the separate acts of perception he had experienced; houses and other solid objects were depicted as the artist had conceptualized them after a long series of perceptions" (14). Hemingway's narrator's observations begin with his attention to the sun, proceed mostly metonymically through a number of otherwise unconnected images (each is connected only by its contiguity with the next image), and conclude with the sun, again underscoring how it cannot be escaped. The sun directs his eye to the half-full beer bottles it shines upon; the beer is cold in contrast to the sun; he looks out the open window from where the sun is coming and sees the road; the road is contiguous with the trees (and they are dusty because of the sun);

his eye carries past this sight to the field and stream; the stream is contiguous with the other trees and a mill; the mill is connected to the log and saw (note that he doesn't try to explain why the saw is rising and falling); his eye catches the four crows in the field; his eye picks out another crow in a tree (a second observer); the movement of the cook from the porch to the kitchen redirects his attention back inside; and the sunlight is still shining through the glasses. Although each observed object is the conceptualization of many impressions, Hemingway strips them down to one striking visual detail each (as Cézanne did with color and shape), thus creating the illusion that each is being perceived for the first time. During this passage, he and John finish their beers, but he doesn't state this directly because he can omit the information and still convey it (an example of what I have termed *implication omission*), and because it would interfere with the seemingly free associative report of the images. (It would show you the narrator's mind actively processing the scene.)

This technique, which novelist Russell Banks terms "the logic of the eye," has had an incalculable influence on subsequent writers. Banks notes that Hemingway learned it by "studying Cézanne" but that he himself learned it "from reading Hemingway":

> Look at "Hills Like White Elephants," or almost anything. Look at the physical description, how he moves from background to foreground. It's the logic of the eye. It's not the logic of the paragraph. And it's not the logic of exposition. It's the logic of the eye. The eye moves from distance to middle ground to foreground. And he will describe a scene in exactly the same way. Or it moves from foreground to middle distance to background. It doesn't swirl around. Or follow any other logic. It's a very physical way of setting a scene.
>
> And that was because the logic of a Cézanne painting is the logic of an eye. (qtd. in Paul 117)

Terry Tempest Williams also makes this connection between Hemingway's impressionism, "the logic of the eye," and the influence of Cézanne: "What I can tell you as a writer of natural history, a storyteller of the American West, is that Ernest Hemingway has been a powerful mentor, in terms of what it means to create a landscape impressionistically on the page, to make it come alive, pulse, breathe, to 'make the country so you could walk into it.'" She, too, concludes, "Hemingway studied Cézanne. We study Hemingway" (11). In the passage from "An Alpine Idyll," we move from the foreground to the middle ground to the background, then back to the middle ground and finally return to the foreground. This logic of the eye is completely impressionist. The logic of an expository paragraph, on the other hand, is always retrospective—a logical arrangement of the impressions after they have been gathered. Such a logic can never accurately represent the moment as it is being experienced.

For example, a more formally organized passage opens "Che Ti Dice la Patria?" as the narrator and a friend drive through fascist Italy toward Spezia:

> The road of the pass was hard and smooth and not yet dusty in the early morning. Below were the hills with oak and chestnut trees, and far away below was the sea. On the other side were snowy mountains.
>
> We came down from the pass through wooded country. There were bags of charcoal piled beside the road, and through the trees we saw charcoal-burners' huts. It was Sunday and the road, rising and falling, but always dropping away from the altitude of the pass, went through the scrub woods and through villages. (SS 290)

In this tableau, note the strategies Hemingway employs to emphasize the visual: the prominence of location markers ("Below were," "far below were," "On the other side were," "beside," "rising and falling," "dropping away"), the location/verb/subject forms of the sentences, and making the road rather than the passengers the real subject of the passage. Because the car is speeding along the road, however, the narrator hasn't the luxury of allowing his eye to wander lazily across the scene, as in "An Alpine Idyll," and so the images recorded are sparse and depicted in less detail: road, hills, oak and chestnut trees, snowy mountains, bags of charcoal, huts, villages. They are also less the result of contiguity than of the narrator's summary recollection of what he has seen along the way, which creates a pattern out of many individual images. As opposed to four specific crows in a field and one specific crow in a tree watching them, we have a more consciously ordered pattern of bags by the road, huts glimpsed between trees, and villages. Although the narrator tries to give the impression of the report being simultaneous with the images seen—note the interjected mention of its being Sunday, which has no necessary connection to the sentence or paragraph—nevertheless the passage is more formally composed, indicating that his mind has processed them.

Although highly atypical for him, Hemingway could also seem to write expressionistically, but his discourse differs markedly from Crane's or Cather's. In "A Way You'll Never Be" (which, in the present context, could aptly be called "A Way You'll Rarely Write"), a previously wounded Nick Adams is bicycling from Fornaci in an American uniform, ostensibly to demonstrate that America is about to enter the war and thereby improve the morale of the Italian troops. He comes across his former outfit, and his friend, Captain Paravicini, realizes that Nick is shell-shocked and has him lie down to rest. Nick's thoughts ramble incoherently as he recalls his wounding outside of Fossalta on the Piave River, including a recurrent reminiscence that he can't understand. In the following passages, taken from Nick's lengthy interior monologue, Hemingway's mode is as close to expressionism as it would ever get:

> . . . those were the nights the river ran so much wider and stiller than it should and outside of Fossalta there was a low house painted yellow with willows all around it and a low stable and there was a canal, and he had been there a thousand times and never seen it, but there it was every night as plain as the hill, only it frightened him. That house meant more than anything and every night he had it. That was what he needed but it frightened him especially when the boat lay there quietly in the willows on the canal, but the banks weren't like this river . . . If it didn't get so damned mixed up he could follow it all right. That was why he noticed everything in such detail to keep it all straight so he would know just where he was . . .

> He never dreamed about the front now any more but what frightened him so that he could not get rid of it was that long yellow house and the different width of the river. Now he was back here at the river, he had gone through that same town, and there was no house. Nor was the river that way. Then where did he go each night and what was the peril, and why would he wake, soaking wet, more frightened than he had ever been in a bombardment, because of a house and a long stable and a canal? (SS 408–409)

In his pioneering study of Hemingway, Philip Young insightfully ties this passage to the woundings near Fossalta experienced by Frederic Henry in *A Farewell to Arms*, Richard Cantwell in *Across the River and into the Trees*, and Hemingway in real life. Young also sees it as the key to what feelings Nick is repressing (and Hemingway omitting) in "Big Two-Hearted

River" and why Nick in that story is afraid to enter the swamp where the river narrows (*Reconsideration* 50–54, 120–21). I should add that Hemingway's wounding is also represented in the combination of Chapters VI and VII from *In Our Time;* in the first, Nick is wounded, and in the second an anonymous soldier is in a trench being bombarded at Fossalta. What we have here, Young suggests (165–71), is a repetition compulsion deriving from Hemingway's wounding at Fossalta di Piave near midnight on 8 July 1918, thirteen days before his nineteenth birthday, when, as Kenneth Lynn summarizes it, "he rode his bicycle far out along the west bank of the Piave to see what he could do for the morale of the men in a forward listening post" and, while he was passing out chocolate in a trench, a mortar shell hit, filling his leg with shrapnel (79).

From a technical viewpoint, however, do we really have expressionism of the sort I earlier delineated? Although the passage addresses Nick's subjective state and the repressed feelings caused by his trauma, nevertheless, even here, Hemingway focuses on the objective data producing those emotions. In lieu of the metaphors Crane employed to depict pure feeling ("an engine of annihilating power"; "tormentors were flies sucking insolently at his blood") or his abstractions ("made his rage into a dark and stormy specter"; "faces in pitiful plights"), and instead of Cather's metaphors ("playful like a big puppy that pawed you") and her lyricizing of the emotions ("the throb of it, the light restlessness, the vital essence of it everywhere"), what we get from Hemingway is a selection of remembered objects (the low yellow house, the willows, the long stable, the change in the width of the river). These images unnerve Nick, not only because they are associated in his unconscious with the site of his wounding but also because the remembered images are different from the scene he saw when he returned to the location. His attempt to solve the puzzle does *not* lead him to examine his feelings but to try to rectify the discrepancy by focusing on the objective data—noticing "everything in such detail to keep it all straight so he would know just where he was." What recurs may be a subjective feeling on the part of the narrator and author, but what occur in the passage are the repeating physical images, which reproduce that subjective feeling of turmoil in the reader. This is superbly effective writing, but it is not expressionism.

Scott Fitzgerald learned expressionism from Cather, impressionism from Conrad and Hemingway, and both modes from Crane. From the outset of his career, his instincts were almost fully expressionistic and his

mature style was heavily so. In his 1926 review of *In Our Time,* after crit-
icizing other American authors, he offered a dictum as a preamble to his
positive assessment of Hemingway: "Material, however closely observed,
is as elusive as the moment in which it has its existence unless it is puri-
fied by an incorruptible style and by the catharsis of a passionate emotion."
Addressing "Big Two-Hearted River," he notes the seeming lack of incident, "but I read it with the most breathless unwilling interest I have experienced since Conrad first bent my reluctant eyes upon the sea." The easy
explanation of the adjectives "unwilling" and "reluctant" is that Fitzgerald was no more fond of trout fishing than he was of the sailor's world, but
there is a more substantial reason for his statement about how the excel-
lence of Hemingway's prose compelled his interest in spite of his own reading preferences. Speaking of how Nick Adams's father in "The Doctor and
the Doctor's Wife" is "backed down" by Dick Boulton "after committing
himself to a fight," Fitzgerald observes: "The quality of humiliation in the
story is so intense that it immediately calls up every such incident in the
reader's past. Without the aid of a comment or a pointing finger one knows
exactly the sharp emotion of young Nick who watches the scene." (In fact,
there is no evidence that Nick witnesses this scene, a testament to the intensity of Fitzgerald's reader response.) In contrast to the "raw food" served
up by other writers, this ability to invoke an intense emotion in the reader
is what is rendered by Hemingway's "incorruptible style," and that style, as
Fitzgerald depicts it, is impressionism ("How to Waste" 120, 121, 122).

To Fitzgerald's great credit, he could appreciate fiction that did not accord with his own writing style nor even with his personal reading tastes
(would that all literary critics could emulate him), and although committed to expressionism, he was also willing to expand his artistic palette.
In 1934 he wrote to Hemingway: "Save for a few of the dead or dying old
men you are the only man writing fiction in America that I look up to
very much. There are pieces and paragraphs of your work that I read over
and over—in fact, I stopped myself doing it for a year and a half because
I was afraid that your particular rhythms were going to creep in on mine
by process of infiltration" (*Fitzgerald Letters* 309). Fitzgerald was writing
Tender Is the Night during this period in which he stopped reading Hemingway, but in that novel he demonstrated that he could shift easily from
one mode to the other, which is something we don't see in the earlier, more
fully expressionistic *The Great Gatsby.* Two randomly chosen consecutive
sentences, respectively impressionist and expressionist, nicely make the

point: "In the square, as they came out, a suspended mass of gasoline exhaust cooked slowly in the July sun. It was a terrible thing—unlike pure heat it held no promise of rural escape but suggested only roads choked with the same foul asthma" (*Tender* 86). Fitzgerald had made a place for impressionism in his expressionist art, but Hemingway was tenacious in his commitment to just the one mode.

T. S. Eliot first offered a theory for the impressionist rendering of emotion in his 1919 essay, "Hamlet and His Problems," in which he coined the term *objective correlative*: "The only way of expressing emotion in the form of art is by finding an 'objective correlative'; in other words, a set of objects, a situation, a chain of events which shall be the formula of that *particular* emotion; such that when the external facts, which must terminate in sensory experience, are given, the emotion is immediately evoked . . . The artistic 'inevitability' [of the emotion] lies in this complete adequacy of the external to the emotion" (92). The problem with what I am terming *expressionism,* for both Eliot and Hemingway, is that in the absence of the necessary "external facts" and the impressions these make on the experiencing subject, the "affect," or subjective response to the external, seems disproportionate. As Eliot puts it, the emotion expressed is not "inevitable" because the external facts are inadequate to it. He continues: "The intense feeling, ecstatic or terrible, without an object or exceeding its object, is something which every person of sensibility has known; it is doubtless a study to pathologists. It often occurs in adolescence: the ordinary person puts these feelings to sleep, or trims down his feeling to fit the business world; the artist keeps it alive by his ability to intensify the world to his emotions" (93). We need not, of course, go so far as Eliot as to proscribe the aesthetics of such authors as Cather, Virginia Woolf, Thomas Wolfe, and William Faulkner, not to mention the original target of Eliot's critique, Shakespeare's *Hamlet.* Nor should we ascribe the employment of expressionism to the pathology of the author. Eliot never denies the reality of the emotion; he only insists that it be the logical result and consummation of sensory experience, and that these objective data be represented in the work of art. "Intensifying the world" is perhaps a phrase more relevant than the objective correlative to Eliot's and Hemingway's aesthetics. The latter is the method but the former is the *purpose* of that method—to make the representation of the external world intense enough that it will be equal to the emotion (for Eliot) or create the emotion (for Hemingway).

A few years before writing "Hamlet and His Problems," Eliot had demonstrated his theory of the objective correlative in "The Love Song of J. Alfred Prufrock." Instead of having the narrator of this dramatic monologue express his feelings of boredom with the insipid conversations he will shortly be hearing at a party, and his despair and self-disgust with the way he is wasting his life in such social pursuits, Eliot offers as a refrain the correlative: "In the room the women come and go / Talking of Michelangelo" (*Poems* 4). Worth noting, though, is that Eliot also employs expressionism; the third stanza describes Prufrock's subjective feelings about his buried self in a metaphor of smoke, which is itself metaphorically depicted as behaving in the manner of a cat. In other words, Eliot had no objection to the metaphorical expression of emotions so long as there was enough of the external depicted in the work of art to serve as the "formula" for those emotions being expressed. But Hemingway rejected metaphors just as he rejected directly expressed emotions, for when you employ a metaphor, however illuminating, you are not paying strict attention to the object you are supposed to be depicting.

Hemingway had read Eliot's Hamlet essay, and Pound discussed with him Eliot's theory of portraying emotion in art while the two were reading through *The Waste Land*. As countless critics have observed, Hemingway's own theory—"the sequence of motion and fact which made the emotion" (*DIA* 2)—was virtually identical to Eliot's, and his method of depicting the external phenomena that evoke the otherwise omitted emotion is the single most central element of his fictional technique. It was likely this, in fact, which led Eliot to praise him in 1933 as a "writer of true sentiment": "Mr. Hemingway is a writer for whom I have considerable respect; he seems to me to tell the truth about his own feelings at the moment when they exist" ("Commentary" 471).

Despite their similar aesthetic theories, however, there were significant differences in their practices. Comparing Eliot's with Hemingway's use of objective correlatives, Carlos Baker offers a telling point:

> Eliot's most frequent practice, as distinguished from his theoretical formulation, is to fashion his objective correlatives into a series of complex *literary* symbols. These are designed to elicit a more or less controlled emotional response from the reader . . . depending to some degree on the extent of his cultural holdings. With Hemingway, on the other hand, the objective correlatives are not so much inserted and adapted as observed and encompassed. They are to be traced back, not to anterior literature

and art objects, but to things actually seen and known by direct experience of the world.

Hemingway's method has this special advantage over Eliot's—that one's ability to grasp the emotional suggestions embodied in an objective correlative depends almost solely on two factors: the reader's sensitivity to emotional suggestion, and the degree of his imaginative and sympathetic involvement in the story which is being told. With Eliot these two factors are likewise emphatically present, but a third is added. This third, which in a measure controls and delimits the first two, is the factor of "literary" experience. (*Artist* 56–57)

In other words, Eliot's literary allusiveness—in addition to his use of expressionism, symbol, and metaphor—complements his impressionist depiction of the objective.

The employment of the objective correlative predates Hemingway and Eliot and was "in the air" in the 1920s. But Hemingway made it his own and practiced it with such unprecedented single-mindedness that it can be found everywhere in his work. For example, in "Soldier's Home," Harold Krebs's resentment toward his mother's lecturing him at breakfast is depicted in the sentence, "Krebs looked at the bacon fat hardening on his plate" (*SS* 151; see Lamb, "Love Song" 34, n. 9). In "Cross-Country Snow," as George and Nick sit drinking at an inn, Nick reveals that he and his wife will be returning to America to have their baby. George's feelings about the impending change in their camaraderie are expressed in the sentences: "George sat silent. He looked at the empty bottle and the empty glasses" (*SS* 187). In "Hills Like White Elephants," the woman's fears that her desire for love and a family are threatened by her mate's wish to remain unencumbered by responsibilities are conveyed through her view of the landscape: "Across, on the other side, were fields of grain and trees along the banks of the Ebro. Far away, beyond the river, were mountains. The shadow of a cloud moved across the field of grain" (*SS* 276). And the man's hedonistic desires are depicted by his view of their luggage: "He did not say anything but looked at the bags against the wall of the station. There were labels on them from all the hotels where they had spent nights" (*SS* 277).

Other objective correlatives are more complex, as, for instance, one from a story that Hemingway directly linked to what he had learned from Cézanne. In the deleted ending of "Big Two-Hearted River"—a text that self-reflexively addresses Hemingway's feelings about his vocation as an author (see Lamb, "Fishing")—Hemingway says of Nick, his autobiographical persona, "He wanted to write like Cezanne painted." Employing an appositive to create some separation between himself and his protagonist, he continues, "He, Nick, wanted to write about country so it would be there like Cezanne had done it in painting" (*NAS* 239).[6] Emily Stipes Watts has identified four Cézanne techniques that influenced Hemingway's landscape depictions: "the use of a series of planes often cut across by a diagonal line, the careful delineation of even the most distant mountains and ridges, the emphasis upon volumes of space with the use of simple geometrical forms as the basis of definition, and the occasional use of color modulation" in which colors define the geometric forms the artist perceives in the scene rather than merely duplicating the various colors, lights, and shades present in the actual landscape. As Watts observes, these techniques reduce "the complexity of nature" to "a series of planes or geometrical forms. Mountains become pyramids, ridges become rectangles, trees become 'solid islands'" (40). Both artists use these techniques to demonstrate the solidity of the natural world.

Hemingway wrote to Gertrude Stein that in "Big Two-Hearted River" he was "trying to do the country like Cezanne and having a hell of a time and sometimes getting it a little bit" (*SL* 122). One of the best of these Cézanne passages occurs near the beginning, as Nick starts uphill through the burned landscape around Seney, Michigan:

> The road ran on, dipping occasionally, but always climbing. Nick went on up. Finally the road after going parallel to the burnt hillside reached the top. Nick leaned back against a stump and slipped out of the pack harness. Ahead of him, as far as he could see, was the pine plain. The burned country stopped off at the left with the range of hills. On ahead islands of dark pine trees rose out of the plain. Far off to the left was the line of the river. Nick followed it with his eye and caught glints of the water in the sun.
>
> There was nothing but the pine plain ahead of him, until the far blue hills that marked the Lake Superior height of land. He could hardly see them, faint and far away in the heat-light over the plain. If he looked too steadily they were gone. But if he only half-looked they were there, the far-off hills of the height of land. (*SS* 211)

The scene is composed as a painting, with Nick standing at mid-height (typical for the viewer in many of Cézanne's paintings), above the pine plain and below the distant hills. The winding road, or *route tournante*, takes us into the scene, as it does in Cézanne's late landscapes and their literary equivalents in Hemingway's fiction.[7] The picture is framed on the left by the range of hills and the line of the river, and on the top by the far blue hills. Nick's view spans to the left, suggesting that his perspective is from the right side of the frame. Each of the three main areas of the painting is distinguished by a particular quality of light: the left by the glints of sunlight reflecting off of the river (which contrast with the darkened burned country and the range of hills), the top by the faint blue hills in the heat-light, and the center by the pine plain that is lighter than the burned country but darker than the blue hills. Each element of the scene is distinct, but they work together to establish an overall effect. What Hemingway says of the far-off hills at the end of the passage is also true of each of the other components of the scene; if you look too closely at any one of them it disappears (as in an Impressionist painting, none has enough specificity of detail to sustain it in isolation), but if you only half-look, it is there. In other words, the particular shapes and planes matter only insofar as they contribute to the totality of the painting, and each is essential to that larger effect.

Ron Berman observes that viewers in the 1920s understood Cézanne through the ideas of Roger Fry, his leading critic and champion. Four elements of the painter's art that Fry emphasized were "the motif of the road, the organization of detail into harmony, the warning that there are elements in his work that outrange our 'pictorial apprehension,'" and "the conception of landscape as a dominant idea." Berman also explains that, in Hemingway, "the winding road is by no means a still, formal part of a described scene. It is an entry into a divided realm." In Cézanne, the *route tournante* provides only limited access to the natural world. "The roads," Berman notes, "are everywhere, yet there are in all these canvases areas that cannot be fully explained. On this, the painter was adamant, even stating that a blank space would be preferable to inserting something that would fake comprehension" (25–27, 32). This is what Fry meant when he spoke of elements beyond our "pictorial apprehension." Berman concludes that Cézanne's notion of limited access (and thus epistemological roadblocks) is one of the major lessons Hemingway learned from the painter and incorporated into his landscape depictions: "The premise of roads and also of inquiries is that they go somewhere. *Routes tournantes* invariably fail to reach certain symbolic objects on their horizon . . . We move from

perspective to a point beyond viewing, and from technique to meaning—
we now know the tendency of the story, from known to unknown. It is
characteristic in Hemingway to begin on a straight road or roadway, then
to experience an entirely different kind of locus of movement—and also of
the mind" (29).

When the *route tournante* in the quoted passage from "Big Two-Hearted
River" comes to its terminus, it leaves Nick with his view of the pine plain
and the far blue hills. But it has led him only to a vista, not to a destina-
tion; the symbolic blue hills remain on the distant horizon. In addition, his
knowledge of their physical reality, his access to them, is limited to what he
makes of them solely through his sense of sight, an epistemological conduit that is further undercut by their faintness and by the fact that he can
perceive them only by not focusing on them, that is to say, only by viewing
them within the entire scene.[8]

Here is where we see a different sort of movement "from technique to
meaning," from the external landscape to the internal terrain of the mind.
In this objective correlative of Nick's emotions about his vocation, his
mood in the scene is expressed purely through the depiction of the landscape, without any mention of what Nick is thinking or feeling. The burned
country, signifying Nick's past, is behind him. He has reached a certain elevation, or realization of his writing abilities. In the distance he can barely
make out the Lake Superior height of land, which resonates symbolically
as the sort of true writing he wishes to achieve but, at this point, can only
glimpse. Between those hills and where he now stands is the vast pine plain
with its islands of dark pine trees, indicating so many steps along the way.
The road he has traveled to this point has risen and dipped but has steadily
climbed. Now, however, it has ended, and he is on his own. He will have to
keep "his direction by the sun" (SS 212). Cézanne had continually urged
his fellow painters to "not be content with the fine formulas of . . . illustrious forebears" and to "free [their] minds" through "contact with nature,
and with the instincts and with the artistic sensations within" (*Letters* 310–
11, 291–92, 303–4). As Cézanne before him, Nick has learned all that can
be learned from others; from now on he will have to teach himself. Both
he and his author realize, if you want to do in writing what Cézanne had
done in painting, "You had to do it from inside yourself" (NAS 239).

Let us conclude by looking at "A Canary for One," in which the narrator,
his wife, and an older American woman share a train compartment from
southern France to Paris. Hemingway employs innovative first-person ex-

ternal focalization (see chapter 4), and so the narrator never expresses his feelings. Nor are we even aware, until midway through the story, that this is a first-person narrative or that, until the story's final two words, the couple is returning to Paris to begin a separation. The story's entire purpose is to make the reader *viscerally feel* the emotional state of the husband/narrator during the train ride to Paris. Hemingway is not concerned that the reader "understand" the husband's emotional state. He only wants to convey impressionistically the texture of the narrator's feelings in a manner preliminary to any sort of conscious understanding on the part of readers, or, to put it in Hemingway's own words, to make readers "feel something more than they under[stand]" (*MF* 75).

Throughout the story, he accomplishes this goal by employing a series of extended correlatives that convey the character's emotions without telling the reader the reason for those feelings. For example, between Marseilles and Avignon, they pass a burning farmhouse and see "bedding and things from inside" spread across a field as people watch the house burn. Although the reader is unaware of the narrator's situation, or even of the existence of a first-person narrator, this scene serves as an objective correlative of the narrator's own marital conflagration, right down to the curiosity of the passersby. Once in Avignon station, the narrator observes "negro" soldiers on the platform and reports that "they were too tall to stare," a statement that makes no sense except for indicating his own sensitivity to every touch of the anomalous, produced by his own internal feelings of defamiliarization (*SS* 338). As the train enters Paris, the narrator observes:

> The fortifications were levelled but grass had not grown. There were many cars standing on tracks—brown wooden restaurant-cars and brown wooden sleeping-cars that would go to Italy at five o'clock that night, if that train still left at five; the cars were marked Paris-Rome, and cars, with seats on the roofs, that went back and forth to the suburbs with, at certain hours, people in all the seats and on the roofs, if that were the way it were still done, and passing were the white walls and many windows of houses. Nothing had eaten any breakfast. (*SS* 340)

The narrator's description of the passing landscape becomes completely a correlative of his own emotional turmoil. Just as he exists between two states of being (marriage and separation), Paris is a city in transition between wartime (the grass has not yet grown back) and peacetime (the fortifications are leveled). To analogize further, with the fortifications that are necessary in war (and marriage) down, will the grass (and his life) regenerate? We may assume from the "if" clauses, which Hemingway added in the final draft (Donaldson, "Preparing" 209), that the narrator once knew his way about the city, yet it now seems strange. His impending separation has defamiliarized Paris, and the way he describes the city, as the train hurtles him into it, is entirely due to how he is experiencing his marital identity. The narrator focuses on details that signify domesticity and contrast with his experience of impending domestic loss: restaurant cars and sleeping cars, cars that carry suburban husbands home from work and suburban wives home from shopping, the veiling walls and revealing windows of people's domiciles. The Paris-Rome cars stand ready to make a symbolically ironic journey that reverses the trip he and his wife have just made. All of this seems so alien to him; he wonders "if that train still left at five" (Do people still fall in love and travel to Rome?) and "if that were the way it were still done" (Do people still return to their families in the suburbs?). Moreover, no sign of life exists, just empty trains, white walls, and blank windows. The question that looms behind the scene, as described, is: Does life still go on? The passage concludes with yet another odd declarative sentence ("Nothing had eaten any breakfast.") that makes sense only as an expression of the narrator's nostalgia for his lost domestic life. Nowhere does the narrator tell us how he feels; the reader must infer it from the details he reports.

Rarely in the Hemingway canon does one encounter a narrator—first person or disembodied third person—stating emotions directly. In those few places where this does occur, such feelings are conveyed by vague words that tell us little: for example, "swell," "lousy," and "fine." The key point here is that *no other author,* not even Eliot, made the impressionist depiction of the objective into the aesthetic dogma that Hemingway did. Nor has any other writer ever put that principle into practice as rigorously. For Hemingway, the narrator's and characters' subjective feelings were the real omitted element of fiction, present in their absence, evoked by carefully selected details, and filled in by readers who, as Fitzgerald observed, recall similar such experiences from their pasts.

4

Who Sees and Who Speaks

HEMINGWAY'S ART OF FOCALIZATION

The artist in his work must be like God in his creation—invisible and all-powerful: he must be everywhere felt, but never seen.
—Flaubert to Mlle. Leroyer de Chantpie (1857),
The Letters of Gustave Flaubert

Never think one story represents my viewpoint because it is much too complicated for that.
—Hemingway to Ivan Kashkin (1939), *Ernest Hemingway: Selected Letters*

No fields of literary theory have contributed more to our understanding of the writer's craft than narratology and reader-response criticism. But these fields have led to a proliferation of new terms that are unnecessary for the practical analysis of fictional texts and that leave the general reader bewildered. For instance, where once stood, or sat, the reader, we now have a narratee and a small army of other such "readers"—including implied, intended, inscribed, postulated, average, informed, naïve, model, ideal, actual, and empirical readers—not to mention members of interpretive and discourse communities. Without getting sidetracked in the labyrinthine world of narrative theory, I wish to extricate two particularly useful terms: *focalizer* and *focalization*. These terms replace *point of view,* that nineteenth-century warhorse that still lives on in high school, college, and creative writing curricula.

The problem with point of view is that it fails to distinguish between the narrator and the character through whose perspective the narrative is, at any given point in the text, being related. As Gérard Genette states, studies of point of view have suffered "from a regrettable confusion between . . . the question *who is the character whose point of view orients the narrative perspective?* and the very different question *who is the narrator?*—or, more simply, the question *who sees?* and the question *who speaks?*" (*ND* 186). For example, in third-person limited point of view, the narrator tells the entire story from the perspective of one of the characters and limits the text's access of information to what that character perceives, feels, and knows. But in some third-person limited texts the narrator confines himself or herself entirely to that character's consciousness and understanding of events; in others, the narrator accesses the character's consciousness but understands both it and events better than the character; and in some third-person limited texts the narrator does not access the character's consciousness and thus seems to know less than the character. Nor does the term *third-person limited point of view* address whose voice is relating the information: the character's, the narrator's, or some combination of the two. Because the term doesn't take into account these important differences, it remains vague and is incapable of discerning the text's perspective. Drawing upon the work of Genette and others, but not fully adhering to any one particular system, I divide point of view into two categories: focalization and voice. These categories give us the tools we need to understand Hemingway's use of perspective in his stories.[1]

Focalizer means two specific things to me: through whose eyes we see and to whose mind we have access. First, the focalizer is the character who situates the action at any given point in the narrative. Thinking in terms of the cinema, we might call the focalizer's view the camera angle. Sometimes, that camera angle is through the focalizer's eyes, and sometimes it is the focalizer who is being sighted by the camera. Sometimes, the camera pulls back into a pan shot, but with the focalizer as a part of that larger view. Second, and especially important, the focalizer is the character whose consciousness the writer allows himself or herself access to. For instance, in a story where X is the focalizer, if Y enters the room that X is in, the author will write "Y entered the room" or "Y came into the room," but never "Y went into the room," because the latter is not the way X would have experienced the action or sighted it. Nor will the author tell you what Y is thinking. The author will either tell you what X assumes Y is thinking or will let Y reveal thoughts through direct speech or through an action or gesture. On the other hand, if X is not the focalizer throughout the story, the author might shift the focalization from one character to another at different points in the text, but at any one point there will be one focalizer (either an individual or a group), with the exception of nonfocalized narratives, which I will explain in a moment.[2]

There are three categories of focalization in fiction: nonfocalized narratives (or zero focalization), internal focalization, and external focalization.[3] In *nonfocalized narratives,* also known as omniscient narratives, the narrator tells more than any of the characters know. That is, we get information that no one character can know or that all of the characters together can know. The perspective at such moments is that of the narrator, and the formula for the text's "knowledge" is: Narrator > Character(s). When a narrative has *internal focalization,* the narrator tells us only what one or more of the characters can know. Whether the text has one focalizer or many, at any given time we only get what the focalizing character(s) can tell us and the formula is: Narrator = Character(s). In *external focalization,* the narrator may use a focalizer or focalizers to sight the action of the text but never gives us access to their thoughts; that is, the narrator may or may not take advantage of the focalizer to sight the action (the first quality of a focalizer) but refrains from telling us what anyone is thinking or feeling (the second quality of a focalizer). Here the formula is: Narrator < Character(s).

Within internal focalization, we have three subcategories: fixed internal focalization, variable internal focalization, and multiple internal focalization. In *fixed internal focalization,* the narrator limits the text to one focalizer and the entire narrative is related through that character. The text is either a first-person narrative or else has the features of a first-person narrative as told in the third-person. The latter, third-person fixed internal focalization, is the equivalent of what used to be third-person limited point of view, with the focalizer acting as what Henry James termed "the central consciousness."[4] In *variable internal focalization,* the text has more than one focalizer. At any given point in the narrative, we have fixed internal focalization, but over the course of the narrative this shifts among two or more characters. *Multiple internal focalization* is a kind of variable internal focalization, except that we have different focalizers viewing the same event or events from their own perspectives. We see multiple internal focalization in epistolary texts or in a novel such as William Faulkner's *Absalom, Absalom!* The line between variable and multiple internal focalization is thin, the main difference being that in the former we have a chronological narrative in which focalization changes from one character to another along the way, but in the latter we get a more circular narrative in which different focalizers revisit the same action to give their own perspectives on it.

Hemingway doesn't employ nonfocalized narration in his stories. Such narration is at odds with his aesthetics of an effaced author, the use of the objective correlative, his impressionism, and his heavy reliance on dialogue. Every bit as much as Faulkner, Hemingway's narrative methods were opposed to omniscience, for the notion that anyone has the sort of knowledge necessary for omniscient narration is anathema to the spirit of modernism. As he told Maxwell Perkins, "I don't like to write like God. It is only because you never do it, though, that the critics think you can't do it" (*SL* 515).

External focalization most suited his aesthetics. When Cleanth Brooks and Robert Penn Warren launched the first attempt to define point of view more rigorously, they divided it into four categories: (1) "Main character tells own story," (2) "Minor character tells main character's story," (3) "Author tells story as external observer," and (4) "Analytic or omniscient author tells story, entering thoughts and feelings" of characters (148). They labeled categories 1 and 4 *internal* and categories 2 and 3 *external*. Although this schema is unsatisfactory—for instance, it's difficult to see how category 2, which describes Nick Carraway's narration of *The Great Gatsby,* is external—nevertheless, Brooks and Warren were the first to use the term *focus of narration* as synonymous with point of view and the first to observe that it matters whether that focus is internal or external. They didn't have the term *external focalization,* the appropriate descriptor for their category 3, but they described it perfectly in regard to Hemingway's "The Killers": "In this story the author tells us everything that happens in the objective physical sense, and everything that is said, but he does not tell us what passes in the mind of any of the characters" (659). To put it in our terms, in "The Killers" Hemingway does not make use of the second quality of a focalizer—access to consciousness—and this completely effaces the narrator and forces the reader to fill in what the characters must be thinking and feeling. In other words, external focalization is a perfect narrative perspective for Hemingway's impressionist aesthetics. He also employs external focalization throughout "Hills Like White Elephants" and for long stretches of many other stories, such as "The Sea Change," that seldom delve into the thoughts of a character.

Hemingway's heavy use of external focalization had its genesis in his reportage for the *Kansas City Star* and the *Toronto Star* before and after the war, for in such dispatches the writer hasn't access to the minds of characters, only to their spoken words and observable actions. Although he felt it to be "the height of silliness" for critics "to go into the newspaper stuff I have written, which has nothing to do with the other writing [starting with the vignettes of *in our time*]" (*CR* epigraph), nevertheless, the techniques he consciously adapted from his newspaper days do have a bearing on the style he created, and the pervasive employment of external focalization in his fiction is an excellent example of this journalistic influence.

Looking at the fifty-three stories that Hemingway completed between 1922 and 1939—the lifespan of his significant work in the genre—we see twenty-three first-person narratives (which is a kind of fixed internal focalization, with the focalizer serving as the narrator); two examples of pure external focalization; and twenty-eight third-person narratives that employ either fixed or variable internal focalization, often with long stretches that are externally focalized.[5] Hemingway's stories were completed during five distinct periods, separated by the time he devoted to producing novels and other full-length books. The periods are:

(1) February 1922 through March 1925—from "Up in Michigan," the first story completed for *Three Stories and Ten Poems* (1923) through "The Battler," the last story completed for *In Our Time* (1925). This period, which also includes the eighteen vignettes of *in our time* (1924), ends as he works on *The Sun Also Rises* (1926).

(2) November 1925 through May 1927—from "Fifty Grand" through "Che Ti Dice la Patria?" "Ten Indians," and "Hills Like White Elephants," the last three stories completed, all in May 1927, for *Men Without Women* (1927). This period ends as he works on *A Farewell to Arms* (1929).

(3) May 1930 through August 1933—from "Wine of Wyoming" through "Fathers and Sons," the first and last completed of the fourteen stories for *Winner Take Nothing* (1933). Over half of these (eight stories) are completed in 1932, as his work on the stories is broken up by writing *Death in the Afternoon* (1932). This period ends as Hemingway works on *Green Hills of Africa* (1935).

(4) February through April 1936—three longer stories: "The Capital of the World," "The Short Happy Life of Francis Macomber," and "The Snows of Kilimanjaro." This period ends as Hemingway goes off to cover the Spanish Civil War and works on the pro-Loyalist documentary film, *The Spanish Earth*.

(5) April 1938 through February 1939—the six stories about the Spanish Civil War, from "Old Man at the Bridge" through "Under the Ridge." This period ends as Hemingway devotes himself to working on *For Whom the Bell Tolls* (1940).

I have periodized the stories according to the dates of completion. The date of first publication tells little about when he was working on a story and the date of commencement is often unhelpful in the case of stories, such as "Cat in the Rain" and "Wine of Wyoming," that had a lengthy period between when he started and when he concluded writing them. See the appendix to this book for a full chronological listing of his stories from 1923 through 1939, with their dates of commencement, completion, first publication, and first publication in a book collection. The number of first-person stories in each period is: period 1 (two of seventeen); period 2 (seven of thirteen), period 3 (nine of fourteen), period 4 (zero of three), and period 5 (five of six). From this pattern, four questions arise: Why did he eschew first-person narration in the early period? Why did he employ it in 60 percent of the stories in the middle periods of *Men Without Women* and *Winner Take Nothing*? Why did he drop it in the three 1936 stories? Why did he resume it two years later?

In the stories published in *Three Stories and Ten Poems* in 1923, Hemingway used first-person narration once. In "My Old Man," he employed an unreliable narrator who discovers that his jockey father, whom he greatly admires, has won money on a fixed race, and who later must confront the possibility, after his father is killed in a racing accident, that the man's entire career was marred by such corruption. Although a good enough story to be republished in *In Our Time,* critics pointed out that it was influenced by a 1919 story by Sherwood Anderson, Hemingway's early mentor. In "I Want to Know Why," Anderson used a similar naïve first-person narrator who also hangs around race tracks and whose admiring friendship with an older male figure, a trainer named Jerry Tilford, is ruined when he discovers Tilford cavorting with prostitutes and taking credit for the victory of their horse Sunstreak. Both stories leave the readers in no doubt as to the characters of the older male figures but deposit their boy narrators is a state of perplexity. After "My Old Man" was rejected by the *Pictorial Review,* Hemingway responded by getting drunk and wondering if the story was any good (*SL* 82). He felt vindicated when Edward J. O'Brien selected it for *The Best Short Stories of 1923* and dedicated the volume to him. But he was a bit defensive in a letter to Edmund Wilson about the connection to Anderson, asserting: "No I don't think *My Old Man* derives from Anderson. It is about a boy and his father and race-horses. Sherwood has written about boys and horses. But very differently . . . I don't think they're anything alike. I know I wasn't inspired by him" (*SL* 105). Two years later, he asked Fitzgerald why he had left out "My Old Man" in rating the stories of *In Our Time* (*SL* 180), and he must have bridled, some months later, when Fitzgerald, in a review praising that volume, termed "My Old Man" the book's least successful effort, noting, "there is an echo of Anderson's way of thinking" ("How to Waste" 121). As late as 1927, Hemingway would misremember in a letter to Maxwell Perkins that "My Old Man" had "been turned down by every magazine except Scribner's and The Atlantic" (*SL* 256), but what bothered him most was the link to Anderson.

More than the irksome question of his debt to the unreliable first-person narrators of Anderson, whom he had come to consider an inferior writer, were other problems inherent in first-person narration. "My Old Man" was pure fiction, even if it resonated with Hemingway's feelings of disappointment in his own father, and although nine of the eighteen *in our time* vignettes were in the first person, the autobiographical elements in these vignettes were not terribly revealing. But the new *In Our Time* stories drew heavily on autobiographical material—characters modeled on family members and friends, his marriage, real-life events, his feelings about the war, his return home, and himself. Anxious about his family's potential disapproval and reluctant to expose himself to a gadding world, he may have embraced exclusively third-person narration for the new stories of *In Our Time* in order to provide himself with the enabling distance he felt necessary in order to write them. The creation of Nick Adams as a persona—what Philip Young calls "a projection of certain kinds of problems Hemingway was deeply concerned to write about, and write out" (*Reconsideration* 62)—along with writing in the third person gave him a kind of protection from having his privacy invaded and from wounding the feelings of others, at the same time as it allowed him to transmute his past into fiction. As he protested in the original ending of "Big Two-Hearted River," which he deleted because it was too autobiographically revelatory (see Lamb, "Fishing"): "Nick in the stories was never himself. He made him up" (*NAS* 238). The pronoun *himself* has an interesting double reference here. If Hemingway is the antecedent, then it means that "Nick was never Hemingway," which is certainly true, no matter how closely Nick represented Hemingway. But in the context of its original inclusion as the end of "Big Two-Hearted River," the final story of *In Our Time*, "himself" would have attributed the stories of that book, and the material upon which they were based, to Nick rather than to Hemingway, adding yet another layer of distance between the author's life and his texts. (For a reading of Nick as the implied author of *In Our Time*, see Moddelmog, "Unifying.")

Until scholars, starting in the 1950s, began feeding on the connections between his fiction and his life, the strategy partially succeeded. For instance, although the father in "The Doctor and the Doctor's Wife" comes off as cowardly in his dealings with the three Indians and as henpecked by his wife, Dr. Clarence Hemingway actually liked the story, and in 1925 Ernest could write to him that he had used "Dick Boulton and Billy Tabeshaw as real people with their real names" as though changing the names of Dr. and Mrs. Hemingway to "the doctor" and "the doctor's wife" made a difference. But his anxiety was always there. In that same letter he betrayed his hurt that his mother had returned her copy of *in our time,* protesting: "When you see anything of mine that you don't like remember that I'm sincere in doing it and that I'm working toward something. If I write an ugly story that might be hateful to you or to Mother the next one might be one that you would like exceedingly" (*SL* 153). In the deleted ending of "Big Two-Hearted River," he has Nick think about how the best of his fiction was pure invention and how: "That was what the family couldn't understand. They thought it was all experience" (*NAS* 237–38). In 1952, he claimed in a letter to biographer Charles Fenton, whom he was trying to dissuade from writing about his family, that he "had a wonderful novel to write about Oak Park" but "would never do it because I did not want to hurt liveing people. I did not think that a man should make money out of his father's shooting himself nor out of his mother who drove him to it . . . When I started I wrote some short stories about actual things and two of them hurt people. I felt bad about it" (*SL* 764).

Because first-person narration resembles personal memoir, readers are more apt to search for real-life counterparts; the "I" of such narratives excites readers' tabloid curiosities. But, of course, that first-person narrator is every bit as much the artful construction that a third-person narrator is, as Hemingway angrily asserted in that same letter to Fenton. Claiming that Harold Loeb, upon whom the character of Robert Cohn in *The Sun Also Rises* was based, had asked him "Why did you make me cry all the time?"—Hemingway responded: "Listen, if that [Robert Cohn] is you then the narrator [Jake Barnes] must be me. Do you think that I had my prick shot off [Barnes's war wound] or that if you and I had ever had a fight I would not have knocked the shit out of you? We boxed often enough so you know that. And I'll tell you a secret: you do cry an awful lot for a man" (*SL* 764). By then Hemingway was well aware, from personal experience, of the liabilities of first-person narration, but even at the start of his career he sensed it and was loath to deal with the complications, in fiction and in life, that it was prone to cause.

Although much scholarship exists on the eighteen vignettes of *in our time*—as part of the structure of *In Our Time,* as material for biographical studies, and as conveniently short texts for examining narrative—their real importance as experiments in which Hemingway first honed his focalization techniques demands further exploration. These techniques, used in the fifteen third-person stories up through "The Battler," were first worked out in the vignettes, a close examination of which demonstrates how very much Hemingway's uses of focalization contribute to his distinctive style. (Please note that I am using the *iot* versions of the vignettes, several of which were slightly revised in *IOT*.)

The "chapter 7" vignette ("Chapter VI" *IOT*) well illustrates Hemingway's innovative use of third-person fixed internal focalization:

[1] Nick sat against the wall of the church where they had dragged him to be clear of machine gun fire in the street. [2] Both legs stuck out awkwardly. [3] He had been hit in the spine. [4] His face was sweaty and dirty. [5] The sun shone on his face. [6] The day was very hot. [7] Rinaldi, big backed, his equipment sprawling, lay face downward against the wall. [8] Nick looked straight ahead brilliantly. [9] The pink wall of the house opposite had fallen out from the roof, and an iron bedstead hung twisted toward the street. [10] Two Austrian dead lay in the rubble in the shade of the house. [11] Up the street were other dead. [12] Things were getting forward in the town. [13] It was going well. [14] Stretcher bearers would be along any time now. [15] Nick turned his head carefully and looked down at Rinaldi. [16] "Senta Rinaldi. [17] Senta. [18] You and me we've made a separate peace." [19] Rinaldi lay still in the sun breathing with difficulty. [20] "Not patriots." [21] Nick turned his head carefully away smiling sweatily. [22] Rinaldi was a disappointing audience. (*iot* 15)

To immerse the reader in the scene, Hemingway begins with external focalization and sights Nick from a slight distance. Rather than access Nick's consciousness, he allows the impressions to do the work in the first eleven sentences. Sentence 1 sets the physical action of the scene: Nick sitting against the wall. Sentence 2 presents an unexplained physical detail of his posture before sentence 3 provides the reason for it, thus allowing the reader a direct visual impression before appealing to the rational sense. The subjects of sentences 4, 5, and 6 are Nick's face, the sun, and the day, again placing the reader in the scene to observe its physical phenomena rather than delving into how Nick is apprehending these phenomena—

in other words, Hemingway is using impressionism. Also note how we get three external details about Nick's face (sweaty, dirty, the sun shining on it) before the conclusion that the day was hot—an example of delayed decoding. Sentence 7 introduces Rinaldi with three perfectly chosen details—big backed, equipment sprawling, face downward—again as an element in the scene sighted from a slight distance. So far, then, we have external focalization that sights the text's two main characters from a point outside of those characters and places the reader in the scene by appealing to sensory impressions of sight, sound (the machine gun fire), touch (heat, sweat), and, perhaps implicitly, smell (the dirty street, the sweat).

The camera angle of the focalization pivots seamlessly in sentence 8. "Nick looked straight ahead brilliantly" is sighted from outside of Nick, but the fact of his looking prepares our segue to Nick's perspective as the camera angle in sentences 9 through 11. If Hemingway had continued the perspective of sentences 1 through 7, he would have had to take the reader away from Nick and Rinaldi to depict the building across the street, but by transferring the camera angle to Nick, he can use Nick's perspective to describe the larger scene. All the previous information on Nick was observable from the outside, but now we move into what Nick sees—the house across the street, the dead, the movement of the Italian army through the town. This, then, prepares the way for the second aspect of focalizing through Nick—access to his consciousness. What is he making of this scene? Here is where voice comes into play.

Let me briefly digress. Genette observes that all narrative is divisible into two categories: a "narrative of events" and a "narrative of words." That is, fiction uses words either to represent physical phenomena or to report words spoken or thought. When one reads that a woman "walked down a path" or that "the sky was cloudy and gray," physical reality is being signified by words, but these words can only point to what they are signifying; they can never reproduce it. Everyone understands this, and, except for deconstructionist critics who choose to elevate the obvious into a philosophy of life, everyone learns to live with it. When it comes to words, spoken or thought, however, these can be represented in fiction exactly as they would have occurred in real life; the text can reproduce that part of the fabula. If a man thinks to himself, "I am tired," the author can write: "he thought to himself, I am tired," and here the words "I am tired" are exactly what they signify.

There are three ways a writer can choose to represent words in fiction:

direct speech, free indirect speech, and summarized speech. Let's say that, in the fabula, an employee enters his boss's office and says: "You can take this lousy job and shove it. I'll be damned if I'll work for a hypocritical coward like you anymore. I quit." In the text, if the author writes these exact words, then we have *direct speech*. If, on the other hand, the author were to write: "He told his boss how he felt about both him and the job, and resigned," then we have *summarized speech*. The gist of the character's words has been summarized by the narrator in his own words, and we have no idea what the character's actual words were. Between these extremes, however, we have a vast middle ground—*free indirect speech*—which combines the character's and narrator's words. Sometimes, free indirect speech is closer to the character, as in: "He told the head where he could shove his lousy job. He'd be damned if he'd work for a hypocritical coward anymore, and he quit." This gives a lot of the flavor of what the character actually said, but it merges the narrator's voice with the character's. On the other hand, free indirect speech can be closer to the narrator than to the character, as in: "He told his boss where he could put his lousy job and also just what he thought of liars and cowards, and then resigned." Here, too, the voices merge, but the narrator's voice is stronger. In addition to these three ways of rendering thought or spoken words from the fabula, there is another technique that is a subset of direct speech, *immediate speech,* which eliminates the narrator entirely by removing the identification tag (e.g., "He said" or "He thought"). This technique, closely associated with James Joyce, who even removed the quotation marks that indicate direct speech, has the effect of "obliterating the last traces of the narrating instance and giving the floor to the character right away" (Genette, *ND* 164–75, quotation on 173).

To return to our analysis, in sentences 9 through 11, the camera angle is Nick's perspective, what he sees, but the voice is more that of the narrator (as it has been since the start of the text). Nick may indeed see that "two Austrian dead lay in the rubble in the shade of the house," yet it is highly unlikely that these are the words he would be thinking. But it is impossible to tell if sentence 12—"Things were getting forward in the town."—are Nick's thoughts in his voice (except for the verb tense) or Nick's thoughts in the narrator's voice (it can be free indirect or summarized speech). By the time we get to sentences 13 and 14, however, we are clearly in Nick's consciousness, with Nick thinking that it is going well and that the stretcher bearers will be along shortly. As for voice, only the verb tenses keep this from being direct speech; Nick would have conjugated "to be" in the present ("Things are" and "It is"). Other than that, we would have direct speech, and Hemingway indicates this by employing the gist of immediate speech, eliminating identification tags (e.g., "It was going well."). This use of immediate speech for mostly free indirect speech continues to keep the narrator effaced and the reader's absorption in the moment intact. In sentences 15 through 21, Nick is fully the focalizer, and Hemingway employs immediate speech to report his words to Rinaldi, but once again he maintains his impressionism by not telling us what Nick feels, instead conveying Nick's pain and discomfort by using the perfectly selected adverb in the repeated phrase "turned his head carefully" (sentences 15 and 21).

Although he has technical access to Nick's consciousness, Hemingway refrains from using it, so as to keep the narrator completely effaced and the reader fully immersed in the scene. He reveals Nick's feelings about his situation through his sardonic words to Rinaldi (sentences 16–18 and 20) and, even more, in the superbly rendered ending. Sentence 21 has two verbs and two adverbs: "turned" his head away "carefully" and "smiling sweatily." The main thing being conveyed here is Nick's physical condition (pain, discomfort, sweating), but that unobtrusive second verb—*smiling*—points to something else. The mystery of Nick's smile is revealed in the final sentence, the wonderful understatement that "Rinaldi was a disappointing audience." Had Hemingway not handled his focalization with such a perfect touch, had he allowed the narrator to hold forth on Nick's thoughts and feelings, had he not, within a narration that is technically fixed internal focalization, done all he could to make it closer to external focalization, this last sentence would have been less effective because it could just as easily have been attributed to the narrator as to Nick. But Hemingway kept his narrator hidden, gave us our glimpse into Nick's mind through immediate speech, and, with the word *smiling*, set up our attribution of the final sentence to Nick's sense of irony rather than the narrator's. This Spartan restraint of the third-person narrator, as much as any other technique, is a sine qua non of Hemingway's unique style, a style that has impressed but baffled so many readers. Only two of his fifty-three stories are fully in external focalization. Nevertheless, in his internally focalized stories, in third-person and even in first-person, we find a preponderance of external focalization, the effect of which is to give the stories a new kind of immediacy by removing the narrator from sight and allowing readers to pick up on the impressionist details Hemingway has carefully—as carefully as Nick turns his head—left for them. The heart of this style was first worked out in the 1923 vignettes.

The sheer variety of focalization experiments in the vignettes is equally impressive, and I wish we had space to analyze more of them as closely as we have "chapter 7." Of the eight other third-person vignettes, some interesting points stand out. Among these, "chapter 2" ("Chapter IX" *IOT*), "chapter 6" ("Chapter V" *IOT*), "chapter 12" ("Chapter X" *IOT*), and "chapter 14" ("Chapter XII" *IOT*) are externally focalized throughout, even though Hemingway employs the second-person pronoun at the start "chapter 14" and may possibly have used a bull as an internal focalizer at the end of "chapter 12." In "chapter 9" ("Chapter VIII" *IOT*), we get the ultimate rarity in Hemingway—a nonfocalized narrative—as the information that the dead crooks were Hungarians and not Italians is something no character in the text, other than the dead crooks, could know. This information is crucial to the irony of the vignette, which ends, "Wops, said Boyle, I can tell wops a mile off" (*iot* 17). In "chapter 10" ("A Very Short Story" *IOT*), he employs variable internal focalization; in two pages the focalization shifts five times from the protagonist and his girlfriend Ag, to him, back to him and Ag, to him, back to Ag, and then to him.[6] In "chapter 12" ("Chapter X" *IOT*), whether the focalization can be considered fully external or partly fixed internal depends upon one's ecocritical orientation—can an animal be employed as an internal focalizer? The vignette concludes: "He [the gored horse] was nervously wobbly. The bull could not make up his mind to charge" (*iot* 22). The focalization of "chapter 16" ("Chapter XIV" *IOT*) is fixed internal, but the focalizer is the dying matador Maera; the text ends when the focalizer does. We get another example of this near external focalization, a trademark Hemingway technique, in "chapter 17," ("Chapter XV" *IOT*), the story of the hanging of Sam Cardinella, in which pure external focalization is undercut only by two brief sentences possibly accessing the minds of minor characters, one about three men awaiting hanging—"They were very frightened."—and another about the guards holding Sam when he loses control of his bowels—"They were both disgusted"(*iot* 28).

In the eleven new stories for *In Our Time,* all written in the third person, Hemingway learned how to maintain fixed internal focalization over the course of longer narratives, often improvising in order to finesse moments when strict focalization might be threatened. A case in point is his first story masterpiece, "Indian Camp," written between November 1923 and February 1924. In the deleted original opening that he removed from the typescript before sending the story out for publication, his rage to explain rather than dramatize had led him to a series of interruptive flashbacks within flashbacks, moribund psychological analysis, stilted dialogue, and numerous focalization blunders. In what was supposed to be fixed internal focalization using young Nick Adams as the focalizer, he reports a conversation between Nick's father and Uncle George on the lake while Nick is back in the tent, thus destroying the story's point of view. Worse, during that conversation, still clinging to the idea that Nick is the focalizer, he writes the sentence: "Uncle George was an enthusiastic fisherman and his father's younger brother" (*NAS* 14). The pronoun "his" obviously refers to Nick, but Nick's absence from the scene opens up a ridiculous possibility.

In the final version, however, the focalization is nearly flawless. Hemingway goes to great lengths to ensure that Nick remains the focalizer. Even the narrator uses the sort of language that would be found in a small child's vocabulary, as when he states that the Indian woman "had been trying to have her baby" (*SS* 92) rather than, say, "had been in labor." Later, we get no details about the Caesarean operation Nick's father performs because Nick is unable to comprehend what is going on and is probably looking away. But Hemingway's major challenge comes when he has to report the Indian father's suicide while still holding to Nick's fixed internal focalization. At this point, Nick has last been seen carrying a basin into the kitchen; since then, his father has checked the sleeping woman, announced his intention to return in the morning, and engaged in a conversation with Uncle George. As Dr. Adams exults and Uncle George sulks, Nick begins to fade from the narrative, a danger heightened when Dr. Adams makes his grisly discovery:

> [1] He pulled back the blanket from the Indian's head. [2] His hand came away wet. [3] He mounted on the edge of the lower bunk with the lamp in one hand and looked in. [4] The Indian lay with his face toward the wall. [5] His throat had been cut from ear to ear. [6] The blood had flowed down into a pool where his body sagged the bunk. [7] His head rested on his left arm. [8] The open razor lay, edge up, in the blankets. (*SS* 94)

This paragraph, deceptively simple, is told entirely in short declarative sentences of action and description, each of which begins with the subject of the sentence. Every sentence leads perfectly into the next, but no sentence gets ahead of itself in anticipating what will follow (we glimpse here something Hemingway learned from Gertrude Stein, as we'll see in chapter 5, and adapted to his impressionist technique). For instance, sentence 5 reports the discovery of the Indian's cut throat but does not anticipate the obvious assumption—once the facts are processed—that he committed suicide. In fact, by putting the sentence in the passive voice, Hemingway not only impressionistically represents *exactly* how the discovery would have felt to the doctor at the precise moment he made it, he also suggests the naturalist environmental forces that have sapped the Indian of his autonomy and victimized him. In this way, he employs delayed decoding to mimic the moment-by-moment nature of the doctor's discovery and conveys that quality to the reader. In addition, the paragraph contains eighty words: sixty-seven are monosyllabic; eleven have two syllables; and only two, necessary uses of the word *Indian,* have three syllables. The words selected would all be found in a small child's vocabulary. In rendering this scene, then, Hemingway was determined not to let anything, whether a complex word (which would undermine the focalization) or a subjective one (which would undercut the impressionism), stand between the reader and the object being perceived.

Although Nick is the story's focalizer, the character upon whom the Indian's suicide has the most revealing effect is the doctor. In a speech immediately prior to the discovery—"Ought to have a look at the proud father."—he vaguely reveals a sense of identification with the Indian who, like him, is a father. The discovery subtly suggests another link between the two men. While the doctor was successfully performing surgery in the lower bunk in order to bring forth life, the Indian, directly above him, was operating in an equally successful effort to end life. The assumption of the Caesarean is that life, no matter how painful and difficult, is worth the effort. The assumption of the suicide is that it is not. (These two assumptions not only form the metaphysical frame of the story but also forecast the antipodal shift in Hemingway's own existential perspective during the next three and a half decades.) It is the assumption of the suicide, acted upon by the character to whom he feels some tie, that emotionally unnerves the doctor. Not only does the suicide deny the values that define the doctor, but the very process by which he discovers it, which imitates a birth, serves to humiliate him further. In this mock birth, the upper bunk sags like a womb from the weight of the Indian's body, and it is filled with blood. The doctor pulls back the blanket to reveal the Indian's head and stands on the edge of the lower bunk, lamp in hand, to look into the upper bunk. The Indian lies dead, like a stillborn baby, and the metaphor is extended even to the point of narrating sentence 5 in the passive voice, which seems to strip his death of the aspect of volition. Between the personification of the surgeon's "hand," in sentence 2, and the surgical instrument, the open razor in sentence 8, lies the dead Indian. The doctor's hand is separated from the instrument by five sentences describing the dead Indian. The doctor stands on the "edge" of the bunk staring at the "edge" of the open razor, staring at the implement of a death that implicitly negates his sense of worth and meaning. In that shocking moment, his feelings of accomplishment and power vanish, and he is reduced to mortal dimensions.

Upon making his discovery, and the unconscious self-discoveries that arise from it, the doctor's first thought is of his son, who has been absent from the minds of the doctor and the reader throughout the passage:

> "Take Nick out of the shanty, George," the doctor said.
> There was no need of that. Nick, standing in the door of the kitchen, had a good view of the upper bunk when his father, the lamp in one hand, tipped the Indian's head back. (SS 94)

"There was no need of that" is an unnecessary authorial intrusion, one that in style and content is at odds with Nick as focalizer. It is also a rather silly sentence. Would it be better to allow Nick to remain in the shanty to continue to stare at the gruesome sight? The sentence seems like an accusation by the author: Why did the doctor not have Nick taken out of the shanty long before this? Embedded in a passage otherwise scrupulously devoid of all authorial comment, in which even the Indian's throat is not directly explained as having been cut by his own hand, this sentence stands out. In the absence of any possible narrative purpose, we might conclude that it gauges the depth of the author's complex and often accusatory feelings toward the real-life father upon whom he based the character of Dr. Adams. Moreover, there is just enough of a sense of pity in the narrator's voice, which is so unlike the rest of this dispassionate prose, to make us wonder if Hemingway is giving way, for just an instant, to self-pity as well.

The passage's final sentence depicts Nick's view of the dead Indian and leads us to why I selected this scene for an example. Who was the focalizer when the suicide was discovered? The discovery paragraph seems, on careful reading, to be perilously close to being focalized through the doctor. Yet, there are sound reasons for why this has to be. First, the most effective way to present the scene is through the sequence of observations that the doctor makes as he discovers the dead Indian. Second, the character most directly and immediately affected by the suicide is not Nick, but his father. Last, Hemingway wanted Nick to remain vaguely absent in order to maximize the effect when his father shifts back into his paternal role and orders Uncle George to take the boy away. In other words, he wanted the reader to be shocked by the discovery first, and then suddenly to realize, along with Dr. Adams, that Nick has seen it too.

But it is a mark of Hemingway's art that this potential focalization problem is so well finessed that, until now, no critic has ever even wondered how a small boy can observe the precise details of what occurs in an upper bunk that must certainly be above his eye level as well as somewhat in the distance. How did Hemingway accomplish this? First, as noted, the vocabulary is exceedingly simple. The camera eye may be Dr. Adams but the vocabulary is Nick's. Second, because the discovery paragraph is purely impressionist, the reader, rather than either the doctor or Nick, supplies the emotional response to the scene. Third, in the final paragraph, Hemingway directly states that Nick "had a good view of the upper bunk," which sounds reasonable enough, though actually not very likely. Fourth, he then repeats exactly a phrase from the discovery paragraph ("the lamp in one hand"). This phrase subtly links Nick's "good view" to the focalization in the discovery paragraph. Significantly, the detail he chooses to repeat suggests that the upper bunk is well lit. Last, he adds one small piece of exposition, that "his father . . . tipped the Indian's head back." This powerful image, which logically would have taken place in the discovery paragraph between sentence 4 (where the Indian is facing the wall) and sentence 5 (where the cut throat is revealed), is a part of the doctor's sequence of action in that paragraph but is removed and relocated to the next paragraph in order to give the impression that Nick is able to observe the entire sequence. In this manner, by employing what I have termed his *technique of sequence displacement,* Hemingway manages, in effect, to focalize through the doctor—reaping the dramatic benefits enumerated above—while making it seem as though he is focalizing through Nick. That critics have not noted it amply demonstrates that he succeeded.

During this same period, Hemingway also continued to experiment with variable internal focalization. Take, for instance, two stories written in March 1924. In "Cat in the Rain," a husband and wife are confined by a downpour to their second-floor hotel room in an Italian town. He reads a book while she, looking out the window, spots a cat huddled under a table. She goes outside to find the cat, accompanied by a maid whom the padrone dispatches to assist her, but is unsuccessful and returns to the room. It is clear throughout the story that her husband is insensitive to her needs and that her desire for the cat possesses enormous symbolic significance. Following what I term a tonal opening paragraph (see chapter 6), the second paragraph commences, "The American wife stood at the window looking out." This is a favorite Hemingway tactic, as we saw in sentence 8 of the Nick vignette above, for establishing or shifting the focalization—having the impending focalizer look, stare, see, or perform some other visual action. Indeed, from that sentence on, the wife is the focalizer in both senses: Hemingway sights the action through her and delves into her consciousness and feelings. In addition, he goes to pains to prevent George, her husband, from being mistaken for a focalizer. He never accesses George's thoughts or feelings, though he briefly uses him as the camera eye once to sight the wife, and he keeps George on the bed immersed in his book and silent except for a few perfunctory responses to his wife and minor actions: "The husband went on reading"; "resting his eyes from reading"; "George was reading again"; "George looked up and saw the back of her neck." The story concludes:

[P1]   "Oh, shut up and get something to read," George said. He was reading again.

[P2]   His wife was looking out of the window. It was quite dark now and still raining in the palm trees.

[P3]   "Anyway, I want a cat," she said, "I want a cat. I want a cat now. If I can't have long hair or any fun, I can have a cat."

[P4]   George was not listening. He was reading his book. His wife looked out of the window where the light had come on in the square.

[P5]   Someone knocked at the door.

[P6]   "Avanti," George said. He looked up from his book.

[P7]   In the doorway stood the maid. She held a big tortoise-shell cat pressed tight against her and swung down against her body.

[P8]   "Excuse me," she said, "the padrone asked me to bring this for the Signora." (SS 170)

In terms of focalization, Hemingway twice underscores that George is not the focalizer by having him "reading again" and "reading his book" (paragraphs 1 and 4). He also distances George from her emotions by having him tell her to shut up and by stating that "George was not listening." Hemingway fully reestablishes the wife as the camera eye in the two mentions of her looking out the window (paragraphs 2 and 4). But in paragraph 6 he suddenly shifts the focalization to George by having him answer the knock on the door and look up from his book. It is therefore George, not his wife, who sights the maid holding a cat. But is it the same cat, the one she wanted? As David Lodge shrewdly demonstrates (29), by shifting the focalization to the husband at the last moment, Hemingway ends the story on a note of ambiguity. Had the wife remained the focalizer, then the indefinite article ("a cat") might indicate a *different* cat, but since George has never budged from his bed, our new focalizer has no way of knowing whether this is the same or a different cat ("a cat" or "the cat"). Nor can the reader know because the story abruptly ends.

   Critics can, of course, speculate on this, and they have: this is a big cat and the original cat seemed smaller; but the first cat only seemed smaller because she "was trying to make herself so compact that she would not be dripped on" by the rain (SS 167); but having the wife receive a different cat is so Hemingwayesque in its irony; but the real irony is that the padrone is sensitive to the wife while her husband is not; but tortoise-shell cats are almost always female and the initial cat is described by Hemingway as a "her"; but that initial cat was focalized through the wife and, in the absence of a physical examination, cats are customarily referred to using the female pronoun; and so on. This speculation is all well and good, but what matters most is the story's purposeful and rich ambiguity, made possible by the focalization shift. In short, it is from technique that textual richness (and critical debates) arise. Incidentally, let me throw one more piece of information into this tempest in a teapot, in a perverse effort to prolong it. Tortoise-shell cats are indeed nearly all female, as the orange gene in the tortoise-shell coat is linked to the gene that determines the female cat's sex. But there are occasionally male tortoise-shell cats, and in these cases the cat is invariably sterile (Fogle 263).[7] Since Hemingway was a cat aficionado, perhaps he knew this and thus it has some bearing on a story in which the wife wants a baby but can't have one (for reasons not specified). In light of the many critical discussions about the theme of sterility in this story, this fact seems relevant.

Another interesting use of variable internal focalization is found in "The End of Something," a story in which Nick breaks up with his girl-friend Marjorie during a nighttime fishing episode. Following an opening paragraph that sets the five-page story's mood and theme, the conscious-ness Hemingway accesses is not the protagonist Nick's, but Marjorie's: "She was intent on the rod all the time they trolled, even when she talked. She loved to fish. She loved to fish with Nick" (SS 108). Hemingway does not delve into Nick's feelings because he is setting up the suspense of the im-pending break-up by having Nick's inexplicable coldness toward Marjo-rie come out in his dialogue and actions until, at the bottom of the fourth page, he reluctantly tells her, "It isn't fun any more." With this, Heming-way at last gives us access to Nick's consciousness: "He was afraid to look at Marjorie." Nick is now the focalizer, both in terms of sighting the ac-tion ("Then he looked at her"; "He looked at her back"; "He looked on at her back") and access to consciousness ("He could hear Marjorie rowing on the water"; "he heard Bill coming into the clearing"; "He felt Bill com-ing up to the fire"). With Marjorie gone and Bill entering the story, the fo-calization shifts again in the final sentence. After Nick, lying face down on the blanket, tells Bill to go away, we read, "Bill selected a sandwich from the lunch basket and walked over to have a look at the rods" (SS 110–11). Nick is in no position to see Bill, and so the information of Bill's inten-tion to look at the rods must come from accessing Bill's consciousness. In a story about something turning into nothing, about the replacement of feeling with emptiness, the shifts in focalization enforce the theme; we go from a focalizer full of feeling to one who's lost feeling, or thinks he has, to one who is devoid of feeling. (Note, in this regard, how effectively Bill's in-difference is depicted in the verbs *selected* and *to have a look*.)

After eschewing first-person narration in all but one non-vignette story up through March 1925, in his next two story-writing periods—from No-vember 1925 through May 1927 and May 1930 through August 1933—six-teen of Hemingway's twenty-seven stories were in the first-person. Why this sudden shift? Perhaps his growing mastery of craft alleviated his anxi-eties about readers mistaking a first-person narrator for the author. In this period even Nick Adams is a first-person narrator in as many as nine stories, including "Now I Lay Me," in which Hemingway's familial and psychological problems are used for material.[8] It's also possible that his employment of first-person narration in his first two serious novels—*The Sun Also Rises,* written just before the second story-writing period, and *A Farewell to Arms,* written before the third—made him more comfortable with this method. Both first-person narration and fixed internal third-person focalization limit themselves to the perspective of one character within the text. The advantages of first-person narration (i.e., fixed internal first-person focalization) are that it effaces the author in the reader's consciousness, although it may cause the reader later to conflate the author and narrator, and that the narrator/character's palpable presence leaves no question about where information is coming from. It is also harder for the writer to commit focalization blunders. In third-person fixed internal focalization, if the author accesses another character's consciousness, the reader may grow suspicious of the intrusion, but in the first-person the reader assumes the narrator is merely guessing at what someone else thinks or feels. Furthermore, first-person narration comes with a built-in unity because everything is filtered through the consciousness of the text's only focalizer. A first-person narrator can freely express his or her thoughts and feelings about anything at any time. The main potential disadvantage of first-person narration, however—unless the author is using it for a purpose—is the reader's hypersensitivity to the narrator's unreliability, which is less likely to occur with a disembodied third-person narrator.

As with his third-person narratives, Hemingway's use of the first person was initially worked out in the focalization laboratory of the *in our time* vignettes. In four of the nine first-person vignettes, all war episodes— "chapter 1" ("Chapter I" *IOT*), "chapter 3" ("Chapter II" *IOT*), "chapter 4" ("Chapter III" *IOT*), and "chapter 5" ("Chapter IV" *IOT*)—the real-life events upon which the vignettes were based can be dated and located (Hagemann 192–93). The "chapter 5" vignette takes place on 23 August 1914 at the battle of Mons in Belgium, "chapter 4" is probably at the same location at a different time of day, and "chapter 1" is in late September or early October 1915 at the battle of Champagne, in which the Allies, mostly the French, lost 145,000 men in a tactical victory. Hemingway was still in high school when these battles took place, and his first-person narrator for "chapter 4" and "chapter 5" is actually Lieutenant Eric Edward Dorman-Smith of the Royal Northumberland Fusiliers, later Hemingway's friend, to whom he dedicated *in our time*. In "chapter 5" he imitates Dorman-Smith's Anglo-Irish locutions, perhaps overdoing it a bit: "It was a frightfully hot day. We'd jammed an absolutely perfect barricade across the bridge. It was simply priceless."; "It was absolutely topping"; "we potted them"; "It was an absolutely perfect obstacle. Their officers were very fine. We were frightfully put out" (*iot* 13). The "chapter 4" vignette is less Monty Pythonesque, but once again the enemy is "potted" (shot) and a soldier is referred to as "Young Buckley" (*iot* 12). The "chapter 1" vignette, although it can be located and dated, is an invention, and the narrator, a kitchen corporal, is possibly French.

In "chapter 3," Hemingway rewrote as fiction a dispatch titled "A Silent Ghastly Procession" that he had filed on 20 October 1922 as a correspondent for the *Toronto Star* at the end of the Greco-Turkish War. With the Turkish occupation of eastern Thrace, thousands of Greek Christians filed through Adrianople along the twenty-mile road to Karagatch. As he reported it, the main column of refugees crossing the Maritza River at Adrianople consists of "twenty miles of carts drawn by cows, bullocks and muddy-flanked water buffalo, with exhausted, staggering men, women and children, blankets over their heads, walking blindly along in the rain beside their worldly goods." The "mud-splashed Greek cavalry herd them along like cow-punchers driving steers." Marching alongside this "ghastly procession," Hemingway spots a husband spreading a blanket over his pregnant wife in a cart to protect her from the rain while "her little daughter looks at her in horror and begins to cry" (*DT* 232). The dispatch is in the third person and concludes with a near plea for the Christian world to help the half a million refugees in Macedonia.

Two years later, in "chapter 3," Hemingway tells substantially the same story, but the dispatch's lengthy sentences are now short, each containing a specific image so that we get a Crane-like series of impressions rather than a stylistically elegant narrative (i.e., the form is more mimetic of the content and more immediate). Also, "their worldly goods" is given detailed specificity, replaced with, "Women and kids were in the carts crouched with mattresses, mirrors, sewing machines, bundles." The vignette concludes: "There was a woman having a kid with a young girl holding a blanket over her and crying. Scared sick looking at it. It rained all through the evacuation" (*iot* 11). Hemingway compresses this image from the dispatch, making it more compact and dire; no husband is present, the frightened girl is responsible for helping, and the woman is giving birth rather than pregnant. Unconcerned with the formal style of journalism, he can have the vernacular repeated *it* between the last two sentences. In the final sentence, the dispatch's plea for help is replaced by the statement that it "rained all through the evacuation." *Evacuation* refers to the movement of the refugees but, juxtaposed with the woman under the blanket, it resonates as a description of the childbirth. In circumstances where humans have been stripped of their dignity and rendered into figurative cattle, childbirth is equated to a bowel movement. Most interesting is that, except for the penultimate sentence, he maintains the third-person narration of the dispatch and even transforms its nonfocalized (omniscient) narration into external focalization. Yet, technically, the text is in the first person, a fact obfuscated by his elision of the words "I was" at the opening of that penultimate sentence ("Scared sick looking at it."). It is, of course, possible that the sentence is in the third person and the narrator is accessing the consciousness of the girl as the one feeling "scared sick" (an earlier draft used the pregnant woman as the focalizer; see Cohen). But such a reading is at odds with the panoramic vista of the entire text.

What Hemingway has discovered here is that even in the first person he can efface the narrator and employ impressionism to give readers direct contact with the objective data, allowing them to produce the subjective response on their own. He would push this method to its limits in "A Canary for One" (1926), in which, halfway through the text, we suddenly realize that what we thought was a disembodied third-person narrator using an elderly woman as his focalizer is really a first-person narrator. He has been reporting the objective data but so scrupulously not telling us his thoughts that we have been unaware of his presence. To efface a third-person narrator is one thing; to efface a first-person narrator is little short of remarkable. Although "A Canary for One" is an extreme case of simulating the effect of external focalization, in many other first-person stories written between 1925 and 1933, Hemingway gives the effect of external focalization by presenting the external data and not having the first-person narrator offer his subjective responses. This technique is a major innovation.

"After the Storm" (begun April 1928, completed June 1932) is narrated by a rough vernacular character from the margins of society in the Florida Keys who makes his living looting sunken ships. He comes across a sunken liner, tries but fails to ransack it, and in the end loses its contents to other scavengers. The narration is indebted to Twain's *Adventures of Huckleberry Finn*, which Hemingway would shortly proclaim "the best book we've had" and the one from which "all modern American literature" has emerged (*GHA* 21). Here are two passages about the discovery of a sunken boat by a protagonist who wishes to loot it, the first related by Huck Finn and the second by the first-person narrator of "After the Storm":

> It was a steamboat that had killed herself on a rock. We was drifting straight down for her. The lightning showed her very distinct. She was leaning over, with part of her upper deck above water, and you could see every little chimbly-guy clean and clear, and a chair by the big bell, with an old slouch hat hanging on the back of it when the flashes come.
>
> Well, it being away in the night, and stormy, and all so mysterious-like, I felt just the way any other boy would a felt, when I see that wreck laying there so mournful and lonesome in the middle of the river: I wanted to get aboard of her and slink around a little, and see what there was there. (80)

> I could see something looked like a spar up out of the water and when I got over close the birds all went up in the air and stayed all around me. The water was clear out there and there was a spar of some kind sticking out just above the water and when I come up close to it I saw it was all dark under water like a long shadow and I came right over it and there under water was a liner; just lying there all under water as big as the whole world. I drifted over her in the boat. She lay on her side and the stern was deep down. The port holes were all shut tight and I could see the glass shine in the water and the whole of her; the biggest boat I ever saw in my life laying there and I went along the whole length of her and then I went over and anchored and I had the skiff on the deck forward and I shoved it down into the water and sculled over with the birds all around me. (*SS* 373)

This sort of narration, in which an uneducated character speaks in his own idiom, is atypical for Hemingway, whose first-person narrators are usually either Nick Adams or other Hemingway persona. But here he uses methods similar to Twain's in *Huck Finn*. Note the unliterary vernacular discourse with its inelegant repetitions—"something looked like a spar" and "there was a spar of some kind"; the five uses of "water" in the second sentence; "as big as the whole world" and "the biggest boat I ever saw." Twain does this throughout *Huck Finn*, though not in the above first passage; for example, Chapter 18 concludes: "We said there warn't no home like a raft, after all. Other places do seem so cramped up and smothery, but a raft don't. You feel mighty free and easy and comfortable on a raft" (155). Also observe the attention Hemingway's narrator pays to function, to specific actions in a progressive sequence ("I drifted over her"; "I went along"; "and then I went over and anchored"; "I had the skiff on the deck forward"; "and I shoved it down"; "and [I] sculled over"). As Leo Marx observes, "The vernacular style bears many marks of its plebian origin. For example, it has been peculiarly useful in expressing a preoccupation with process, with the way things are done. By its very nature a genteel style implies an invidious distinction between intellectual and manual work. But the vernacular hero does not honor the distinction, and moreover his practical rhetoric denies its significance" (15). Marx analyzes this aspect in Twain's depiction of Huck's escape from pap's cabin, noting: "What we have here is a meticulous rendering, one by one, of physical actions or manipulations. A series of verbs . . . is strung together, largely by the word 'and,' and the total effect is an immediate impression of a process." He concludes by comparing this style to Hemingway's when "describing how Nick Adams baits a fish-hook" (15).

Despite the many similarities, however, there is one glaring difference between these narrations, both in the quoted passages and throughout the texts. Twain has Huck report his feelings upon seeing the sunken boat, and these subjective responses are linked to Huck's inner emotional state as he has directly expressed it earlier (for example, in the first quarter of the novel he describes himself as "lonesome" seven different times before describing this boat as "lonesome" in the above passage). Hemingway's first-person narrator, however, tells us virtually *nothing* about his feelings. Even when he attempts to, it comes out vague and unrevealing; for example, later on he says, "It made me shaky to think how much she must have in her" and "It was a hell of a thing all right" (*SS* 374, 376). If the Twain passage were rewritten in the third person, it would come out as third-person fixed internal focalization, but the Hemingway passage would be essentially unaltered and would remain mainly external focalization. Throughout "After the Storm," we have no difficulty knowing what the narrator is feeling; it is implicit in the depiction of his actions. This is true even when our subjective responses to the story differ from his, as when he discovers through a porthole a dead woman floating inside and his only concern is whether he can get the rings from her fingers. I cannot make the point too strongly or too often. The key to Hemingway's style is his strict adherence to impressionism (as I have defined it) and, concomitant to this, his making all forms of focalization as close to external focalization as possible.

In the remaining five first-person vignettes of *in our time,* we have a "peripheral" first-person narrator, one who is not the main character of the narrative. The most interesting of these is "chapter 8" ("Chapter VII" *IOT*), the story of the frightened soldier in the trench at Fossalta who prays to Jesus and later goes upstairs with the prostitute. This vignette would be in the third person with the soldier as the focalizer except that in the eighth sentence Hemingway writes: "*We* went to work on the trench and in the morning the sun came up and the day was hot and muggy and cheerful and quiet" (emphasis mine; *iot* 16). "We" changes the story from fixed internal third-person focalization to peripheral first-person focalization and raises the question: What is gained by this strategy? As Robert Scholes observes, were the story told by the frightened soldier in the first person then it would be "a confession, a telling at last of previous untold sins" (*Textual* 37). Thus it would be formally akin to, say, Edgar Allan Poe's "A Cask of Amontillado." If told in the third person with that frightened soldier as the focalizer, it would be a representative story of someone "finding religion in the trenches" and then forgetting about it once the danger passed. Because it is a peripheral first-person narration, however, the reader is intrigued by this focalizer suddenly revealed in sentence 8: Who is this narrator whose only trace in the text is that first-person plural pronoun? Is he a comrade to whom the frightened soldier confessed? Is he a soldier relating a "war story" he heard and assuming a stance of authority in the retelling by claiming he was there? Are the frightened soldier and the first-person narrator the same person, with the narrator making a confession under the cloak of ascribing his story to someone else, an anonymous frightened soldier? Given that the bombardment occurs at Fossalta, where Hemingway himself was wounded, is this Hemingway confessing to his own fears at the time behind the double screen of an anonymous frightened soldier and an anonymous first-person narrator? Did Hemingway find religion by that trench where he was blown up and later lose it when out of danger? None of these questions can be answered, but that so many questions can now be asked is a mark of how the shift in focalization in sentence 8 deepens the interpretive terrain of the text and, in Hemingway's parlance, makes the reader feel something more than he or she can understand. In other words, the shift in focalization creates the omission (Who is this narrator?) that produces the text's effect.

We see a peripheral first-person narrator in four other vignettes: "chapter 11" ("The Revolutionist" *IOT*), "chapter 13" ("Chapter XI" *IOT*), "chapter 15" ("Chapter XIII" *IOT*), and "chapter 18" ("L'Envoi" *IOT*). Hemingway would also employ it in the initial story of the second period of his story-writing career, "Fifty Grand," when he turned to exploring the first-person. Other first-person peripheral narrations in the stories include "Wine of Wyoming" and "Old Man at the Bridge."

There are, however, several stories that I wish to define as variants of first-person peripheral narration. I term this variant the *Conradian split* because Joseph Conrad's *Heart of Darkness* is (along with *The Great Gatsby*, which it influenced) one of the texts best known for employing this focalization technique. In a Conradian split, the subject is one character (Kurtz), the first-person narrator is another character (Marlowe), but both the subject and the narrator are of equal interest in the text. That is to say, in such a text, readers are equally drawn to the story of the subject character, to the effect of that story on the first-person narrator, and to the way that the subject's story as we come to know it is conditioned or even determined by the nature of the narrator. The first of these interests is ontological (Who is this subject?), the second is reader-response (How do we respond to the subject in comparison to how the narrator responds to him/her?), and the third is epistemological (How do we know what we know about the subject?).

Faulkner's *Absalom, Absalom!* is a complex example of a Conradian split, divided among several narrators in multiple internal focalization with a huge time span between the fabula and the time of narration. The ontological interest is the story of Thomas Sutpen and his clan; the reader-response interest is how we process this story in comparison to how Rosa, Mr. Compson, Quentin, and Shreve process it; and the epistemological interest is how do we get our information about the Sutpen family? Other Conradian splits in novels include Ishmael/Ahab in Herman Melville's *Moby-Dick*, Nick Carraway / Jay Gatsby in *The Great Gatsby*, and Nellie Birdseye / Myra Henshawe in Willa Cather's *My Mortal Enemy*. The Conradian split is a frequent focalization technique in the short story, for example in Poe's "The Fall of the House of Usher," Melville's "Bartleby, the Scrivener," and Sherwood Anderson's "Death in the Woods." Hemingway employed the Conradian split to great effect, most especially in "A Canary for One," (the narrator / the "American lady"), "In Another Country" (the narrator / the Italian major), "God Rest You Merry, Gentlemen" ("Horace"

/ Dr. Fischer), "The Light of the World" (Nick/Alice), and "The Mother of a Queen" (Roger/Paco).

The categories "first-person main" (first-person narrator telling his or her own story), "first-person peripheral," and "Conradian split" are not always easy to determine, but they are useful tools for thinking about focalization technique in the short story. Among Hemingway's seventeen first-person narratives completed between November 1925 and July 1933, we have a clear first-person narrator telling his own story in "Now I Lay Me," "After the Storm," and "A Way You'll Never Be"; a clear first-person peripheral narrator in "Fifty Grand"; and a Conradian split in "A Canary for One," "In Another Country," "God Rest You Merry, Gentlemen," "The Light of the World," and "The Mother of a Queen." "An Alpine Idyll" is not easily classified. Is it a first-person main focalization, or is the story of the peasant who hung a lantern from his dead wife's mouth enough to make him the subject of the story in a Conradian split? "Che Ti Dice la Patria?" seems a first-person main narrative, but could it instead constitute a Conradian split with the subject being, as the text's final sentence identifies it, "how things were with the country or the people" (SS 299)? Is "A Day's Wait" really about the father, his sick child, or both? Ultimately, it comes down to one important question that readers must decide for themselves—"Whose story is this?"

In *The Lonely Voice*, Frank O'Connor relates the following incident:

> One night in a Dublin street I watched an extraordinary scene between a tramp and a prostitute whose sad little affair had broken up—his hope of a home, hers of a husband. Bit by bit she stripped off the few garments he had bought for her, threw them at his feet, and stood in the cold night air shivering. Suddenly I looked around and saw a beautiful girl who was also watching the scene and realized that she was easily the most interesting figure in the little group. On her face was a look that I can describe only as one of exultation. Maupassant would have followed that girl to her home. (69)

Had O'Connor written a story based on this fabula, he could have employed a Conradian split, with the tramp and prostitute as the subjects and the girl who observes them as the focalizer. It might be told by the girl in the first person. But it could also be narrated using the girl in third-person fixed internal focalization. In that case, it would have the form of Hemingway's "A Clean Well-Lighted Place," in which two waiters in a café converse about an old man who sits alone drinking and who recently tried to hang himself. Although mostly in dialogue, the story is focalized through the older waiter, and Hemingway allows himself access to that character's consciousness, especially at the end when he enters the waiter's mind in a lengthy passage of immediate speech. I bring up the O'Connor anecdote to make two points. First, a narrative need not be in the first person to be a Conradian split; the split can be between the subject and the focalizer. We see examples of Conradian splits in such third-person stories as "Indian Camp" (Nick / Dr. Adams), perhaps "The Battler" (Nick / Ad and Bugs), and "A Pursuit Race" (Mr. Turner / William Campbell). Even the externally focalized "The Killers" possesses a near Conradian split (Nick / Ole Andreson).

The second point is a general one about the relationship between focalization and storytelling. My friend Marc Dolan and I occasionally used to play a game; when one of us related a recent incident from his life, afterward we would ask, "Whose story is this?" That is, if one were to write a story based on this incident, which character would present the most interesting, the richest, point of view? Often, after some discussion, we would find that the best focalizer was not necessarily the person who, in the real-life incident, was the main character. (It was never me, or even my girlfriend, but always some utterly irrelevant person who just happened to be present!) Since we all want to think of ourselves as the heroic first-person narrators of our own lives, I came to resent rarely even being the focalizer of mine. As would, I'm sure, the tramp or the prostitute from the O'Connor anecdote, I felt the focalizer should be me and not the young woman across the street. But this little exercise taught me something. The Jamesian dictate that the fixed internal focalizer, his "central consciousness," be the person most finely aware and best positioned to get the most out of the material is a principle relevant to the novel but not to the short story. In one of his many pronouncements on the subject, James defines what sort of character best serves as the central consciousness:

> The person capable of feeling in the given case more than another of what is to be felt for it, and so serving in the highest degree to *record* it dramatically and objectively, is the only sort of person on whom we can count not to betray, to cheapen or, as we say, give away, the value and beauty of the thing. By so much as the affair matters *for* some such individual, by so much do we get the best there is of it, and by so much as it falls within

the scope of a denser and duller, a more vulgar and more shallow capacity, do we get a picture dim and meagre. (Preface to *The Princess Casamassima* 1093)

Don't be misled by James's use of the word *feeling* here; what he means is that the best fixed internal focalizer, or central consciousness, is the character with the broadest perspective and deepest capacity for understanding the events being related. As his friend Edith Wharton summed it up, James believed "that the mind chosen by the author to mirror his given case should be so situated, and so constituted, as to take the widest possible view of it" (*Writing* 45–46). For James, this meant the character with the greatest capacity for awareness.

In the short story, in which the material is less spacious and diverse, the best focalizer is usually not the character possessed of the greatest capacity for awareness, but the character who is most interestingly *emotionally affected* by that material. No one would deny that the character with the widest perspective in "Indian Camp" is Dr. Adams, who must perform a Caesarean operation with fishing equipment; that the most important character in the real-life sense is the pregnant Indian woman; or that the least relevant character is Nick, who also has the narrowest perspective. But Nick, who has little capacity for understanding the events he witnesses, is by far the best focalizer for the story. If we were present for the events of "In Another Country," the object of our concern and principal character would be the Italian major, who has lost his wife and who also has the broadest perspective, but the young narrator has the more interesting emotional perspective if not the most emotionally wrenching one. Hemingway's best stories proceed obliquely, by indirection, and such fixed internal focalizers, although not necessarily possessing the widest perspective or greatest awareness, get us to the heart of the story in the most illuminating way.

For the reader, focalization is epistemological—it determines how we know what we know. But for the writer, it is structural—the choice of focalization determines the form of the story. As Robert Scholes and Robert Kellogg observe: "Point of view is the primary way he [the writer] controls and shapes his materials. Once made, his choice of point of view and the mode of language appropriate to it will influence his presentation of character, incident, and every other thing represented. For the reader, however, point of view is not an esthetic matter but a mode of perception" (275).

We read stories after the fact and do not tend to ponder what possibilities of narration the fabula presented before the story was made. To understand what the writer confronted at the start, though, one can take a story and posit alternative methods of focalization and different focalizers and then explore what might have emerged from those choices. It is—similar to playing "Whose story is this?"—a game, but one that greatly enriches our understanding of focalization, the form of the story, and the relationship between them.

In this chapter, I've tried to illuminate Hemingway's methods of focalization and, concurrently, to examine the significance of the *in our time* vignettes, in which he first worked out many of the focalizing techniques he would further develop in the thirty-nine new stories he wrote for his first three story collections. Upon completing the stories of *Winner Take Nothing* in 1933, he had not only employed the types of narration we've explored here, he had also written stories in the form of a play ("Today Is Friday"), almost fully in dialogue ("Hills Like White Elephants"), in the form of a personal essay ("A Natural History of the Dead"), in the form of an epistle ("One Reader Writes"), and a postmodern story told three times with variation in each telling ("Homage to Switzerland"). In by far the best criticism of the latter, Michael Reynolds demonstrates how it ingeniously dramatizes Einstein's theory that time and space are not absolute values. Although the story is utterly atypical in Hemingway's opus, Reynolds concludes, only partially tongue-in-cheek, "If James Joyce had written 'Homage to Switzerland,' its study would have produced a book, 15 articles, and 30 dissertations" ("Homage" 258).

By the time Hemingway wrote the three third-person stories completed in 1936, and the one third-person and five first-person stories completed in 1938 and early 1939, he was running out of innovative things to do with focalization in the genre. The two long African stories of 1936 are interesting experiments. In "The Short Happy Life of Francis Macomber," he successfully uses extended variable focalization that verges on the nonfocalized Tolstoyian omniscience he had hitherto eschewed (some critics think he did cross into omniscience). Although he doesn't necessarily reveal anything beyond what can be accessed through the minds of the characters, and the bulk of the focalizing is done through the hunter Robert Wilson and Francis Macomber, nevertheless, at different points he focalizes through Macomber's wife Margot, the lion Macomber wounds and Wilson finishes off, one of the gun-bearers (briefly), and, from outside of the text, the Macombers' social set and an anonymous society columnist.[9]

Aside from the ecocritically problematical question of focalizing through the lion, the two places where the text flirts with (or crosses over into) omniscience are when the narrator reports how the Macombers "were known" to society (*SS* 22), and when he says of Macomber, "lying alone, he did not know the Somali proverb that says a brave man is always frightened three times by a lion; when he first sees his track, when he first hears him roar and when he first confronts him" (*SS* 11). (He also reports what Macomber "did not know" in several other places.) But the former is knowledge that the Macombers might presumably have had, and the latter is something that Wilson surely might have known. In fact, what most sets this story apart in Hemingway's opus is the full-blown repertoire of cinematic camera techniques and the deft orchestration of voices in words spoken and thought (each of which represents a different ideology and set of values). As Wallace Martin observes, the story includes a "dazzling display" of "panoramic views, close-ups, track shots . . . and zoom-ins." Martin also notes that the story is, in the Bakhtinian sense, heteroglossic, that the narrative "highlights rather than smoothing over the linguistic differences" in the speech and thoughts of the characters (144, 149). Whether or not "Francis Macomber" is omniscient, the story is certainly an ambitious attempt at highly complex focalization, and in this it reveals Hemingway's desire to move into such forms of narration on a larger scale.

The other African story of 1936, "The Snows of Kilimanjaro," in which a writer named Harry is dying from gangrene during a safari, is mainly told through third-person fixed internal focalization but occasionally and at the end is focalized through his wife Helen. The experiment here is seen in the series of Harry's lengthy flashbacks, set against his impending death in base time, and in passages of immediate speech in the present that report Harry's thoughts.

Hemingway drew upon the focalization techniques of both African stories in the novel he completed the following year. In *To Have and Have Not* (published in 1937, with sections previously published as stories in April 1934 and February 1936), he innovatively employs variable focalization and immediate speech, and even mixes first- and third-person narration, though not altogether successfully. Three years later, he achieved striking success in complex focalization in his greatest novel, *For Whom the Bell*

Tolls (1940), the first full-length book in which he did not employ any first-person narration. Written mainly using third-person fixed internal focalization through the protagonist, Robert Jordan, it occasionally varies its focalizer for specific scenes, as in the stunning portrayal of El Sordo's last stand against the Fascists; it is heavily in dialogue; it employs flashbacks as Jordan recalls earlier events in his life; and it makes such perfect use of immediate speech with its access to Jordan's thoughts that it sometimes feels as if it's a first-person narrative. In terms of focalization, then, *For Whom the Bell Tolls* was the inevitable result of Hemingway's ambition, one that he partially fulfilled in the African stories but that required a novel-length narrative for consummation.

The thematic material of the six published stories of the Spanish Civil War written between April 1938 and February 1939, his final story-writing period, also fed into the writing of *For Whom the Bell Tolls*. But in terms of focalization, little here is new. Six months after the war commenced in July 1936, Hemingway contracted to write dispatches for the North American Newspaper Alliance (NANA). During the next two years, he made three extended visits to that war-torn country (March–May 1937, September–December 1937, March–May 1938), filing thirty reports for NANA and writing the commentary and providing the narration for *The Spanish Earth*, a pro-Loyalist documentary written by Archibald Mac-Leish, John Dos Passos, and Lillian Hellman. With his gift for concision, he also annunciated the truest political line of the day in seven short words when he appeared at the American Writer's Congress on 4 June 1937 and stated, "Fascism is a lie told by bullies" (qtd. in Reynolds, *1930s* 270).

Perhaps because the dispatches were in the first person, so too were five of the six stories, as well as a seventh he completed but never published. The six first-person stories take place in Spain, mostly in Madrid, and the one third-person story, "Nobody Ever Dies," is set after the war in Cuba. The first-person narrations are mostly first-person peripheral, akin to the narration of a dispatch, and the narrator is a character who greatly resembles Hemingway. In "The Denunciation" and "The Butterfly and the Tank," the narrator is an American fiction writer named Enrique Emmunds (resonating with "Ernest" and "Hem"); he stays at the Florida Hotel (where Hemingway stayed); he frequents Chicote's Restaurant (Hemingway's favorite Madrid bar); he has Hemingway's memories of New York, Chicago, Key West, and Marseilles, as well as his memories of George, the chasseur at the Ritz in Paris (actually Georges, later immortalized in *A Move-*

able Feast); and, most of all, he has Hemingway's attitude right down to an ironic self-revelation—"But I had given him the shortest cut to having Delgado arrested in one of those excesses of impartiality, righteousness and Pontius Pilatry, and the always-dirty desire to see how people act under an emotional conflict, that makes writers such attractive friends" (*CSS* 426). In "Night Before Battle," "Under the Ridge," and the unpublished "Landscape with Figures," the narrator is, as Hemingway was, a member of an American film crew making a war documentary.

Clearly, Hemingway was emotionally too close to the material to digest it and transmute it into art. The fabulas of the stories are almost contemporaneous with their time of narration, and he was still in the correspondent's mode. From Paris on 22 October 1938, he sent off "Night Before Battle" to Arnold Gingrich, editor of *Esquire,* and wrote: "Christ it is fine to write again and not to have to write pieces [dispatches]. I was really going nuts with that." Confiding that he was offered "a staff captain's commission with the French to go with what they were going to move into Spain," he claimed, "Things [the impending Loyalist defeat by Franco] are so foul, now, that if you think about them you go nuts." The answer is to get back to writing: "You have to climb up into that old tower to do your work . . . A writer has to write and beyond all other things it can make you feel good when it comes out right." He also mentions having "two chapters done on a novel" (*SL* 472–73). By February 1939, he had completed six stories about the war and wrote Maxwell Perkins from Key West that he wanted to combine five of them with "three very long ones I want to write" (one of which would, over a decade later, become *The Old Man and the Sea*) for a new story collection to come out in the fall (*SL* 479). A month later, he wrote Perkins that instead of the three long stories, he had written "Under the Ridge" and "then started on another [story] I'd had no intention of writing for a long time and working steadily every day found I had fifteen thousand words done; that it was very exciting; and that it was a novel." Although he did not discard the idea of a story collection, he declared his intention to finish the novel and that "it will be as good as I can write." Significantly, he stated that the novel was "20 times better than that Night Before Battle," and, in a phrase that aptly describes all his civil war stories, he said that the story "was flat where this [the novel] is rounded and recalled where this is invented." He added, "I find I know a lot more than when I used to write and think that is maybe what makes it easier . . . I feel as happy and as good as when I was going good on A Farewell to Arms"

(*SL* 482). Two months later, in May, he was two hundred pages into the manuscript of what would be his longest novel and mistakenly assuming that he was over halfway done (*SL* 485).

The Spanish Civil War stories, though far below Hemingway's standards, performed an important enabling function. As Allen Josephs notes, because they were so autobiographical and political, they helped "to purge the real war and the real loss of the Spanish Republic from Hemingway's fiction" and "became a kind of cathartic, fictional memoir" ("Civil War" 325). In the end, he was so wrapped up in his novel that he never even bothered to mail out "Landscape with Figures." His career as a story writer was, for all intents and purposes, over.

Although he would write a handful of stories in the years after *For Whom the Bell Tolls,* in his last two decades Hemingway continued to seek new challenges in the novel, as he had, during the previous two decades, in short fiction. He had accomplished everything he had wanted to do in the story genre and in the process had changed it forever. He might have done the same for the novel, but *For Whom the Bell Tolls* turned out to be his high water mark. His future efforts were undermined by physical injuries, failing health, the effects of years of serious alcohol drinking, the strain and distraction of celebrity, and a losing battle with the emotional depression he had fought off for years by whatever means necessary so that he could do the one thing he most loved—writing. It wasn't for lack of ambition—the sheer generic variety of his longer works and the experimentation revealed in the unpublished manuscript of *The Garden of Eden* disproves that. He just wore down. After writing a fictional death for Richard Cantwell, the protagonist and persona of his 1950 novel *Across the River and into the Trees,* eleven years later Hemingway followed suit. If he could no longer write, he would no longer live. The rest he left to the readers, critics, and others who continue to hover about the remains.

5

Repetition and Juxtaposition

FROM STEIN TO HEMINGWAY

Immature poets imitate; mature poets steal; bad poets deface what they take, and good poets make it into something better, or at least something different. The good poet welds his theft into a whole of feeling which is unique, utterly different from that from which it was torn; the bad poet throws it into something which has no cohesion. A good poet will usually borrow from authors remote in time, or alien in language, or diverse in interest.
                    —T. S. Eliot, "Philip Massinger"

Something else I learned to consider—judiciously—for myself, from Hemingway, was the use of repetition: we need to coin another term to honor him, conveying repetition transformed in his hand as a special term for emphasis; used well, repetition becomes the Beethoven note, a knell laden with resonant meaning.
                    —Nadine Gordimer, "Hemingway's Expatriates"

Acknowledging Gertrude Stein's influence on Hemingway has become obligatory when discussing his use of repetition, but the extent of her influence has been exaggerated and misunderstood. It was Hemingway's nature to learn quickly from mentors and, once he got what he needed, to drop them just as quickly. This process was partly the result of temperament— he was too competitive and independent to remain in thrall to anyone— and partly it was because, however much others influenced him, he always transmuted that influence into his own craft. One rarely sees Hemingway imitating anybody else, and when he does, it's unexceptional.

Stein influenced Hemingway as a maternal figure, a teacher, and a writer. During their brief relationship, she served as a surrogate mother who physically and emotionally had much in common with Grace Hall Hemingway but, unlike her, took his literary ambitions seriously and encouraged him at a time when he desperately needed such support. In a letter to her biographer written after her death, Hemingway also admitted having had a strong sexual attraction to Stein (*SL* 650); as Jeffrey Meyers observes, Hemingway "tried to work out" with her some of "the strong

Oedipal feelings" he had for Grace (77). Second, just as Pound guided his reading of literature, so Stein extended the art education Grace had provided by introducing Hemingway to the Impressionists and Cubists. The walls of her Paris apartment were covered with paintings by Paul Cézanne, Henri Matisse, Georges Braque, Juan Gris, and Pablo Picasso, including Picasso's famous portrait of Stein (which resembled Picasso).

Stein told Hemingway she had written *Three Lives* sitting in front of Cézanne's *Portrait de Madame Cézanne,* and the prose of that book, as James Mellow notes, imitates "Cézanne's method, with its infinitely patient repetition of one stroke laid next to another." Mellow summarizes what Stein discovered in Cézanne and passed on to Hemingway: "the sense of overall composition in which each part, each sentence, was as significant as any other part, a composition in which nothing seemed to happen, but one which, through reiterative phrases and shifting emphases, moved forward to the culminating paragraph" (150). Hemingway took her instruction to heart, began regularly visiting the Musée du Luxembourg and the Louvre, developed into an art aficionado, and translated Cézanne's methods into his own literary techniques of landscape depiction (Reynolds, *Paris* 40). Stein also introduced him to another of his passions, the bullfights, talking to him about the great matador Joselito and encouraging him to travel to Spain (*DIA* 1–2). The influence of Stein's own writing, however, is a complicated matter, for she was more a philosopher of language and narrative than a teller of stories; her methods of narration in such works as *Three Lives* and the highly opaque *The Making of Americans* are so utterly different from even the most avant-garde types of modernist fiction that any disciple would, of necessity, have to adapt rather than adopt them.

At the time Stein influenced Hemingway, she was trying to do in fiction what her friend Picasso was doing in painting. As she explained, before Picasso "no one had ever tried to express things seen not as one knows them but as they are when one sees them without remembering having looked at them." Picasso tried "to express not things felt, not things remembered, not established in relations but things which are there, really everything a human being can know at each moment of his existence and not an assembling of all his experiences." When we view a person in profile, we "see" only one eye, but we "know" from memory and experience that a second eye exists hidden from our sight, "and everybody is accustomed to complete the whole entirely from their knowledge, but Picasso when he saw an eye, the other one did not exist for him and only the one he saw did exist for him and . . . he was right, one sees what one sees, the rest is a reconstruction from memory and painters . . . concern themselves only with visible things and so the cubism of Picasso was an effort to make a picture of these visible things." Yet, by 1914, "there were less cubes in cubism" because "after all one must know more than one sees and one does not see a cube in its entirety" (*Picasso* 15, 35). Picasso moved from cubes to flat surfaces when he realized that a cube still implies an unseen portion of the object. With that shift, Stein believed, Picasso created a purely objective art (however subjective it might seem to viewers) in that it was entirely based on what could be seen at a given moment. Stein, too, in this period between *Three Lives* and the publication of *The Making of Americans,* committed herself to an aesthetics of pure objectivity, removing from her fiction anything known from memory or experience and instead relying exclusively on what can be perceived through the senses at any given moment. This is a fiction of surfaces, so different from anything that came before that it barely seems to fit the category of narrative.

From this effort to write fiction based only on what the senses perceive at a moment in time, five elements of Stein's aesthetics derive. First, she believed that writers should not draw upon their own lives because this subject matter is so saturated with memory that it is difficult to recover it exactly as it existed at the moment of being experienced. Second, she developed techniques for writing a "continuous present"—narratives in which each sentence presents only what was experienced at that precise moment, divorced from the memory of previous moments and not anticipating what might come next. She thereby eliminated linearity from narrative. One favorite Stein technique was to employ verbs in progressive tenses and gerunds, which present action as continuing rather than completed (in the past). She also tended to eschew nouns because nouns represent objects that build up significance over time, whereas ongoing verbs locate their significance in the moment they are taking place. Third, with linearity eliminated, it became necessary in each sentence, and even in each clause, to repeat information from previous sentences and clauses because the sentences are discreet and do not build upon each other (although there is still a cumulative effect). She called this "beginning again," with each sentence starting from scratch in presenting that particular moment. Fourth, this necessarily led to "repetition" because she had to repeat phrases of information for each sentence and clause in order to prevent sentences from connecting with one another, which would occur if the reader needed to process the text in the usual way by carrying that information forward from earlier sentences. But Stein called her form of repetition *insistence,* stating that "there is no such thing as repetition." By *insistence* she meant that even when something is repeated, "emphasis can never be the same"—in other words, nothing (including words) can ever really be repeated because each moment, and the sentence or the clause representing it, is unique: "if anything is alive there is no such thing as repetition" ("Portraits" 165, 171, 174). (Stein used as an analogy the cinema in which each frame slightly differs from adjacent frames.) Fifth, since selection, plot, linearity, and all other elements of traditional narrative depend upon memory and experience—what must be eliminated if we are to focus exclusively on perception in the present in its purity and integrity— then Stein must use all the material she treats. In other words, there are no available criteria to determine what material is important; all perceptions and sensations at the moment they are experienced are equally important (neither anticipated in advance nor sorted out in memory). And each sentence or page, too, is equally important; no hierarchy of significance exists among them. These principles create the flatness of her narratives, which one can almost read by starting anywhere in the text rather than going from beginning to end. Using the Great War as an analogy, she states: "Really the composition of this war, 1914–1918, was not the composition of all previous wars, the composition was not a composition in which there was one man in the centre surrounded by a lot of other men but a composition that had neither a beginning nor an end, a composition of which one corner was as important as another corner, in fact the composition of cubism" (*Picasso* 11). These, then, were the fundamentals of her aesthetics at the time she influenced Hemingway. As she summed it up, "Continuous present is one thing and beginning again and again is another thing. These are both things. And then there is using everything" ("Composition" 518).

As we've seen, Hemingway also wanted to represent moments as they are being experienced rather than retrospectively after they've been processed; this aim is central to his impressionism. But he wanted no part of Stein's elimination of linearity; he only sought to give his fiction immediacy. Although on occasion he employed Stein's technique of using progressive tenses and gerunds to give the impression of ongoing action, he did so selectively and did not make it the keystone of his art that it was for hers. Stein emphasized verbs and adverbs, and used as few nouns as possible, but Hemingway used few adverbs and very basic verbs—his favorite being different forms of *to be*. Furthermore, his verbs are often intransitive, and he frequently introduces verbs with an expletive so that the sentence is in the passive voice, further vitiating the power of the verb. His style is diametrically different from Stein's—heavily noun based, with a few carefully selected adjectives, weak verbs and verb forms, and nearly no adverbs. As Harry Levin once noted, "Hemingway puts his emphasis on nouns because, among parts of speech, they come closest to things. Stringing them along by means of conjunctions, he approximates the actual flow of experience" (79).

Nouns build up meaning from their appearance in different contexts throughout a narrative, from the qualities that accrue to them over time (what Roland Barthes terms the "semic code"), and this accretion necessarily involves memory. By his noun-based style, Hemingway subordinated Stein's pure representation of a given moment to the exigencies of story and the cumulative meanings that build up during a narrative. In Hemingway you get the perceptions (and infer the sensations) of the moment as it is experienced, but that experience is also conditioned by the memory of what went before and by the anticipation of what might come next. These latter two elements were, for him, *also* a part of the experience of any particular moment and could not be separated out from it. For Stein, a deconstructionist before there was deconstruction, another problem with nouns was that the signifier could never equal the signified—*cat* was only a word and never a real cat. Not coincidentally, in much of her writing, one might say that nothing exists for her outside the words of the text. But Hemingway was not terribly concerned with signifier slippage or the philosophical implications of such proto-Derridean epistemological skepticism. He wrote *cat* and assumed the reader would fill in a specific cat from personal experience.

As for his own experiences, he purposely based his fiction on events he had participated in or observed directly—wars, hunting, fishing, bullfighting, travels, relationships with family, friends, and women—the material of his own life. For Stein, subject matter should not come from one's own experience because that involved memory; for Hemingway, to write about what one didn't know from experience was anathema. With reference to Stein's trinity of the continuous present, using everything, and beginning again, Hemingway's present was both the moment and the extended context of the moments in which it occurred; he used selection rather than everything; and he had no need to begin again since his narratives were linear. There was yet another fundamental difference in their aesthetics. As Kirk Curnutt (citing Shari Benstock) points out, Stein's automatic writing was an attempt to free up language by resisting mastery, by keeping words from having to submit to her will. But Hemingway "was incapable of appreciating this resistance [of mastery], for will, mastery, and control for him were integral measures of craftsmanship . . . Because he imagined writing as a centripetal quest to arrive at the 'one true sentence,' he could only misread Stein's centrifugal hermeticism as indifference to" the responsibility of writers to revise and to make their writing intelligible (127).

What, then, did Hemingway learn from Stein's writing if their aesthetics were so different? Although he would say many cruel things about her, his posthumous memoir contains a genuine moment of appreciation: "She had also discovered many truths about rhythms and the uses of words in repetition that were valid and valuable and she talked well about them" (*MF* 17). In *The Making of Americans,* sections of which Hemingway proofread, copied as her amanuensis, and even helped get published, Stein explains and demonstrates her theory of repetition. In a person's unique existence, each repeats the feelings, perspectives, ways of being, and other characteristics that make them who they are: "Repeating then is in every one, in every one their being and their feeling and their way of realising everything and every one comes out of them in repeating" (284). By writing sentences that focus exclusively on the perceptions she has at each moment of observing a character, Stein's repetition is really "insistence," as each sentence, despite the repetition, adds something perceived in that particular moment (since no two moments can ever be the same). The total effect of all of these sentences depicting the perceptions of a string of moments, rather than summing them up with adjectives in retrospect, is a painting created in the same manner as the Cézanne portrait Stein stared at while she wrote, brushstroke by brushstroke: "repeating then makes a complete history in every one for some one sometime to realise in that one. Repeating is in them of the most delicate shades in them of being and of feeling and so it comes to be clear in each one the complete nature in each one, it comes to be clear in each one the connection between that one and others to make a kind of them, a kind of men and women" (*Americans* 184). Gradually, through a person's repetitions, their "complete nature" becomes

clear, as well as their similarities to others whom they resemble. Stein acknowledges the existence of these types or "kinds," but because of her deep
sense of the particularity of each individual person she refuses to sum up
these "kinds" with categorical adjectives.

Here is a brief example from *The Making of Americans* of Stein's
method, which I have literally snatched at random from a novel she called
"almost a thousand pages of a continuous present" ("Composition" 518):

> She was to mostly every one a completely honest one. She was to
> mostly every one an earnest, an excited and an ambitious one, she was
> to mostly every one fighting to be successfully a winning one by steady
> fighting all her living, by courage in resisting being worn out by any one
> else's attacking, she was to every one one being one leading in all fight-
> ing she was doing all her living, she was one having complete conviction
> that thinking and working and being an interested one in everything was
> something giving meaning to her being in all of her living. This is to be
> now some description of the way some were realising being in Julia Deh-
> ning. (*Americans* 626)

Note how the brushstrokes are laid down in the clauses of the long middle
sentence, how the portrait builds with each particularity but although cumulative does not require the reader to link the sentences and clauses together. Also note the importance of gerunds and progressive tenses in conveying perceptions of Julia Dehning's feelings and states of being without
attaching these to specific concrete actions in a temporal sequence. Last,
note how this is both the way Stein describes Julia and also the manner by
which others come to know Julia (or how anyone comes to know anyone,
for that matter). The final sentence has a wonderful double meaning that
states Stein's major premises. This is *the way* some people realize "being"
in Julia (how they realize the nature of Julia), and it is also *why* they realize (because these qualities are in Julia). Insistence is epistemological and
ontological: the *process* by which we perceive the object and the *nature* of
the object.

But what has this to do with Hemingway? Stein's insistence was different from his repetition, and when he tried to ape her, it was mannered and
mostly ineffective. His early story, "Up in Michigan," which she found "*in-
accrochable*" for its sexual explicitness (*MF* 15), has a Stein-like paragraph,

although critics disagree over whether it was written before or after Stein met and influenced him (Smith, *Reader's Guide* 5–6):

> Liz liked Jim very much. She liked it the way he walked over from the shop and often went to the kitchen door to watch for him to start down the road. She liked it about his mustache. She liked it about how white his teeth were when he smiled. She liked it very much that he didn't look like a blacksmith. She liked it how much D. J. Smith and Mrs. Smith liked Jim. One day she found that she liked it the way the hair was black on his arms and how white they were above the tanned line when he washed up in the washbasin outside the house. Liking that made her feel funny. (*SS* 81)

This passage effectively conveys Liz's feelings toward Jim, but it draws attention to itself and is stylistically at odds with the story. Somewhat more felicitous is the paragraph in "Cat in the Rain" in which Hemingway uses *liked* in six consecutive brief sentences to convey the wife's feelings about the hotel padrone (*SS* 168). Most effective was his use of *like* in "Soldier's Home" to convey the wax and wane of Krebs's attraction to the hometown girls he watches from his mother's porch after returning from the war:

> He liked the girls that were walking along the other side of the street. He liked the look of them much better than the French girls or the German girls. But the world they were in was not the world he was in. He would like to have one of them. But it was not worth it. They were such a nice pattern. He liked the pattern. It was exciting. But he would not go through all the talking. He did not want one badly enough. He liked to look at them all, though. It was not worth it. Not now when things were getting good again. (*SS* 148)

Here he does not overdo it (five uses of *like* spread over thirteen sentences), with the *likes* countered by opposing feelings about the girls, so that rather than a pattern of declarative "he liked" sentences, we have an internal monologue demonstrating Krebs's ambivalence. Effective or not, however, these passages are atypical in Hemingway's opus, although repetition is a major technique of his art.

Many writers were working with repetition in narrative after the war, and, as Michael Reynolds points out, Hemingway had experimented with it in the journalism and stories he wrote for the *Toronto Star* (*Young* 191, 213–14). Jeffrey Meyers notes that Hemingway was even playing with repetition in a story he wrote for the *Kansas City Star* in April 1918 before going off to war, a brief sketch in which he repeats—at the start, middle, and end—three slightly varied sentences about a woman walking along the wet, lamp-lit sidewalk (Meyers 25–26; *CR* 56–58). Furthermore, his mature use of repetition, as Frank O'Connor observes, was much closer to Joyce's than to Stein's (*Lonely* 116, 118–19, 156–60). So what were the "truths about rhythms and the uses of words in repetition" that Stein taught him and that he thought "were valid and valuable"?

Something Hemingway surely learned from her is that by repeating a word in a different context you can foreground a different denotation or connotation and change that word's meaning. This sort of repetition with variation, a variation produced by different contexts, is central to Hemingway's use of repetition in his nondialogue prose (we'll deal with his innovative use of repetition in dialogue in chapter 8). Let's look at three exemplary instances of this technique, each of which illuminates a different function of Hemingway's use of repetition.

The initial example is the third paragraph of "Che Ti Dice la Patria?"— it occurs after the opening paragraphs we analyzed in chapter 3, as the narrator and his friend drive through fascist Italy on their way to Spezia:

> [1] Outside the **villages** there were **fields** with **vines**. [2] The **fields** were <u>brown</u> and the **vines** course and thick. [3] The **houses** were <u>white,</u> and in the streets the men, in their Sunday clothes, were playing bowls. [4] Against the **walls** of some of the **houses** there were **pear trees**, their branches candelabraed against the <u>white</u> **walls**. [5] The **pear trees** had been sprayed, and the **walls** of the **houses** were stained a <u>metallic blue-green</u> by the spray vapor. [6] There were ***small clearings*** around the **villages** where the **vines** grew, and then the woods. (<u>SS</u> 290; boldface, italics, and underlining mine)

Five of the ten verbs in this passage are forms of *to be,* three of which are employed in a passive construction introduced by the expletive *there were* (sentences 1, 4, and 6). The other two uses of *to be* are also inactive: as linking verbs joining a subject with a complement, in this case noting the color of the fields and the houses (sentences 2 and 3). Two of the remaining five verbs are in the passive voice ("had been sprayed" and "were stained" in sentence 5), so that the subjects of the sentence (the trees and walls) are being acted upon. In both cases, the "actor" is omitted (i.e., we do not know who sprayed the trees and thus stained the walls). The second case comes close to being a linking verb, with "stained a metallic blue-green vapor" acting as an adjective clause. The second verb of sentence 4 (*cande-labraed*) may seem transitive because Hemingway has elided the auxiliary *were*. But even if it is transitive, the nature of this unusual verb (and perhaps neologism) makes it seem inactive, more a description of the shape of the tree branches than an action they are performing. It is also possible that *candelabraed* is coined here as an adjective. The only two active verbs in the passage depict the men's actions, "playing bowls" (the Italian game of *bocce*) in sentence 3, and the vines' actions, "the vines grew," in the last sentence. The past progressive tense of the former indicates a continuing action, which keeps it in the present moment (a Stein technique), and these two verbs indicate the only real action taking place in the scene: the men playing and the vines growing. This juxtaposition invites a contrast between the two activities; the only subject performing a useful action are the vines, upon whose growth the village's economy, and the men's leisurely bowling, depends. There are no adverbs in the passage, and the general effect of the verbs is to describe a static scene, a painting rather than a narrative, one that functions as part of a three-paragraph tonal opening to set up the narrator's subsequent representation of the people in these villages as passive underneath the veneer of Italy's Fascist government. The vines continue to grow, governments come and go, but the village's way of life abideth forever.

Nouns perform the real work in this passage, and Hemingway employs them in his own form of repetition. There are fourteen different nouns: villages, fields, vines, houses, streets, men, clothes, bowls, walls, pear trees, branches, vapor, clearings, woods. (I designate *pear trees* as a noun rather than an adjective and noun because *pear* signifies a species of tree rather than modifying *trees*.) Six of these fourteen nouns are repeated: three mentions of *walls* and two mentions each of *villages, fields, vines, houses,* and *pear trees.* Also, *fields* is signified a third time in the synonym *small clearings* in sentence 6. The nouns are generic, or "category nouns," modified by only a few adjectives that are either primary colors (*brown* and *white* and the more exotic *metallic blue-green*) or else fairly general (*course, thick, small*). These category nouns and the adjectives that modify them imitate elements of Cézanne's paintings of similar such towns: the highlighting of particular shapes by uniform and basic colors that work in juxtaposition with one another. In this case, we have brown fields, white houses, and metallic blue-green stains, which define the main shapes in the portrait, although in real life many more colors would be present.

Hemingway disperses the repeated nouns across the paragraph in the manner of a painting, forming the visual structure of the passage. If we break down the paragraph into three groups of two sentences each, then each group in the triptych contains five of the repeated nouns, with the third group also containing a sixth conceptual repetition in its use of *small clearings* as a substitute for *fields*. In sentences 1 and 2, we are approaching the villages, and the five repetitions are nouns from this location: outside the villages, fields, vines, fields, vines. In sentences 3 and 4 we are in the villages: houses, walls, houses, pear trees, walls. In sentences 5 and 6, we are leaving the villages, and the repeated nouns go from the triad of pear trees, walls, and houses in sentence 5 to the triad of small clearings, around the villages, and vines in sentence 6. The picture is framed by another favorite Hemingway technique, which I term *recapitulation with variation*. Sentence 6 gathers up the images of sentence 1 but repeats them in a slightly different manner. Instead of "Outside the villages" we get "around the villages"; in place of "fields" we get the synonym "small clearings"; and in both we get "vines." Hemingway used recapitulation with variation for many purposes. Here, it provides the frame for the tableau. Elsewhere, as in the sixth paragraph of "A Canary for One," he employs the technique in order to emphasize the actions of one of the characters. The second sentence of that paragraph reads: "In the night the American lady lay without sleeping because the train was a *rapide* and went very fast and she was afraid of the speed in the night." The final sentence reads: "There was a blue light outside the compartment, and all night the train went very fast and the American lady lay awake and waited for a wreck" (*SS* 338). In recapitulation with variation, he slightly alters what is being repeated so that the repetition does not call attention to itself, as it so manifestly does in Stein's repetitions. This type of repetition without literal repetition enables him to eat his cake and have it, too.

In sentence 6, something new appears—"and then the woods"—which takes us past the frame and out of the picture, preparing us for the next paragraph in which we are suddenly in a specific "village, twenty kilometres above Spezia" (*SS* 290). The narrator and his friend are traveling the country, but Hemingway wants to present, in the paragraph we've been analyzing, a representative landscape. Moreover, he wants this painting to apply to all the villages the narrator passes through, which means it is a most un-Stein-like retrospective reconstruction of several points of time conflated into one description. By this method, he presents the repeated experiences of passing through villages as a static painting of one moment, but the repeated nouns carry us through (and across) the painting so that we still have motion, something emphasized in the additional "and then the woods"—which adds a degree of suddenness to our movement away from the composite village. The pattern of repeated nouns is also akin to how Cézanne would lead the viewer through his painted landscapes by following the natural path of the scene. By his use of repetition, then, Hemingway presents a tableau characterizing the composite village and still maintains the narrative movement of the car, carrying the focalizer through the paragraph.

In the above passage, Hemingway employs juxtaposition only in the contrast of colors and between the men bowling and the vines growing. Juxtaposition, however, was one of his major techniques and especially important to his short story art. Sometimes he uses juxtaposition to undercut a character's speech. In "Indian Camp," the doctor tells his son, "I don't hear them [the pregnant woman's screams] because they are not important." The next sentence is, "The husband in the upper bunk rolled over against the wall" (SS 92). Juxtaposing the husband's action with the doctor's words exposes the doctor's insensitivity without Hemingway intruding to assert that the screams are important—to the woman, her husband, and the doctor's son. Similarly, in "In Another Country," the doctor tells the wounded narrator, "You will be able to play football again better than ever." The next sentence begins, "My knee did not bend and the leg dropped straight from the knee to the ankle without a calf" (SS 268).

Hemingway's juxtapositions are not solely for such indirect commentary; they are also employed more subtly. The first paragraph of "In Another Country" is a classic Hemingway tonal opening and a perfect piece of fictional prose. It caused Frank O'Connor, who disliked Hemingway's stories and his techniques, to characterize the paragraph as the work of "an old magician sitting over his crystal ball, or a hypnotist waving his hands gently before your eyes" (Lonely 158), and its first sentence led the critically sober Fitzgerald to call it "one of the most beautiful prose sentences I've ever read" and later to exclaim, "God, what a beautiful line" (Fitzgerald Letters 300, 301). The passage not only imparts to the reader a sense of foreboding that sets the mood for the story, it also provides an excellent example of Hemingway's use of repetition and juxtaposition:

> [1] In the **fall** the war was always there, but we did not go to it any more. [2] It was **cold** in the **fall** in Milan and the dark **came** very early. [3] Then the electric lights **came** on, and it was pleasant along the streets looking in the windows. [4] There was much game hanging outside the shops, and the snow powdered in the fur of the foxes and the **wind** blew their tails. [5] The deer hung stiff and heavy and empty, and small birds blew in the **wind** and the **wind** turned their feathers. [6] It was a **cold fall** and the **wind came** down from the mountains. (SS 267; boldface mine)

In looking at this passage as carefully as we would a poem, we can see why Wallace Stevens called Hemingway "the most significant of living poets" (*Letters* 411–12), why Hemingway himself claimed that the "secret" of his fiction is that it is "poetry written into prose" (qtd. in Mary Welsh Hemingway 352), and why I insist on examining short story passages through the formalist close readings that are the hallmark of poetry criticism rather than fiction criticism.

The first sentence presents the proposition the story will subsequently disprove: that one can choose whether or not to go to war, with war here standing as a metaphor for untimely death. The first part of the sentence is passively constructed with an anapest followed by three iambs ("In the fall the war was always there"), whereas the second part has an active construction underscored by four consecutive stresses, an iamb followed by a spondee followed by a trochee ("we did not go"). Thus, in both the sentence's content and prosody, "the war" is inert while "we" are active and have the power of choice. By the story's end, "the war," as a metaphor for death, will be active—the Italian major's wife, whom he had not married until he was safely invalided out of the war, one assumes to protect her from widowhood, dies unexpectedly, and "we" are passive, looking helplessly out a window and at a set of meaningless photographs. Even the lack of a pattern of stresses—the last sentence of the story is deliberately written to make it impossible to scan—serves to emphasize the narrator's confusion, undercutting his certainty in the first sentence: "The photographs did not make much difference to the major because he only looked out of the window" (SS 272).

Even as the paragraph provides thematic fodder for the critic, however, it also indirectly prepares us for the subsequent reversal. The language is exceedingly simple: 106 words totaling 421 letters, with the average word slightly less than four letters long. Of these 106 words, 88 are monosyllabic, 17 have two syllables, and only one (*electric*) has three syllables. The paragraph scans as iambic ("the fall the war was always there") or anapestic ("It was cold in the fall in Milan"), but several double and triple stresses serve to emphasize the darkness, death, and irresistible force being carried down from the mountains where the war is being fought ("dark came"; "game hanging"; "snow powdered"; "wind blew"; "deer hung stiff"; "birds blew"; "wind turned"; "cold fall"; "wind came down"). The sixth sentence is a recapitulation with variation. It gathers up the words and phrases from the paragraph and repeats them in a different arrangement that summarizes the sense of the passage, whose sense is at odds with the first sentence.

Four important words are repeated: two mentions of *cold*, three each of *fall* and *came*, and four of *wind*. The first *fall* merely denotes the season when the story takes place and associates it with *war*. The second *fall* is still a season but is doubly modified by *cold* and *Milan*. Thus, *fall* is denoted as a season and linked to *war, cold,* and *Milan* (an action, climate condition, and location). After this, two related things come ("came"), first the "dark" and then, in response to the dark, the "electric lights." These are, along with the wind blowing, turning, and coming down, two of the three active verbs in the passage. The "snow powdered in the fur of the foxes" is either intransitive or else, if Hemingway purposely elides the auxiliary in "was powdered," the real actor in the clause is not the snow but the wind; that is, what we have here is the passive voice of "the wind powdered the snow in the fur of the foxes." As for the "we" who do not go to the war in the first sentence, this construction is active, but the use of the negative and the fact that this assertion will be undone by the story vitiates that construction. Of the three subjects attached to active verbs, then, the dark and wind are actors, whereas the electric lights are agents whose human actors are absent from the passage. Beginning in sentence 4, we get the drum roll of "winds." As inescapable as the sun in "An Alpine Idyll" or the rain at the start of "Cat in the Rain," the wind powders the snow in the fox fur, it blows the foxes' tails, it blows the birds about, and it turns the birds' feathers. (Note how the effect would be ruined had he written, "the birds flew in the wind" instead of "blew in the wind.")

Arriving at the recapitulation with variation of the sixth sentence, we have been amply prepared for the final repetitions of *fall, cold, came,* and *wind.* Although "cold fall" still refers to the season, it also resonates with a darker meaning, one created by the ominously double-stressed words and by the actions of the wind throughout the passage. The "wind came" is linked to the "dark came," creating an image that will set the mood of the narrative. Even thematically, these repetitions resonate. The dark will indeed come "very early" for the major's wife, there will be a "cold fall" for the major (and also for the naïve narrator), and no one will possess the sort of agency claimed in the first sentence. Rather, in the same manner as the dead game and the birds blowing in the wind, they are all at the mercy of the naturalistic forces pervading the story.

To return to juxtaposition, note how *cold* and *dark came* in sentence 2 undercut through proximity the claim made in sentence 1, and how *fall* serves as the link in this relation. The *electric lights* are then juxtaposed to the *dark,* leading briefly to a "pleasant" scene, which is immediately undercut by its juxtaposition to the actions of the wind. Even the juxtaposition of *cold fall* and *wind came* works to effect an indirect statement, although this time through concordance rather than dissonance. One could just as accurately say that the "cold came" and the "wind fell."

Hemingway's use of juxtaposition was influenced by Pound's imagism, Cézanne's art, and Stein's continuous present, and it well suits his techniques of impressionism, concision, omission, external focalization, and dispassionate presentation. Addressing the correlation between Pound's imagist pronouncements and Hemingway's writing practices, Peter Messent observes: "Precise observations juxtaposed with one another lead to moments of striking insight, often as a result of implicit metaphoric connection. 'Luminous detail' presented without authorial comment operates as a dominant stylistic mode. This stress on particulars, on concrete objects, leads to sequences of clear and hard images put before the reader with all excess description pared drastically away. Emotional and intellectual complexity come directly from the presentation of the physical image" (21–22). In juxtaposition, directly stated connections are omitted, leading to concision. The omission of such connectives effaces the narrator's presence, which is abetted by Hemingway's frequent use of external focalization, even in first-person narratives. The absence of connectives—akin to Emily Dickinson's use of dashes in her poetry—leaves behind, indeed stresses, only an "implicit metaphoric connection" between the images that are now juxtaposed.

These techniques are made possible by his impressionism, without which those external images would either not exist, or would be inextricably entwined with subjective language mitigating the juxtaposition of concrete images. The repetition of images also creates a spatial form in which multiple types of juxtaposition occur throughout the passage, so that their arrangement on the page—their form—implies the author's judgment (which the reader must infer), a key aspect of Hemingway's modernism. I also mention Stein's continuous present as an influence here—in addition to imagism and the juxtapositions on the canvas—because one result of her recording of distinct moments is that meaning derives from their proximity, from the slight differences that exist between such moments on the page. In Stein, juxtaposition results from the contiguity of the moments and the sentences reporting them, not, as with Pound and Hemingway, from the stark placement of images next to each other. Surely, however, Hemingway must have noticed how juxtaposition functions in Stein as he imitated her in his notebooks. Although his use of the technique was different, he learned about its possibilities from Stein as well as from Pound.

Let us conclude with the first paragraph of "Now I Lay Me," in which Hemingway uses repetition and juxtaposition in a different and particularly innovative way, linking these to the operations of consciousness and the unconscious. This highly autobiographical story is based on Hemingway's own wounding and his childhood memories. Nick Adams, fearful of drifting off to sleep in the night because it resembles the experience he had of almost dying, keeps himself awake until light by recalling fishing in different streams, by praying, and then by trying to remember everything that has ever happened to him. The opening paragraph reads:

[1] That night we lay on the floor in the room and I listened to the silk-worms eating. [2a] The silk-worms fed in racks of mulberry leaves and [2b] all night you could hear them eating and a dropping sound in the leaves. [3a] I myself did not want to sleep because [3b] I had been living for a long time with the knowledge that if I ever shut my eyes in the dark and let myself go, my soul would go out of my body. [4a] I had been that way for a long time, ever since [4b] I had been blown up at night and felt it go out of me and go off and then come back. [5] I tried never to think about it, but it had started to go since, in the nights, just at the moment of going off to sleep, and I could only stop it by a very great effort. [6a] So while now I am fairly sure that [6b] it would not really have gone

out, [6c] yet then, that summer, I was unwilling to make the experiment. (*SS* 363)

This does not appear to be, on first reading, a passage with an unusual amount of repetition. The repeated words are less evident than in the paragraph from "In Another Country," perhaps because the passage is longer (176 words versus 106). But perhaps not. Here is the same passage with all the repetitions struck out and boldfaced, including such minor words as articles, conjunctions, and prepositions. Many of these words are exact repetitions, but I also include five instances of words that are close in meaning (*fed* and *eating; listened* and *hear; night* and *dark; living* and *that way; but* and *yet*), different forms of the same verb (*would go out, go off, to go, going off*), and different forms of the same pronoun (*my, myself,* and *me*). The key to Hemingway's use of repetition in this passage is not necessarily that the same word is repeated but that the signification is.

> **~~That night~~** we lay on **the** floor **~~in the~~** room **~~and I listened to the silk-worms eating. The silk-worms fed in~~** racks **of** mulberry **~~leaves and~~** all **night** you **~~could hear~~** them **~~eating and a~~** dropping sound **~~in the leaves~~**. **~~I myself~~** did **not** want **~~to sleep~~** because **~~I had been living for a long time~~** with **the** knowledge **that** if **~~I ever~~** shut **my** eyes **~~in the dark and~~** let **~~myself go, my~~** soul **~~would go out of my~~** body. **~~I had been that way for a long time, ever since I had been~~** blown up **~~at night and~~** felt **~~it go out of me and go off and then~~** come back. **~~I~~** tried **~~never to~~** think about **~~it, but it had~~** started **~~to go since, in the nights~~**, just **~~at the~~** moment **~~of going off to sleep, and I could~~** only stop **it** by **a** very great effort. So while now **~~I am~~** fairly sure **~~that it would not~~** really **~~have gone out, yet then, that~~** summer, **~~I was~~** unwilling **to** make **the** experiment.

I provide this visual image to show just how much repetition there really is in this seemingly nonrepetitive passage. In fact, 126 of the 176 words are repeated, or 71.6 percent (versus 55.7 percent for the "In Another Country" passage). Furthermore, going beyond the repetitions of monosyllabic words in the passages from "Che Ti Dice la Patria?" and "In Another Country," this passage repeats such whole phrases as "I had been living for a long time" and "I had been that way for a long time." Sentence 2 is almost a replay of sentence 1, substituting "all night" for "that night"; and "The silk-worms fed" and "you could hear them eating" for "I listened to the silk-worms eating." The paragraph also contains numerous multiple repeti-tions, such as *night* (five times including *dark*), forms of *to go* (seven times, including three sentences in which it is used twice), and first-person pro-nouns (sixteen times). To what effect are these repetitions working?

To answer this question, let us consider three other aspects of the pas-sage: the buried metaphor in the first two sentences, the time shifts, and the formality of the narrator's discourse. Just as "throwing up" was the buried metaphor in "chapter 2" of *in our time* (see the end of our first chap-ter), the buried metaphor of the first two sentences here is, no pun in-tended, the experience of being buried alive. Literally, the narrator lies on the floor of a makeshift hospital room and hears silkworms outside eat-ing mulberry leaves. But more abstractly and, paradoxically, experien-tially, he lies in an enclosed space and listens to worms eating and drop-ping closer and closer to him. Underscoring this Poesque gothic effect is that the worms are active and he is passive—recumbent and listening. Al-though Hemingway was probably unaware of it, a Romantic belief held that as death approaches, the last sense to disintegrate is that of hearing. For instance, in poem #280, Emily Dickinson imagines herself in her cas-ket and, as her "Being" is now "but an Ear," it is the sound of the mourners "treading," the service "beating," and the noise of the pallbearers' "Boots of Lead" that she apprehends through her one remaining sense (128–29). In poem #465, she imagines herself dying and, after the "Windows failed" (her eyesight goes), the last sense she has before death is hearing the fly's buzz (223–24).

Death is not, as is commonly said, the end of life; it is the moment *after* the final moment of life. Death is wholly other than life; in it, temporal-ity ceases to have meaning. A philosophical empiricist, in #280 and #465 Dickinson tries to imagine the experience of death, but in both cases she cannot. The first poem ends, "And Finished knowing—then—"; the sec-ond concludes, "I could not see to see—" (i.e., I could not sense to under-stand). In both poems, the effort to grasp empirically the experience of death causes her to keep backing up in her narrative. For example, in #465, she begins at the moment of her death, then flashes back to moments be-fore death, then to an earlier time when she wrote her will, then to the mo-ment before death, and then back to her death again. Death not only un-does the temporal frame we employ to understand our lives, it also undoes the chronology of the narrative.

In contrast to Faulkner, Hemingway did not typically employ narrative time shifts. Occasionally, a character reflects on the past—as in "The Snows of Kilimanjaro"—but his stories, including "Snows," proceed chronologically. Not so, however, the opening of "Now I Lay Me." Sentence 1 begins in the base time of "that night" with the simple past tense ("we lay" and "I listened"). Sentence 2 also starts in base time using the simple past ("silkworms fed") but shifts the subject from the narrator ("I") to the silkworms. The second part (2b) extends the duration of the action by changing *that night* to *all night* and employing the second-person with the modal *could,* which asserts confidence (i.e., if you had been there, you would have heard it too) and also subtly shifts the emphasis to the activity of the worms, which is depicted using the past progressive ("eating"). The shift to the past progressive, as does the change to "all night," also acts to extend the duration of base time. Sentence 3, too, begins in the simple past but then (3b) suddenly moves to an indefinite period of time preceding base time ("I had been living for a long time with the knowledge"). The first part of sentence 4 reiterates that indefinite time period preceding base time, but the second part (4b) moves us back to the most distant specific point in past time, when the narrator was "blown up at night," which is the experience that caused the entire paragraph.

The disclosure of this information also defines the start of the indefinite period of time indicated in sentence parts 3b and 4a. Sentence 5, as do sentence parts 3b and 4a, covers the entire time period from the moment he was blown up to base time. Sentence part 6a flashes forward to the moment of narration ("now I am fairly sure"), part 6b shifts to the indefinite period of time between the wounding and base time ("it would not really have gone out"), and part 6c concludes with a further extension of base time ("then, that summer" rather than "that night" or "all night"). These are a lot of time shifts for a six-sentence paragraph, especially for one by Hemingway. Put in chronological order, the paragraph would read: 4b (the night he was blown up); 3b, 4a, and 5 (the indefinite period of time between when he was blown up and the specific night of the story); 6c (the summer in which the night of the story takes place); 2b, 3a, and 6b (the slightly extended night of the story); 1 and 2a (the night of the story, or base time); and 6a (the present time of narration).

A final point is that the narrator's diction and tone seem unusually formal for a Hemingway story (especially one related by Nick Adams). Note the use of the appositive construction *I, myself,* which is unnecessary for purposes of identification. Also note such verbosity as: "I had been living for a long time with the knowledge that if ever I" instead of, say, "I'd known for a long time that if I"; or "just at the moment of going off to sleep" instead of "as I was falling asleep." Last, note the almost clinical distance of the final sentence: "now I am fairly sure" and "yet then, that summer, I was unwilling to make the experiment" (as opposed to, say, "but that summer I didn't want to try it").

Why, then, the metaphor of being buried alive, the wild time shifts held together by an inordinate use of time markers ("that night," "all night," "for a long time," "for a long time," "ever since," "in the nights," "just at the moment," "now," and "then, that summer"), and the unusually formal diction? In chapter 8, we will explore how, in real life and in Hemingway dialogue, each speech simultaneously demonstrates conscious calculation and unconscious self-revelation. In first-person narratives such as "Now I Lay Me," the same holds true, for this paragraph is a speech act, although a written one. Nick consciously asserts that, even though he was once beset by feelings of panic, he was able to control those anxieties. His formal diction and discursive distance from the experiences he relates are an attempt to seem in control, as is his qualified statement that he is "now fairly sure that" his soul would not have gone out of him that summer (the equivalent of saying, "I'm all right now"). But the force of his anxieties, then and now, is involuntarily revealed as well. When he tries to describe his feelings that night, it unconsciously comes out as a metaphor of being buried alive. His attempt to explain his state of mind wreaks havoc upon the chronological order of the passage as he resists revealing, until halfway through, the reason for his anxieties.

These considerations bring me at last to the two kinds of repetition that occur in the passage. The first centers on Nick's trauma and the repetitions of *night* and *going out,* the two phenomena his unconscious associates with being suddenly wounded. (This is akin to the way his unconscious associates the low yellow house, the long stable, and the change in the width of the river with his wounding in "A Way You'll Never Be," discussed in our third chapter). *Night,* along with one mention of *in the dark,* appears five times. In the first two sentences, it is associated with lying on the floor and listening to the worms eating. In sentence 3, night is the precondition of his soul leaving his body. (Falling asleep, we later learn, is not the problem—he can sleep without anxiety during the day.) In sentence 4, night is associated with being blown up. In sentence 5, it is joined with subsequent anxieties about his soul leaving his body. Similarly, a form of *to go* is used seven times, in each case to describe his soul leaving his body during the wounding or later when falling asleep at night. He says that if "I ever shut my eyes in the dark and let myself go" (fell asleep), then "my soul would go out of my body" (leave). At the time of his wounding, he "felt it go out" (leave) and "go off" (go further away) before coming back. Since that time, it has repeatedly "started to go" (leave) "just at the moment of going off to sleep" (note how he purposely uses "going off" rather than the more common expression "falling asleep"). In the final repetition he consciously tries to assert control in stating that he now knows "it would not really have gone out," yet by unconsciously eliding the rest of the phrase ("gone out of my body"), he makes the "going" seem more permanent, as though a candle going out, a vanishing rather than a leaving, and the addition of "fairly" undercuts his assertion of current certitude. This is the repetition of the unconscious reliving the trauma in which it is trapped— a repetition compulsion.

But another kind of repetition also occurs here, that of the conscious trying to contain its feelings of panic. In a repetition compulsion, the unconscious wants to revisit the trauma, but the conscious masks that unconscious desire in symbolic equivalents and deploys various forms of repression to protect the psyche. By doing so, however, it prevents the subject from recognizing the repetition compulsion, and the subject, in a futile effort to triumph over his phobia, keeps mentally revisiting it and/or repeatedly puts himself in circumstances likely to duplicate the events that caused it (in Hemingway's case, his constant courting of danger). The main means by which Nick tries to control his unconscious fears in this story is consciously to repeat his actions during various fishing trips, to describe them to himself methodically and in detail in order to prevent his mind from panicking. But when he does this, and also when he tries praying for everyone he has ever known or "remembering everything that had ever happened to" him, unpleasant memories sneak into his reminiscences: the salamander whose "tiny feet" tried to hold to the hook when Nick used him as bait and an incident of marital discord between his parents (SS 365, 364). This activity of conscious mental repetition—demonstrated in the subsequent ten paragraphs—is exactly the "very great effort" he refers to in this first paragraph. We therefore have two kinds of repetition at work here: his repetition compulsion, which causes the repetitions of the first paragraph, and his conscious efforts to repeat other memories in order to control that compulsion.

Hemingway thus employs repetition for three purposes: landscape portraiture, emphasis, and depicting the actions of the unconscious and conscious. All three contribute to what Joseph Frank has termed "spatial form," the modernist aesthetic in which texts are designed for readers to apprehend them "in a moment of time, rather than as a sequence" (10). In his landscape depictions, Hemingway undercuts linearity to create a visual image grasped instantaneously, as in his representation of the composite village in "Che Ti Dice la Patria?" or the scene viewed through the window in "An Alpine Idyll." Images repeated for emphasis also create a spatial form, as in the opening of "In Another Country," where a symbolic field emerges from the text that subsumes the linear narrative to its own representation of mood. Last, a hallmark of modernist spatial form is the immersion of the reader in the protagonist's conscious and unconscious in such passages as the opening of "Now I Lay Me"—in which temporality itself is negated. As Frank observes, in "this juxtaposition of past and present": "Time is no longer felt as an objective, causal progression with clearly marked-out differences between periods; now it has become a continuum in which distinctions between past and present are wiped out . . . Past and present are apprehended spatially, locked in a timeless unity that, while it may accentuate surface differences, eliminates any feeling of sequence by the very act of juxtaposition" (63).

As for influence, Hemingway was indebted to Stein for his use of repetition in landscape depiction, for she guided him through the world of art, Cézanne in particular. In the employment of repetition for emphasis, his major influences were first, the King James Bible, and later, James Joyce. With regard to the repetitions of the conscious and unconscious, there is no direct evidence that Hemingway ever read Freud or even any of Freud's popularizers. We also know that he detested critics, for instance Philip Young, whom he felt were trying to psychoanalyze him, in 1952 calling them "a combination of the Junior F.B.I.-men, discards from Freud and Jung and a sort of Columnist peep-hole and missing laundry list school" (*SL* 751). But Freudian thought pervaded Western culture after the war and throughout the 1920s; even many who had not read him casually used terms such as *wish fulfillment, id, projection, transference, repression,* and *repetition compulsion.* In addition, Hemingway had carefully read Stein's *Three Lives* and *The Making of Americans,* the former heavily influenced by William James and the latter by Freudian theory (see Ruddick, chaps. 1–2). And he was a careful reader of Havelock Ellis as well. More to the point than any tracing of direct influence, however, is the simple fact that Hemingway was an astute observer of human behavior, his own included. What matters is not that he produced, in fictions such as "Big Two-Hearted River," "Now I Lay Me," or "A Way You'll Never Be," textbook examples of Freudian repetition compulsions—which he most certainly did—but that he understood the haunted mind, every bit as much as did Poe and Dostoevsky, two other writers who never read Freud. After all, it was Freud who used the works of literary artists to explain his theories and not the other way around.

6

Openings, Endings, and the Disjunctive Bump

I think that when one has finished writing a short story one should delete the beginning and the end. That's where we fiction writers mostly go wrong.
—Anton Chekhov, quoted in Ivan Bunin, *Memories and Portraits*

The arrest of attention by a vivid opening should be something more than a trick. It should mean that the narrator has so brooded on this subject that it has become his indeed, so made over and synthesized within him that, as a great draughtsman gives the essentials of a face or landscape in half-a-dozen strokes, the narrator can "situate" his tale in an opening passage which shall be a clue to all the detail eliminated.
—Edith Wharton, *The Writing of Fiction*

But you have to know where to stop. That is what makes a short story. Makes it short at least.
—Hemingway, "The Art of the Short Story"

In the short story, beginnings are read in anticipation of the end, and the end is read with the beginning still fresh in mind. The reader brings a greater alertness to a story than to a novel, in which one settles in for the long haul and, once done, reflects on the narrative, looking back to a beginning read many hours or days before. Beginnings and endings of stories take up proportionally greater space and are therefore more prominent. A story is a sprint, with no time to recover from a fall. The writer must know how to begin and, as Hemingway suggests, also know when to shut up.

Titles are our initial contact with stories but we rarely understand what they mean at first. When we have finished reading, however, and when we refer to the story afterward, they increasingly function in our sense-making process. Sometimes Hemingway's titles signify a character or characters and are mostly denotative ("My Old Man," "The Battler," "The Killers"). But even such seemingly neutral titles have their effect. Compare these with, say, "The Jockey," "Campfire Incident," and "The Big Swede." Other titles go deeper by choosing a symbolic object ("Cat in the Rain," "A Canary for One," "A Clean, Well-Lighted Place") or a resonant location ("Indian Camp," "Big Two-Hearted River," "The Snows of Kiliman-jaro"). Sometimes the titles are ironic. "An Alpine Idyll" encloses an embedded gothic narrative, "Up in Michigan" and "The Sea Change" can be read as sexual double-entendres, and "A Simple Enquiry" is anything but simple. "The Short Happy Life of Francis Macomber" is ironic if it refers to Macomber's whole life, but perhaps not if it refers to his final moments in which, from one perspective, he finally "lives."

Hemingway's best titles are sometimes literary allusions that enrich the story. "In Another Country" references a passage from Marlowe's *The Jew of Malta* that T. S. Eliot used as the epigraph to "Portrait of a Lady"—"Thou hast committed — / Fornication: but that was in another country, / And besides, the wench is dead" (*Poems* 8)—leading to critical debates about how this relates to the death of the Italian major's wife, Nick's feelings about marriage (here and in other texts), and Hemingway's break-ups with Agnes von Kurowsky and his wife Hadley. "Now I Lay Me" comes from an eighteenth-century child's prayer and is directly relevant to the narrator's fear that his soul will leave his body if he falls asleep at night ("Now I lay me down to sleep, / I pray the Lord my soul to keep; / And if I die before I wake, / I pray the Lord my soul to take"). "Ten Indians" alludes to a nursery rhyme adapted from an 1860s minstrel show song. On the literal level, it can refer to the nine drunken Indians of the opening paragraph plus Prudence, the Indian girlfriend who breaks Nick's heart. The nursery rhyme has two verses, one counting up from one to ten little Indian boys, the other counting back down to one, which corresponds to how Nick's misery over his loss of Prudie builds up in the story and then is virtually gone by morning. The longer minstrel show versions begin with ten Indians and count down, but there are two different endings: "One little Injun livin' all alone, / He got married and then there were none" and "One little Indian boy left all alone; / He went out and hanged himself and then there were none." These endings point to, respectively, the aspiration and despair young Nick feels in the story. "God Rest You Merry, Gentlemen" is the opening line of a traditional Christmas carol. The effect here is purely sardonic, as what happens on Christmas Day in this story—in which a too-literal reading of the New Testament leads to self-mutilation and perhaps death—is at odds with the carol's "tidings of comfort and joy" about how we are protected by God from "Satan's power / When we were gone astray" (see Lamb, "Critique" 27–28). "The Light of the World" quotes Jesus' words to his disciples before restoring a blind man's sight—"As long as I am in the world, I am the light of the world" (John 9:5)—but there is little light in this story's world, in which the narrator "sees" but doesn't really understand.

Not all allusive titles have manifest sources. "Che Ti Dice la Patria?" (What is the news from the fatherland?) was a patriotic slogan of Gabriele d'Annunzio (Meyers 84), the Italian author, Fascist, and prototype for Mussolini whom Hemingway scorned in a 1920–21 poem: "Half a million dead wops / And he got a kick out of it / The son of a bitch" (*Poems* 28). "Big Two-Hearted River" is based on a fishing trip along the Big and Little Fox Rivers above Seney, Michigan, but titled after a river further north that Hemingway had never fished. The title of "A Way You'll Never Be," the story about a shell-shocked Nick, may have been Hemingway's attempt to give confidence to Jane Mason, a friend and perhaps lover, who had recently suffered a mental breakdown—his point being that Nick survives even though he was "much nuttier" than Jane would ever be (*HLS* 228).

Whether allusive or not, Hemingway's titles work with the text to create an effect. "Indian Camp" and "In Another Country" both depict "other countries" for which the protagonists are ill equipped. "Che Ti Dice la Patria?" presents a different sort of news from the fatherland. "Big Two-Hearted River" is in accord with Nick's ambivalence and its formally partitioned text. Nick's traumatized state in "A Way You'll Never Be" is the way most readers "will never be." "The End of Something" perfectly states, in its lack of clarity, Nick's own vague emotions by the conclusion of the story. "Soldier's Home" is a bifurcated story; the exposition of the first half blames Harold Krebs's problems on war trauma while the scenes of the second half fault an overbearing mother. These dueling interpretations also prominently contend in the criticism of several key Hemingway stories, and I have elsewhere labeled them, respectively, the "war wound" thesis and the "childhood wound" thesis ("Fishing" 162–63). In "Soldier's Home," Hemingway deliberately equilibrates these possibilities, beginning with the ambiguity of the title. He categorizes Krebs as "soldier" rather than as son, ex-soldier, student, Oklahoman, American, or just plain Krebs. "Soldier" points to the exposition and the war trauma thesis, "Home" to the scenes and the conflicted mother-son relationship. The two words (and interpretations) are linked by an apostrophe and an *s*. But the nature of this construction is purposefully ambiguous. If it's the possessive case, then the title can be restated as "Home of the Soldier," which emphasizes the home. If it's a contraction, then the title could be rewritten as "Soldier Is

Home," emphasizing the soldier. Increasing the ambiguity is a third possibility; ever since the Civil War, *soldier's home* has been a common term for a chronic care facility administering to physically or emotionally incapacitated veterans.

After we've noted the title, stories can begin with introductory exposition or without it, and they can start at the beginning of the fabula or in medias res. Hemingway employed four different techniques for opening his stories: in medias res without subsequent exposition, in medias res with exposition displaced to later in the text, traditional expository openings, and what I term the *tonal opening* that establishes a mood from which the story organically unfolds.

Opening in medias res without later exposition is familiar now but in Hemingway's day was still somewhat unconventional. "The Light of the World" begins with a one-sentence observation about the bartender by the first-person narrator (Nick) and then proceeds to a scene heavily laden with dialogue. A page and a half later, we get some unhelpful exposition that Nick and Tom came into town on one end and are going to leave on the other, a brief description of the town, and a paragraph describing the inhabitants of the train station they enter. The rest of the story is one scene told in dialogue. We get no exposition on Nick and Tom—who they are, where they are going, or why—and the nondialogue prose merely describes what Nick sees along the way. (In fact, we don't even get Nick's name, but Hemingway scholars have classified this as a Nick Adams story.) The opening of "The Killers" quickly sets the scene, using stage directions: "The door of Henry's lunch-room opened and two men came in. They sat down at the counter" (SS 279). The only significant exposition in this dialogue-driven story comes when one of the gunmen reveals, nearly halfway through the text, their intention to kill the Swede, and later when the Swede vaguely suggests that something he did has led to his predicament. The effect of this in medias res opening and lack of exposition is to make the reader feel the same confusion that the characters in the lunchroom feel in the face of the gunmen's truculent behavior. In contrast to these first two examples, "The Battler" begins with two paragraphs of nondialogue, a depiction of Nick after he's been tossed off a moving train, although the fact that he was tossed is not revealed until a few paragraphs later. But no exposition is offered about why Nick was on the train or where he was going. He is thrown into this story, where he will meet two odd characters, in the same way that the reader is thrown into it.

The second kind of opening is also in medias res, but some exposition (rarely much in Hemingway) is subsequently provided. "Fifty Grand" starts without locating the characters or the setting; even the conversation with which it begins is presented in medias res: "'How are you going yourself, Jack' I asked him." This is a response to the omitted salutation by Jack Brennan to the narrator. The next line is further disjunctive in that Jack doesn't reply to the narrator's question: "'You seen this, Walcott?' he says" (SS 300). The effect is to give the story immediacy by eliminating the framing amenities and to increase the reader's alertness, since there are no clear cues setting up the narrative. The exposition begins on the second page and is subsequently dispersed on a "need-to-know" basis. Similarly, "The Sea Change" opens with a passage of dialogue between a man and a woman, followed by a statement that they are in an empty Parisian bar early in the morning in late summer and a description of the woman's attire. All other exposition must be deduced from the dialogue. In "The Gambler, the Nun, and the Radio," Hemingway begins with a scene and then presents its exposition, he introduces the story's next part with two pages of traditional exposition, and the rest of the narrative alternates between scene and summary.

Hemingway also used traditional openings, presenting the necessary exposition and then letting the story develop from it. His most traditional opening, in "The Capital of the World," gives three pages of exposition about the backgrounds of the young waiter Paco and the matadors, picadors, and bandillero living at the hotel where Paco works. With that general background filled in, Hemingway then presents the exposition for the evening in which the story takes place and finally, after three pages, he is ready to treat the story's events. Other examples of traditional openings include "Up in Michigan," "The Doctor and the Doctor's Wife," "Soldier's Home," "Ten Indians," "An Alpine Idyll," and "A Pursuit Race."

The most interesting and innovative beginning in Hemingway's stories is what I term the *tonal opening*, which establishes the mood and often embodies the theme of the narrative. Linda Wagner-Martin observes that Pound's imagist tenets for poetry can be extended into five principles of prose theory and applied to Hemingway:

(1) the centrality of the image, a concrete representation as opposed to an abstraction; (2) the objectivity of presentation; (3) juxtaposition as a means of connecting single images, the placing of image against image

with no literal transition so that the reader's apprehension of meaning depends on an immediate response to the montage of concrete detail; (4) *organ base,* Pound's notion that every piece of writing has a controlling tone and a shape that reflects its meaning; and (5) simplicity, rooted in directness and in the avoidance of poetic diction and subject matter. (*Modern* 29)

In the tonal opening, he employs all of these principles, especially the first and fourth—establishing a controlling tone through a central opening image. We've examined the tonal openings of "In Another Country" and "Now I Lay Me." Others include "The End of Something," "Cat in the Rain," and "Big Two-Hearted River."

"Cat in the Rain" provides a glimpse into a woman's unhappy marriage, its plot revolving about her attempts to acquire a cat caught in the rain, the symbolic resonances of which critics have debated (see chapter 4). Although the story presents no exposition on the woman, her husband, or their marriage—we don't even know her name—nevertheless it illuminates the dynamics of their relationship. It begins:

[1] There were only two Americans stopping at the hotel. [2] They did not know any of the people they passed on the stairs on their way to and from their room. [3] Their room was on the second floor facing the sea. [4] It also faced the public garden and the war monument. [5] There were big palms and green benches in the public garden. [6] In the good weather there was always an artist with his easel. [7] Artists liked the way the palms grew and the bright colors of the hotels facing the gardens and the sea. [8] Italians came from a long way off to look up at the war monument. [9] It was made of bronze and glistened in the rain. [10] It was raining. [11] The rain dripped from the palm trees. [12] Water stood in pools on the gravel paths. [13] The sea broke in a long line in the rain and slipped back down the beach to come up and break again in a long line in the rain. [14] The motor cars were gone from the square by the war monument. [15] Across the square in the doorway of the café a waiter stood looking out at the empty square.

[16] The American wife stood at the window looking out. (*SS* 167)

As with all Hemingway tonal openings, this carefully constructed montage is designed to evoke a mood. Note the sense of isolation in the phrases "only two Americans" and "did not know any of the people" they passed.

The word *only* deliberately emphasizes their isolation; otherwise, the information "two Americans" would suffice. The seemingly gratuitous modifier *American* to begin the second paragraph further stresses her isolation. Passing people "on the stairs" signifies transience, which is underscored by being in a foreign hotel and by the spaces and people specified in the opening: a public garden, war monument, park benches, gravel paths, Italian tourists, traveling artists, a café, motor cars, a doorway, and a window.

Critics have examined the binary of the public garden and the war monument, but Hemingway has actually set up a ternary that also includes the sea. Both the garden and the monument are public spaces, a point so important that he repeats the word *public* in sentence 5. Between them, the garden and monument represent the continuum of linear time. The garden is a living, growing entity, its "big palms" pointed upwards and toward the future, while the war monument commemorates the dead, points downward, and is oriented toward the past. Beyond them lies the sea, representing cyclical time. It serves the same function as the month of April at the start of Eliot's *The Waste Land,* its eternal timelessness standing in counterpoint to the brief linear span of human life (on the story's intertextuality with Eliot, see Smith, *Guide* 43–47). The rain—mentioned five times in five sentences—feeds the growing palms but merely covers the bronze war monument and stands in stagnant pools on the gravel paths. The rain also renews the sea, a point emphasized by the way Hemingway repeats the phrase about the sea breaking "in a long line in the rain" in sentence 13, which repetition also mimics the motion of the tide along the beach. If the sea resonates as an objective correlative of the flood and ebb of the woman's desires, the gardens and monument correlate, respectively, to her desire to move forward in her life and to her "dead" marriage (which, at this point, is but a figurative monument to what might once have been a happy union).

In sentences 6 through 8, Hemingway employs one of his favorite tactics for conveying a sense of loss—what I term the *present absence*—in which he presents something that once was, engages the reader, and then snatches it away so that the reader feels its absence. (He also does this in the openings of, for example, "The End of Something" and "God Rest You Merry, Gentlemen.") The depiction of the square on sunny days disappears in sentence 9 with the introduction of the rain, but even this sentence participates in the portrayal of the square's aesthetic appeal to the artists— the bronze monument glistens in the rain. So the next sentence announces that it *is* raining (which it has been doing from the start, only Hemingway strategically has deferred telling us). The rain then comes down in figurative torrents on the page, leading to his mention of the absent motor cars. This specific absence is extended through the waiter who stands in the doorway, "looking out at the empty square." The next paragraph begins with the woman "looking out" the window, by what I have termed *implication omission* at that same empty square. Not directly mentioning the "empty square" a second time enables the sentence to resonate even more powerfully; that is, she is also looking out on "emptiness" in a larger sense, a correlative of how she feels about her life.

Let's look at what the woman experiences throughout the story—by turns she is isolated, confined, stagnant, unappreciated, transient, unable to move into the future she desires, lacking control or agency, empty, and frustrated—and note how these qualities are evoked in the tonal opening. She is isolated by her nationality, by her unfamiliarity with the other guests, and by the rain that keeps her in the room. She is confined in one space by the rain, as is the waiter. That isolation and confinement combine to make her stagnant. Hemingway also conveys her stagnancy in sentence 1 in his choice of the verb *stopping* at the hotel instead of *staying*; the pools of rain water standing on the gravel paths in sentence 12 are the objective correlative of the stagnancy she feels. The gardens, monument, and pretty square, as well as the café and its waiter, are unappreciated, since there are no people there to appreciate them—correlatives of how the woman feels unappreciated by her husband. The hotel, the stairway, the doorway, the window, and the mention of tourists signify transience, and the roiling sea represents her unfulfilled desires (akin, say, to the function of the sea for Edna in Kate Chopin's *The Awakening*). Her lack of agency is mirrored by the waiter, who can only "wait" for the rain to cease so he can go back to "waiting." The correlative of her feelings of absence and emptiness are everywhere in the paragraph, from the snatched scene of sentences 6 through 8, to the enormous symbol of the empty square she looks out upon. Her frustrations are mirrored, as well, in the entire paragraph. It would be difficult to establish the mood of a story better than Hemingway has in this tonal opening.

Typical Hemingway stories treat an episode, or a linked series of episodes, that opens out onto the characters' larger lives. Sometimes—as with "Indian Camp," "In Another Country," or "The Killers"—it is a "prologue-story" (previously called an "initiation story"), in which the illusions of the main character are formed, altered, or dashed, pointing toward a future trajectory. In what might serve as an exemplary epigraph for such stories, Frank O'Connor concludes "Guests of the Nation," in which the young Irish narrator finds himself an unwilling party to the execution of two British soldiers: "And anything that happened to me afterwards, I never felt the same about again" (18). O'Connor himself notes a similar line in Gogol's "The Overcoat," terming it a pithy description of what all short stories are about: "and from that day forth, everything was as it were changed and appeared in a different light to him" (*Lonely* 16). Actually, the "from that time on" construction appears four times in "The Overcoat," arguably the founding text of the modern short story; it is applied to the young clerk who is touched by Akaky's pleas, the bullying policeman who confronts a corpse on the street, the government official morally responsible for Akaky's death, and finally to Akaky's corpse (307, 331 twice, 333). Sometimes, the story is an "epilogue-story"—a retrospective on, or concluding episode of, past events. Examples include "Fathers and Sons," "The Snows of Kilimanjaro," and "The Short Happy Life of Francis Macomber."[1] Often, it is a Chekhovian "slice-of-life" story that reveals elements of a character ("Now I Lay Me," "A Way You'll Never Be," "One Reader Writes"), a relationship ("The Doctor and the Doctor's Wife," "Out of Season," "The Sea Change"), a place ("The Gambler, the Nun, and the Radio," "Under the Ridge," "Che Ti Dice la Patria?"), or a way of life ("Fifty Grand," "After the Storm," "The Light of the World"). These categories are not mutually exclusive. For instance, "The Undefeated" is both an epilogue-story and a slice of life that reveals the character of Manuel, his friendship with Zurito, the matador's way of life, and aspects of Madrid in the 1920s.

At the end of all stories, whether an episode or a linked series, the reader is necessarily jarred, suddenly reminded that this has been but a glimpse, however revealing, into the larger story that is the life of the character. Waiting at the end of the Hemingway story, or of any short story, is what I term the *disjunctive bump*—the unavoidable sign of a story's delimited space, what Sean O'Faolain observes is a reminder that a story is but a "convention which makes tiny bits of life speak for the whole of life" (155, 158). All fictional texts, of course, have such limits. As Henry James says of the novel, "Really, universally, relations stop nowhere, and the exquisite problem of the artist is eternally but to draw, by a geometry of his own, the circle within which they shall happily *appear* to do so" (Preface to *Roderick Hudson* 1041). But the novel presents a fuller rendering of the larger lives of its main characters, duration is its keynote, and it occupies a longer stretch of the reader's time, so that the ending is inherently less jarring. The story, on the other hand, stops almost after it starts; the ending is read so soon after the beginning that it is a more important and potentially dangerous element of the text. All story writers must negotiate the disjunctive bump: choosing whether to emphasize it, de-emphasize it, or leave it alone.

The sort of ending that most emphasizes the disjunctive bump is the *open ending.* The story concludes before the narrative sequence has run its full course, leaving the reader to wonder how that sequence will play out. We see examples of open endings in "Cat in the Rain," "A Natural History of the Dead," and "The Undefeated." In the latter, Manuel lies on the operating table, pleading with Zurito not to cut off his *coleta* (the matador's pigtail). Zurito relents, and the story ends:

> Manuel lay back. They had put something over his face. It was all familiar. He inhaled deeply. He felt very tired. He was very, very tired. They took the thing away from his face.
> "I was going good," Manuel said weakly. "I was going great."
> Retana looked at Zurito and started for the door.
> "I'll stay here with him," Zurito said.
> Retana shrugged his shoulders.
> Manuel opened his eyes and looked at Zurito.
> "Wasn't I going good, Manos?" he asked, for confirmation.
> "Sure," said Zurito. "You were going great."
> The doctor's assistant put the cone over Manuel's face and he inhaled deeply. Zurito stood awkwardly, watching. (*SS* 265–66)

The story stops before the sequence is over. We do not know if Manuel will live or die. If he does live, we do not know if Zurito will insist that he keep his bargain and retire from bullfighting (Zurito may have relented temporarily out of pity). The ending thus emphasizes the disjunctive bump by leaving us in the moment of the operation without providing a resolution. As with "A Natural History of the Dead," which also concludes in the midst of an operation—"'Hold him tight,' said the doctor. 'He is in much pain. Hold him very tight'" (*SS* 449)—this type of ending leaves the reader wanting closure.[2]

Such overtly open endings occur infrequently in Hemingway stories. More typical is what I term a *rounded closed ending,* in which the narrative sequence has played out, all the necessary actions of the episode have been reported, and the suspense has been resolved. This sort of ending allows the disjunctive bump its effect: neither increasing it, as in the open ending, nor trying to diminish it by floating the reader off. "The Short Happy Life of Francis Macomber," in which Margot Macomber accidentally shoots her husband in the back of the head while trying to protect him from a charging buffalo, would have had an open ending. But Hemingway closed it off in the last three speeches between the hunter Wilson and Margot:

> "That was a pretty thing to do," he said in a toneless voice. "He *would* have left you too."
> "Stop it," she said.
> "Of course it's an accident," he said. "I know that."
> "Stop it," she said.
> "Don't worry," he said. "There will be a certain amount of unpleasantness but I will have some photographs taken that will be very useful at the inquest. There's the testimony of the gun-bearers and the driver too. You're perfectly all right."
> "Stop it," she said.
> "There's a hell of a lot to be done," he said. "And I'll have to send a truck off to the lake to wireless for a plane to take the three of us into Nairobi. Why didn't you poison him? That's what they do in England."
> "Stop it. Stop it. Stop it," the woman cried.
> Wilson looked at her with his flat blue eyes.
> "I'm through now," he said. "I was a little angry. I'd begun to like your husband."
> "Oh, please stop it," she said. "Please, please stop it."
> "That's better," Wilson said. "Please is much better. Now I'll stop." (SS 36–37)

Margot pleads with Wilson to cease insinuating that she deliberately killed her husband. But on a metafictional level, she is begging the author not to leave the ending open, with the reader questioning her motives. Her eight requests that he (Wilson and Hemingway) "stop it" are finally granted, and the story gets a rounded closed ending that seems to acquit her. Had Hemingway concluded with Wilson's "flat blue eyes," it would have been akin to the open ending of "The Undefeated" (and perhaps a better ending as well).

Other rounded closed endings include "The Battler," "Fifty Grand," "A Simple Enquiry," "An Alpine Idyll," "After the Storm," "The Light of the

World," "God Rest You Merry, Gentlemen," "A Day's Wait," and "The Wine of Wyoming." The narrator of "After the Storm," having failed to loot a sunken ocean liner, concludes the story:

> They never found any bodies. Not a one. Nobody floating. They float a long way with life belts too. They must have took it inside. Well, the Greeks got it all. Everything. They must have come fast all right. They picked her clean. First there was the birds, then me, then the Greeks, and even the birds got more out of her than I did. (*SS* 378)

No bodies are floating, nor will the ending float the reader off past the disjunctive bump. It is a classic Aristotelian denouement, neither more nor less.

Often, however, Hemingway seeds his closed endings, which slightly diminishes the effect of the disjunctive bump. In what I term a *seeded closed ending,* although the narrative sequence has run its full course, some strands remain that merge into something greater: a time outside the text, an element of nature, an ongoing process. These tend to expand the story slightly past its formal conclusion. Examples of seeded closed endings include "Up in Michigan," "Cross-Country Snow," "Hills Like White Elephants," "The Killers," "Ten Indians," "A Pursuit Race," "A Way You'll Never Be," and "Fathers and Sons." In "Up in Michigan," after Jim Gilmore has sexually taken Liz Coates and fallen asleep on the dock, she starts to cry, then covers him with her coat. The story ends: "Then she walked across the dock and up the steep sandy road to go to bed. A cold mist was coming up through the woods from the bay" (*SS* 86). This is still a closed ending, as the sequence begun with Liz's infatuation with Jim concludes with his unexpected aggressive assault and, in its aftermath, her feelings of misery and emptiness. But the camera pans out in the penultimate sentence, carrying Liz away from the scene, and the final sentence shifts the reader's focus to the larger phenomenon of the landscape. It gently floats the reader off from the story so that the final focus is on the bay, thus diminishing slightly the thudding stop of the disjunctive bump. Compare it, for instance, to a more rounded closed ending, that of "The Battler." After Nick Adams leaves Bugs and Ad by their campfire, he climbs an embankment and heads back up the railroad track. The last sentence reads: "Looking back from the mounting grade before the track curved into the hills he could see the firelight in the clearing" (*SS* 138). As with the end of "Up in Michigan," the camera pans away from the scene, but instead of floating us slightly off into the hills, Hemingway has Nick look back at the waning vestiges of the scene (the campfire), leaving the reader in the moment of the story by returning the focus to the episode. These are subtle, and to be honest, very subjective responses; what I'm basing my classificatory system on might cause other readers to view both these endings as either rounded or seeded. Clearly, however, Hemingway is negotiating the disjunctive bump in both stories: in one, ending with a focus on the larger landscape; in the other, returning to the episode. Although I may seem to be parsing the utterly irrelevant, to the writer these subtleties matter because they evoke different responses from the reader.

Sometimes it is impossible to classify a story definitively. Take the ending of "In Another Country." The major snaps at the young narrator and walks off, reappearing to apologize and explain that his wife has just died. After a three-day absence, he returns to the hospital and the therapy machines they've been using for their injured limbs. On the wall are "before and after" photographs of wounds the machines have cured. The story concludes with the narrator wondering where these photographs came from, since they are supposedly the first patients to use the machines. The final sentence reads: "The photographs did not make much difference to the major because he only looked out of the window" (SS 272). Although the narrator has begun to question the machines, still, the narrative sequence has run its full course and so this might be a rounded closed ending. But it could also be viewed as an open ending because the narrator's incipient realization that the doctors have lied to them about the efficacy of the machines might constitute an unfinished sequence. Although the reader fully figures this out, it is not entirely clear that the narrator, by the end of the story, has; he's only pointed out what strikes him as a conundrum. Moreover, some might consider it a seeded closed ending with the major's perspective of looking out the window slightly floating us away and lessening the disjunctive bump.

The ending of "The Snows of Kilimanjaro" is also hard to classify. Helen calls to her dying husband, receives no answer, and cannot hear him breathing. Outside the tent, the hyena who awakened her is still making noises: "But she did not hear him for the beating of her heart" (SS 77). This may appear to be an obvious closed ending, signaled by Harry's death, for which we have been waiting throughout the story. But can we be sure he is dead? If the beating of her heart drowns out the noisy hyena, perhaps it also drowns out Harry's breathing. If he's not yet dead, then technically we have an open ending, even if we know how it will eventually end. Moreover, the two quick shifts in focus—to the hyena outside the tent, and then to the beating of her heart—seem to evade the disjunctive bump by connecting the end of the story to ongoing processes. A powerful effect is rendered here, but one that eludes classification.

It may seem perverse for me to deconstruct my system in the very act of setting it up, but I point to the endings of "In Another Country" and "Kilimanjaro" for two reasons. First, in several stories, Hemingway presents innovative endings that are not easily classified. Second, these stories are exceptions. In the endings of most other stories—for example, "After the Storm"—the boundaries of these classifications are much less permeable. Take two endings that employ the same verb, but in different tenses. In "Wine of Wyoming," an American couple declines a farewell dinner at the home of their French friends and, the next morning on their last visit, discover they've hurt their friends' feelings. As they drive away, the wife says, "We ought to have gone last night" and the story ends: "'Oh, yes,' I said. 'We ought to have gone'" (SS 467). The sequence has concluded and although they have spoken of returning in a few years, the sense is that they won't. No suspense remains. By contrast, in "Fathers and Sons," after Nick's son pesters him about visiting the tomb of his grandfather (Nick's father), the story concludes: "'We'll have to go,' Nick said. 'I can see we'll have to go'" (SS 499). Rather than treating a discreet incident, as in "Wine of Wyoming," this story has been about Nick's ambivalent memories of his father, which is an ongoing process for him, and the verb tense of the final sentence aptly indicates that, although the ending is closed, it is more a seeded closed ending than the rounded closed ending of "Wine of Wyoming."

The endings of "Fathers and Sons," "Cross-Country Snow," and "A Pursuit Race" come close to being a fourth type of Hemingway ending, which I inelegantly christen the *float-off*. In this kind of ending, whether or not the episode is completed, the author floats the reader temporally past the ending into some undefined point in the future (or back into the past, as in Fitzgerald's *The Great Gatsby*) or spatially past the ending onto a larger landscape, which has the effect of undercutting the suddenness of the disjunctive bump by merging the story into something larger outside the sequence. This sort of ending is closely associated with Chekhov, as when, following the protagonist's sea burial in "Gusev," he floats the reader off to the depths of the sea, then to the clouds, and finally ends with the ocean's surface: "The sky turns a soft lilac. Seeing this magnificent, enchanting sky, the ocean frowns at first, but soon itself takes on such tender, joyful, passionate colors as human tongue can hardly name" (*Stories* 121). This is a closed ending with a float-off. But even in a story with an open ending, which normally emphasizes the disjunctive bump, Chekhov could find a way to float the reader off. In "The Lady with the Little Dog," which concludes with Gurov and Anna desperately searching for a way to free themselves from their unhappy marriages so they can be together, Chekhov floats the reader past the open ending with: "And it seemed that, just a little more—and the solution would be found, and then a new, beautiful life would begin; and it was clear to both of them that the end was still far, far off, and that the most complicated and difficult part was just beginning" (*Stories* 376). James Joyce penned the most effective float-off of this type in the history of the short story when, in "The Dead," he managed to merge the end of the story of Gabriel Conroy at a dinner party with the entirety of all the living and the dead of Ireland, not to mention the very seasons of the natural world.

Sometimes the ending, rather than floating the reader off temporally or spatially, appends a moral or provides an ironic commentary. Both techniques undercut the effect of the disjunctive bump by drawing the reader's attention away from the story itself and linking it to some larger idea. In each case, the float-off, by seeming to merge the episode with something larger, lulls the reader into not noticing that the story is but a small episode from which he or she has been rudely ejected. Hemingway does not employ the lyricism of Chekhov or Joyce, but he does use float-offs as a deliberate strategy. Examples of full-blown float-offs into a future time include "Indian Camp," "The Three-Day Blow," "Soldier's Home," "Big Two-Hearted River," "Now I Lay Me," "A Clean, Well-Lighted Place," and "The Gambler, the Nun, and the Radio." Float-offs by way of an appended moral conclude "My Old Man" and "The Mother of a Queen." Examples of float-offs using ironic commentary are "On the Quai at Smyrna," "The Sea Change," and "Che Ti Dice la Patria?" Sometimes, as in "Indian Camp," "Now I Lay Me," and "The Capital of the World," Hemingway floats the reader off by combining a future time with ironic commentary.

Hemingway learned the appended irony ending from Maupassant, who used it frequently. He may have also learned from Maupassant a fifth type of ending—the ironic twist, or what I term the *snapper*, in which some new piece of information is revealed at the very end that forces the reader back into the story to reconsider in a new light what he or she has just read. If a snapper is merely a trick, as in O. Henry's stories, the text will not repay a second reading, and the quality of a snapper can vary widely, as we see when comparing Maupassant's famous "The Necklace" with his much superior "The Jewels of M. Lantin." Hemingway used the snapper only once, in "A Canary for One," when the first-person narrator reveals in the story's final two words that he and his wife are returning to Paris to begin their separation. Addressing such twists in 1932, Hemingway's fictional persona says, "it is years since I added the wow to the end of a story" (*DIA* 182). I refer here to twists at the very end of a story, not to those that occur earlier, which are more properly termed *peripeteia* (reversal), for example, the death of the major's wife in "In Another Country" or the Indian father's suicide in "Indian Camp." Nor am I referring to information withheld and imparted later on in a story for maximum effect, for example, the revelation that Nick's break-up with Marjorie in "The End of Something" was premeditated.

Let's look at some of Hemingway's float-off strategies for mitigating the disjunctive bump. At the end of "The Gambler, the Nun, and the Radio," Mr. Frazer thinks of the Mexican musicians he has met while convalescing in a hospital. The story concludes with a temporal float-off: "They would go now in a little while, he thought, and they would take the Cucaracha with them. Then he would have a little spot of the giant killer and play the radio, you could play the radio so that you could hardly hear it" (*SS* 487). "A Clean, Well-Lighted Place" combines a float-off into the future with general commentary: "Now, without thinking further, he would go home to his room. He would lie in the bed and finally, with daylight, he would go to sleep. After all, he said to himself, it is probably only insomnia. Many must have it" (*SS* 383). "Big Two-Hearted River" has a one-sentence float-off into the future: "There were plenty of days coming when he could fish the swamp" (*SS* 232). The temporal float-off of "Soldier's Home" is more extensive: "He would go to Kansas City and get a job and she would feel all right about it. There would be one more scene maybe before he got away. He would not go down to his father's office. He would miss that one. He wanted his life to go smoothly. It had just gotten going that way. Well, that was all over now, anyway. He would go over to the schoolyard and watch Helen play indoor baseball" (*SS* 153). The string of *he woulds,* although placing the reader inside the protagonist's anticipatory consciousness, also places the reader in the scenes that will occur after the story is over. This would have been a rounded closed ending allowing the disjunctive bump its effect had Hemingway stopped with the sentence that opens this final paragraph: "So his mother prayed for him and then they stood up and Krebs kissed his mother and went out of the house" (*SS* 152). But with this lengthy float-off, Hemingway elides the bump, depositing the reader in the larger story of Krebs's future.

"My Old Man" also would have been a story with a rounded closed ending had it concluded with George Gardner telling the young narrator, whose jockey father has just been killed and who has overheard some people call him a crook: "Don't you listen to what those bums said, Joe. Your old man was one swell guy." Hemingway slightly floats us away, however, with the boy's general observations: "But I don't know. Seems like when they get started they don't leave a guy nothing" (*SS* 205). The ending of "The Sea Change" uses irony to diminish the disjunctive bump. The protagonist fails to persuade his girlfriend to leave her lesbian lover and is crushed; looking in a mirror he tells the bartender, in all sincerity, that he is now "a different man," and the bartender unwittingly provides the irony: "'You look very well, sir,' James said. 'You must have had a very good summer'" (*SS* 401). The ending of "The Capital of the World" is a float-off into the future followed by a float-off into ironic commentary. Paco, whose sisters are at a Garbo film, is accidentally knifed while playing bullfights. After a paragraph describing the quotidian activities of the people in the movie theater and the hotel, the story concludes:

> The boy Paco had never known about any of this nor about what all these people would be doing on the next day and on other days to come. He had no idea how they really lived nor how they ended. He did not even realize they ended. He died, as the Spanish phrase has it, full of illusions. He had not had time in his life to lose any of them, nor even, at the end, to complete an act of contrition.
>
> He had not even had time to be disappointed in the Garbo picture which disappointed all Madrid for a week. (*SS* 50–51)

The penultimate paragraph pulls away from the disjunctive bump by dwelling on what Paco would have known had he not died, giving the impression that we are connected to this hypothetical ongoing process, while the final paragraph further dilutes the bump by giving it an ironic turn.

To sum up, then, open endings emphasize the disjunctive bump and rounded closed endings allow the bump its normal effect. Seeded closed endings diminish that effect a bit because they slightly float us away from the closure of the ending, and full-blown float-offs work to diminish more fully the effect of the disjunctive bump. At the end of *Death in the After-noon,* his joint treatise on bullfighting and writing, Hemingway concludes about fiction that "any part you make will represent the whole if it's made truly" (278). That is a statement of faith that all story writers ascribe to, but to succeed the writer must effectively negotiate the disjunctive bump.

7

The Normative Center, the Illustrative Stamp, and the Joycean Epiphany

And thus, though surrounded by circle upon circle of consternations and affrights, did these inscrutable creatures at the centre freely and fearlessly indulge in all peaceful concernments; yea, serenely revelled in dalliance and delight.

—Herman Melville, *Moby-Dick*

The threads of a story come from time to time together and make a picture in the web . . . which stamps the story home like an illustration.
—Robert Louis Stevenson, *Memories and Portraits*

I wish to begin this chapter by coining two terms: the *normative center* and the *illustrative stamp*. The concept of a normative center is employed in political discourse to signify a cultural mainstream, but I wish to appropriate the term for literary criticism and use it in a completely different fashion. In novels, especially in the sentimentally charged nineteenth century, we often find a moment of time in which tensions cease and the author portrays relationships in the ideal, giving us a glimpse of "how things ought to be." Such scenes offer an ethical standard against which readers may judge, whether consciously or not, other events. The normative center, as I conceive it, is a device of authorial judgment; by giving readers a criterion of relations in the ideal, the author enables them to assess the actual, that is, what transpires throughout the bulk of the novel. Such normative centers are necessarily extremely brief, for if tensions were to cease for too long the novel would be undermined. Novels are about conflict, but normative centers enable us to evaluate that conflict.

Take, for example, normative centers from the following classic American novels of the nineteenth century. Near the end of Nathaniel Hawthorne's *The Scarlet Letter*, Hester Prynne lets down her hair and removes the letter that brands her an adulteress, as she and Arthur Dimmesdale have an intimate conversation in the forest while Pearl plays nearby. For the first time in the novel, we realize something that surely we knew but that had nonetheless eluded our fullest comprehension: these characters are a nuclear family—a mother, a father, and their child. Just before effecting this transformation, Hester annunciates her real feelings about their illicit sexual union—"What we did had a consecration of its own. We felt it so! We said so to each other!" (170)—renouncing the gendered mask of penitence she has been forced to assume for seven years. But this passage lasts only a few pages; when subsequently Pearl does not recognize her mother, Hester must gather up her hair and resume wearing the letter. Nevertheless, the image of this nuclear family serves as a contrast to their shattered relations throughout the novel, and the "higher law" for which Hester speaks stands as an evaluation of the lesser laws of society that pervade the text and determine the lives of its characters.

Likewise, at the end of chapter 87 of Herman Melville's *Moby-Dick,* "The Grand Armada," the whaling boats float into the midst of the "enchanted calm" of a whale nursery and are "visited by small tame cows and calves; the women and children" of the whales they've been hunting. While even such dedicated predators as Queequeg and Starbuck are transfixed by the sight of pregnant whales and mothers nursing their newborn, Melville presents Ishmael and the reader with a vision of what should be our relation to the nonhuman world, delight rather than murder prompted by vengeance or utilitarian pursuits, and this vision further enables Ishmael to discern the joy in himself that lies beneath his eternally "unwaning woe." But, as with *The Scarlet Letter,* the realities depicted in the text resume: a maimed male whale with a cutting-spade protruding from his tail churns through the water, in his agony wounding other whales, and "the submarine bridal-chambers and nurseries" vanish (422–26). There are other normative centers in *Moby-Dick*—e.g., Ishmael's vision of human kindness and validation of hearth and home in "A Squeeze of the Hand"; the metaphor of the Catskill eagle at the end of "The Try-Works." Those occupy only a paragraph each, while the one in "The Grand Armada" is a mere two pages in a novel of over six hundred pages. Despite their brevity, they remain in the reader's memory, serving to condemn the text's many scenes of obsession, rapacity, violence, and waste in the whale hunt. Hawthorne's forest scene and Melville's several normative centers base their authorial judgments in the ethics of "affect"—family, filiation, and sympathy—values that are foregrounded by sentimental writers such as Harriet Beecher Stowe.

In *Uncle Tom's Cabin,* Stowe herself has several normative centers, the first and most telling of which occurs in chapter 13 at Rachel and Simeon Halliday's Quaker home, when a group of people, white and black, gathers to eat, "the first time that ever George [Harris] had sat down on equal terms at any white man's table" (223). In a book about, among other things, homelessness and the social construction of inflexible racial hierarchies, this brief passage affects both the reader and the characters: "This, indeed, was a home,—*home*,—a word that George had never yet known a meaning for; and a belief in God, and trust in his providence, began to encircle his heart" (224). In an insightful cultural reading of this scene, Elizabeth Ammons notes that "Stowe provides a glimpse of the maternal paradise America might be" were it to emulate this Quaker community, which is "agrarian, nonviolent, egalitarian, and, above all, matrifocal" (168). That "glimpse," I'd assert, is a normative center, a deliberate strategy in the craft of the nineteenth-century novel.

The normative center of *Adventures of Huckleberry Finn,* written by Stowe's Hartford, Connecticut, neighbor, is particularly noteworthy. It consists of precisely the first six paragraphs of chapter 19, immediately following the horrifying Grangerford-Shepherdson massacre, in which Jim and Huck lie on the raft, floating down the Mississippi and discussing the stars above. For a brief period of time, even race vanishes, as a black and a white American coexist in perfect harmony in, not coincidentally, the non–socially constructed natural world. Twain even celebrates this melding of black and white in an observation he puts into Huck's mouth. As dawn approaches, Huck sees "a pale place in the sky; then more paleness, spreading around; then the river softened up, away off, and weren't black any more, but gray" (156). This normative center, in which the American vernacular in fiction reaches its apogee, is forthwith dashed when the Duke and King hop aboard: race and social hierarchy return, Jim resumes wearing his minstrel mask, and the ideal vanishes before the actual.

The normative center in *Huck Finn* is exemplary for several reasons: it is extremely brief; it is at odds with the events of the novel; it possesses a nearly epiphanic quality in that an ideal, almost sacred, vision shows forth from the same mundane material of which the rest of the novel is spun; it emerges from a sentimental matrix of values; it concretizes an authorial judgment that the reader incorporates into his or her own sense making; and the scene is memorable way out of proportion to its size in the larger text. The predominant image of this novel in the American mind is of Jim and Huck peacefully floating down the river on their raft—indeed, this very picture adorns the cover of the Mark Twain Library edition. Yet, that appealing image, representing how Americans wish to view the reality of race as well as how they have so often misread this particular novel, is limited in the text to just three pages that are a respite from the conflicts represented throughout the book.

As we move into twentieth-century fiction, normative centers disappear from novels, perhaps indicating the waning of sentimentalism as a force informing literary production, perhaps resulting from the fragmented world of modernism. In the more culturally unified and religiously informed ethos of the nineteenth century, a normative center and common vision of the ideal is more available; in the twentieth century this vision is replaced by the luminous moment, which is the normative center of the fragment. Toward the end of Edith Wharton's *The House of Mirth,* Lily Bart glimpses an alternative to the casualty-strewn mating game of high society in the happy if materially deprived domestic life of the Struther family, but Lily's insight comes almost as an afterthought when it is too late for it to matter. In William Faulkner's *Absalom, Absalom!,* the normative center is a single line of dialogue spoken by a distressed Henry Sutpen to Charles Bon—"*You are my brother.*"—an ideal quickly dashed by Bon's biologically untrue but socially realistic assessment—"*No I'm not. I'm the nigger that's going to sleep with your sister. Unless you stop me, Henry*" (286). And in Hemingway's *The Sun Also Rises,* the notion of a normative center is undercut when the expatriates corrupt the bullfight and is mocked in the novel's final lines. When Brett cries out to Jake, "we could have had such a damned good time together," a traffic policeman raises his baton and Jake replies, "Isn't it pretty to think so?" (251).

The normative center, then, is a powerful device in the nineteenth-century novel, but for Hemingway it is no longer appropriate in the modern world. Moreover, short fiction hasn't enough space to employ such a device. Instead, in the short story, we often see something very different, a phenomenon I term the *illustrative stamp.* I derive this concept from an observation by Robert Louis Stevenson: "The threads of a story come from time to time together and make a picture in the web; the characters fall from time to time into some attitude to each other or to nature, which stamps the story home like an illustration . . . Other things we may forget . . . but these epoch-making scenes, which put the last mark of truth upon a story and fill up, at one blow, our capacity for sympathetic pleasure, we so adopt into the very bosom of our mind that neither time nor tide can efface or weaken the impression" (*Memories* 256–57). Such compelling images can occur in longer narratives—Stevenson himself cites Robinson Crusoe recoiling from the footprint, Achilles shouting at the Trojans, and Christian (in *Pilgrim's Progress*) running with his fingers in his ears, which Stevenson calls, "culminating moments in the legend" that are now "printed on the mind's eye for ever." He sums up, "This, then, is the plastic part of literature: to embody character, thought, or emotion in some act or attitude that shall be remarkably striking to the mind's eye" (*Memories* 256–57).

A few years after Stevenson penned the above passage, Anton Chekhov articulated his own sense of what I'm calling the illustrative stamp: "The short story, like the stage, has its conventions. My instinct tells me that at the end of a novel or a story I must artfully concentrate for the reader an impression of the entire work" (*LSS* 17). Although Stevenson links these moments to longer narratives and Chekhov applies them to all his fiction (which, aside from several novellas, was entirely comprised of short fiction), the phenomenon they address is especially important to, and typical of, the short story, mainly because a story is so often episodic, more limited in scope to the treatment of one idea, and particularly scenic in nature. A well-placed image is therefore more capable in a story than in a novel of gathering up the various strands of the narrative and stamping it home, in Stevenson's words, "like an illustration."[1]

Just as the normative center in a novel is brief but memorable, so too is the illustrative stamp in a short story. It also has a sensory and, often, a pictorial quality; it is more of a moment rather than the fuller scene of the normative center. They differ, however, in several respects. The normative center stands out because it is so different from the rest of the novel. The illustrative stamp, too, is memorable, not because it is different, but because it is so strongly representative that it seems to embody the essence of the entire text. The normative center, as I have posited it, is also a deliberate aesthetic strategy on the part of the author, a means of subtly pointing the reader to a particular authorial judgment without seeming didactic. But the illustrative stamp seems less conscious on the author's part and more the remembered experience of reading a good story. Here I emphasize the word *seems,* not wishing to preclude the possibility of the author's intentionality in employing the illustrative stamp. Last, the normative center typically derives from a sentimental ideology that it concretizes in its action. Not so the illustrative stamp, certainly not in the Hemingway story, although his illustrative stamps often resonate with a sentimental longing that cannot be fulfilled.

Determining a story's illustrative stamp is quite subjective, and the surest definition I can offer is that it is a moment in the text that one recalls long after reading the story, after one has forgotten nearly everything else. It is always a *sensory* moment, when the reader's processing of the text results not in abstraction or conceptualization, but in apprehending a single captured sensory image (which may subsequently be analyzed, of course, but only after it has been felt). It is not merely a snapshot, which appeals to only one of the senses, but an image that emerges from all the elements of the text (though it crystallizes these) and appeals directly to the reader's need to *feel* an experience. And it is a moment that, upon rereading the story, seems to embody in the emotions it evokes the gist of that story.[2]

I would like to return to the anecdote from the introduction, about how I reread Hemingway many years after first reading him. More than just a passage of nostalgia or a tribute to a favorite author, and more than a cautionary tale about not letting the attitude of others co-opt one's own responses to literary texts, this experience demonstrates the power of the illustrative stamp. As I stared at the titles of stories I hadn't read in over a decade, some I didn't remember at all, but others caused me to recall a particular moment in them that had stuck in my mind over the years, images bridging the gulf of time. While rereading the stories—the characters, scenes, plots, and dialogues reemerging in my consciousness—these initially remembered moments still stood out. Somehow, they had stayed with me, but I didn't understand why. Now, three decades later, I think I know the answer, and to explain it I've come up with the term *illustrative stamp*. These moments crystallized the stories so effectively that they ingrained themselves in my memory.

For specificity's sake, let me reconstruct a partial list of the moments I recalled before rereading the stories: young Nick on the lake in the early morning with his father rowing, his hand trailing in the cold water, thinking that he will never die; Nick's father quietly cleaning his shotgun as his wife harangues him; Nick, lying face down on the blanket after breaking up with Marjorie, telling Bill to leave him alone; Nick and Bill drinking and discussing baseball, trying to imitate men; Harold Krebs, leaving home, stopping at the schoolyard to watch his little sister play indoor baseball; the unhappy woman peering down at the cat in the rain; Nick glancing warily at the dark swamp where fishing would be tragic; the crowd raining down debris and laughter on Manuel as he vainly pursues the bull; the Italian major staring impassively out the hospital window beside the faked photographs of restored hands; Ole Andreson lying fully dressed on his bed staring at the wall as he awaits the gunmen from Chicago; an insomniac Nick lying on the floor listening to the silkworms outside eating; the narrator seeing the dead woman's hair floating inside the porthole of the sunken liner; the old man in the café drinking alone in the shaded dark under an electric light; Alice, big as three women, whom Nick realizes has a pretty face as she argues with another prostitute; the papers strewn among the dead that an unhinged Nick finds on his way from Fornaci; Nick driving with his son and remembering his father. So many of these illustrative stamps are of a character staring at something, or staring at nothing, paralyzed, unable to act. Even the ostensibly wholesome ones carry dark undertones. Is this what I have brought to Hemingway, I wonder, or what he has presented to me? Perhaps it's what we have brought to each other, why I first appreciated him and why these moments remained so long in my memory. I am certain, though, that they are an inextricable part of my sense-making process, and I believe that these, or other such moments, are a part of that process for any reader of short stories.

The illustrative stamp need not occur at or near the end of a story, but usually it does, which is why Chekhov locates it at the end and why Stevenson says that it "stamps the story home like an illustration" and puts on it "the last mark of truth." Most of the examples above take place toward the end of the story (the one in "Soldier's Home" will occur after the narrative is over), while others are ongoing actions throughout the text (e.g., the old man drinking in "A Clean, Well-Lighted Place," Nick driving with his son in "Fathers and Sons"). The one exception, which tends to prove the rule, is when Nick comes across the dead amid their papers at the start of "A Way You'll Never Be." Nick performs a mass postmortem, analyzing what must have happened in the battle by reading the debris left in its aftermath, a text consisting of terrain, corpses, personal papers, and pieces of equipment. What were once two coherent fighting forces are now just fragments, and in the remainder of the story Nick struggles similarly to read the debris of his own shattered psyche in an effort to resurrect his own coherence. This initial scene is therefore an objective correlative of Nick's own inner state and also functions as the text's illustrative stamp.

Hemingway's employment of the illustrative stamp may have something to do with the influence of Pound and imagism. In his landmark 1945 essay, "Spatial Form in Modern Literature," Joseph Frank elucidates Pound's notion of the "image":

> "An 'Image,'" Pound wrote, "is that which presents an intellectual and emotional complex in an instant of time." The implications of this definition should be noted: an image is defined not as a pictorial reproduction but as a unification of disparate ideas and emotions into a complex presented spatially in an instant of time. Such a complex does not proceed discursively, in unison with the laws of language, but strikes the reader's sensibility with an instantaneous impact. Pound stresses this aspect by adding, in the next paragraph, that only the *instantaneous* presentation of such complexes gives "that sense of sudden liberation; that sense of freedom from time limits and space limits; that sense of sudden growth, which we experience in the presence of the greatest works of art." (11)

The realignment of modernist texts along spatial lines—in which the totality of the narrative must be grasped by the reader at once rather than processed linearly—has special relevance to Hemingway's stories. They are invariably episodic; plot is subsumed to Chekhovian mood; and they are often "timeless," in that past (memory), present (action), and future (anticipation) all coexist in, and simultaneously impinge upon, the protagonist's consciousness throughout the text. Is it possible, then, that what we recall as the illustrative stamp is the moment in the text that most exemplifies the image manifested by spatial form?

As with objective correlatives, we also see illustrative stamps in premodern stories, I believe for two reasons. First, remembering Edgar Allan Poe's definitions, the story itself is short enough to be apprehended in its totality, so that a part is more apt to exemplify the whole. Second, as readers trained in the classics of modernism, we ourselves might be more apt to seek out, even unconsciously, such unifying images in premodern texts. Moreover, the story genre entered its modern phase long before the novel did. When we think of the distinctive qualities of modernist fiction—for example, alienation, the experience of fragmentation, the use of myth as a structuring device, the subjective response to modernization and modernity, the focus on consciousness and the unconscious, the shift from ontology to epistemology and the consequent focus on reality as multiple, the importance of the subjective in determining what is real—we find these qualities in the stories of Poe, Hawthorne, Nikolai Gogol, and Melville, just as we later find them in those of Chekhov, Ambrose Bierce, Lu Hsun, and Katherine Mansfield.

We also find epiphanies in premodernist stories. Although the illustrative stamp is not synonymous with the epiphany, an epiphany can serve as an illustrative stamp: for example, the beauty of the obese woman's face suddenly manifesting itself in Nick's consciousness in "The Light of the World." The term *epiphany* first entered the study of modern literature through James Joyce and has been loosely employed by critics ever since. The word derives from the Greek *epiphaneia* ("manifestation") and originally had to do with the sudden showing forth of a divinity, as in the climax of a Greek play when a god reveals himself and imposes order. It was, in this same sense, incorporated into Christianity in the festival of the Epiphany, celebrated twelve days after Christmas, which commemorates the manifestation of Jesus's divinity to the Gentiles as represented by the Magi. Joyce appropriated the term and applied it secularly to art, describing it in the second draft of *A Portrait of the Artist as a Young Man* (titled *Stephen Hero*), in which Stephen Daedalus (in later works, Dedalus) presents his theory of aesthetics.

Overhearing an exchange between a young man and woman, Stephen receives a keen impression disproportionate to the triviality of the conversation. He contemplates collecting "many such moments together in a book of epiphanies": "By an epiphany he meant a sudden spiritual manifestation, whether in the vulgarity of speech or of gesture or in a memorable phrase of the mind itself. He believed that it was for the man of letters to record these epiphanies with extreme care, seeing that they themselves are the most delicate and evanescent of moments" (211). Key to this part of the definition is that the epiphany is *sudden*. Second, it *emerges from the trivial,* what would not otherwise appear a likely conduit for a sudden spiritual manifestation making such a keen impression. Third, because it is sudden and emerges from the mundane, it is implicitly *unexpected*. Fourth, as with any such sudden spiritual manifestation, the epiphany is delicate and *evanescent*; it comes and then disappears in the twinkling of an eye, sinking deep down into the unconscious. It is the job of the writer to record it, to keep it tethered to a plane of conscious accessibility even as it also dives down into the soul of the character experiencing it, thus capturing it and transmuting it into literature.

Stephen then expands upon his aesthetic theory to his companion Cranly, who is an unappreciative audience. Stephen takes from Thomas

Aquinas the idea that the "three things requisite for beauty are, integrity, a wholeness, symmetry and radiance." To apprehend "any object, hypothetically beautiful" first "you must lift it away from everything else: and then you perceive that it is one integral thing, that is *a* thing. You recognise its integrity" (212). Next comes analysis: "The mind considers the object in whole and in part, in relation to itself and to other objects, examines the balance of its parts, contemplates the form of the object, traverses every cranny of the structure. So the mind receives the impression of the symmetry of the object. The mind recognises that the object is in the strict sense of the word, a *thing,* a definitely constituted entity" (212). Last, "the mind makes the only logically possible synthesis and discovers the third quality. This is the moment which I call epiphany": "First we recognise that the object is *one* integral thing, then we recognise that it is an organised composite structure, a *thing* in fact: finally, when the relation of the parts is exquisite, when the parts are adjusted to the special point, we recognise that it is *that* thing which it is. Its soul, its whatness, leaps to us from the vestment of its appearance. The soul of the commonest object, the structure of which is so adjusted, seems to us radiant. The object achieves its epiphany" (213).

Joyce describes this phenomenon with difficulty, falling from literary language into philosophical discourse, but for a reason. He is trying to explain an ecstatic experience where some mundane object of everyday life suddenly shows forth a quality in which the object is both distinct in its common appearance and, simultaneously, reveals its participation in something deeper, something spiritual. His prose seems unclear because it is virtually impossible, in language, to describe such a mystical experience. (Make no mistake about it; that is exactly what Joyce is trying to do.) At its best, such an attempt leads to Walt Whitman's employment of a sexual metaphor to describe the ecstatic experience in "Song of Myself"; at its most inept, it's someone on LSD saying, "Like, wow, man, I can see my hands."

William James delineates four elements that define a mystical experience: ineffability, a noetic quality, transiency, and passivity. *Ineffability* means that the experience "defies expression, that no adequate report of its contents can be given in words." He states that "its quality must be directly experienced; it cannot be imparted or transferred to others" and that it is more a state of "feeling" than a state of "intellect" (343). About its *noetic quality,* James says: "Although so similar to states of feeling, mystical states seem to those who experience them to be also states of knowledge. They are states of insight into depths of truth unplumbed by the discursive intellect. They are illuminations, revelations, full of significance and importance, all inarticulate though they remain; and as a rule they carry with them a curious sense of authority for after-time" (343). These two elements "always entitle any state to be called mystical," but the next two, though not absolutely necessary, usually are also part of the experience. *Transiency* means that "mystical states cannot be sustained for long." Moreover, and here I would make the connection to dreams, "when faded, their quality can but imperfectly be reproduced in memory; but when they recur it is recognized; and from one recurrence to another it is susceptible of continuous development in what is felt as inner richness and importance." As for *passivity*, although a mystical experience can be "facilitated" by "voluntary operations" (e.g., the chanting of a mantra, the fixing of one's attention), once the mystical state is realized "the mystic feels as if his own will were in abeyance, and indeed sometimes as if he were grasped and held by a superior power" (343–44).

Here we see what Joyce was up against and, perhaps, why critics have subsequently had so much difficulty using the epiphany in literary analysis, often mistaking any deep revelation or sudden awareness on the part of a fictional character for an epiphany. Joyce is trying to capture and transfer a state of perception and feeling that by definition can neither be described in language nor grasped by others except through their own direct experience. These feelings also elevate the one who has experienced them (Stephen) from the mundane world of their fellows (Cranly among them) and consequently separate the person from those to whom they wish to impart the experience. It was this dilemma that led another mystic, Walt Whitman, to the verge of existential despair in the late 1850s (see Lamb, "Prophet" 429–30). Moreover, the experience fades, which is why both Stephen and Joyce want to record it before this happens. Nevertheless, when Joyce moved from trying to describe the epiphany to embodying it in his fiction, he succeeded. He did so via his own combination of impressionism and expressionism, presenting the impressions that create the emotion and his lyrical probing of the experiencing consciousness, as in his depiction of Gabriel's epiphanic realization of the inner life of his wife Gretta at the conclusion of "The Dead."

I have delved into the epiphany at some length because I want to distinguish it from the illustrative stamp, because it is an important element in the short story (both before and after Joyce), and—since it is so frequently misused in literary criticism—to explain it, I hope with some clarity.

Joyce was the living author whom Hemingway most respected. The two were intimate friends in Paris in the 1920s, and each understood the other's craft better than any of their contemporaries or subsequent critics. Partly because Joyce eschewed writing directly about his craft, critics (except for Robert E. Gajdusek 9–56) have tended to ignore Joyce's influence on Hemingway, who was generally vague about what he learned from others. In Paris, Hemingway often brought Joyce his manuscripts for criticism. Nor was he hesitant to acknowledge his admiration. In 1933 he stated that "no one can write better, technically" than Joyce and that he'd "learned much from him" (*SL* 384). He also asserted that any poet or fiction writer not influenced by, respectively, Pound and Joyce deserved "to be pitied" (qtd. in *HLS* 236). Seventeen years later, he avowed, "Jim Joyce was the only alive writer that I ever respected," and "he could write better than anyone I knew" (*SL* 696). For his part, Joyce said of the younger writer that "giants of his sort are truly modest; there is much more behind Hemingway's form than people know" (qtd. in Ellmann 695).

Despite his admiration for Joyce's art, however, the epiphany played no significant role in Hemingway's story aesthetics. Moments of recognition and sudden awareness abound in his stories, but these are not, technically speaking, epiphanies. One possible exception might be Nick's experience, noted earlier, in "The Light of the World," but I search in vain for others. There are two reasons for this absence. First, whenever Hemingway tried to describe ecstatic moments, he either did so directly, as in his descriptions of the catharsis of the bullfights in *Death in the Afternoon,* sounding—similar to Joyce in the above passages from *Stephen Hero*—more the philosopher than the fiction writer. Or else his strict use of impressionism and omission of the subjective prevented the full treatment of moments that could have developed into epiphanies, as in the passage when Nick hooks the giant trout in "Big Two-Hearted River." Refusing to probe Nick's emotions and develop the potential epiphany, Hemingway instead resorts to immediate speech, reporting Nick's thoughts using the first-person pronoun: "By God, he was a big one. By God, he was the biggest one I ever heard of" (*SS* 227). To employ the epiphany would be, to Hemingway if not to Joyce, to allow the "whatness" of the object to supercede its "thingness"; that is, it would compromise his commitment to the ultimacy of the physical world upon which his entire aesthetics were built.

A second reason for the scarcity of epiphanies in his work derives from Hemingway's own religious temperament. Although he possessed, as Keneth Kinnamon ("Hemingway") and Allen Josephs ("Spanish Sensibility") have both noted, a fully Hispanicized sensibility and would, in the 1930s, convert to Catholicism, he rarely seems to have undergone a mystical experience beyond the catharsis of the bullfight or the joy of the sportsman. Joyce tried to secularize the epiphany, but the ecstatic experience nevertheless carries religious undertones; the spirituality, the "whatness" of the trivial object must partially derive from a realm other than the profane, a sacred realm in which Hemingway had little faith. In fact, the closest Hemingway ever really came to a full Joycean epiphany was when he penned an anti-epiphany toward the conclusion of "A Clean, Well-Lighted Place." Rather than a spiritual essence manifesting itself to the waiter as he watches the old man, a vision of nothingness consumes the text: "It was all a nothing and a man was nothing too" (*SS* 383). This existentialist credo is exemplary of Hemingway, for whom nothing precedes existence or succeeds it. In short, he loved the things of this world, but there is little evidence that he believed in an accompanying spiritual world.

As did so many modernists, Wallace Stevens for instance, the only immortality Hemingway could imagine was one created by perfect art. His son Gregory recalls, "We were brought up Catholics, but he made it clear he didn't believe in an afterlife" (qtd. in Brian 305). Hemingway addressed this question in *Green Hills of Africa:*

> For we have been there in the books and out of the books—and where we go, if we are any good, there you can go as we have been. A country, finally, erodes, and the dust blows away, the people all die and none of them were of any importance permanently, except those who practised the arts, and these now wish to cease their work because it is too lonely, too hard to do, and is not fashionable. A thousand years makes economics silly and a work of art endures forever, but it is very difficult to do and now it is not fashionable. People do not want to do it any more because they will be out of fashion and the lice who crawl on literature will not praise them. Also it is very hard to do. So what? (*GHA* 109)

The first sentence recalls Whitman's claim to readers at the start of "Song of Myself"—"And what I assume you shall assume, / For every atom belonging to me as good belongs to you" (27). For Whitman, what creates this possibility of shared experience is the similar physical existences of people and that everyone contains within themselves the divine Over-Soul. But for Hemingway the only way to experience something is to have that experience directly ("out of the books") or through the art of a writer whose prose can convey it ("in the books"). The true work of art "endures forever," akin to the "earth" that "abideth forever" in the Ecclesiastes quotation that serves as an epigraph to *The Sun Also Rises*. Furthermore, even this small flicker of transcendence available to humanity is threatened—by its difficulty, by the literary marketplace, and by the arbiters of that marketplace, the critics. The concluding "So what?" is Hemingway's affirmation, in the face of difficulty and doubt, of his faith in the act of literary creation. Sadly, where this left him when the Yeatsian circus animals of his art deserted him, the biographies make all too clear.

Having made the point that Hemingway does not employ the epiphany, I'll conclude on a different, somewhat contradictory, tack. Richard Ellmann explains that although Joyce took the term *epiphany* from Catholicism, for him it did not signify the manifestation of the sacred, "although that is a useful metaphor for what he had in mind." Joyce's epiphanies were secular, and the artist "must look for them not among gods but among men, in casual, unostentatious, even unpleasant moments" (83). But Joyce came from the matrix of Catholicism and the epiphany is so saturated with connotations of the holy that it is difficult, in appropriating it for a secular art, to divest it fully of sacramental associations. Even when blasphemously joking, Joyce depends upon Catholic theology, as when he says of Stephen: "Phrases came to him asking to have themselves explained. He said to himself: I must wait for the Eucharist to come to me: and then he set about translating the phrase into common sense. He . . . built a house of silence for himself wherein he might await his Eucharist" (30).

What I am suggesting is that it is exceedingly difficult, even for someone as cosmopolitan as Joyce, to escape the paradigms of the culture in which one was raised. To offer a major example, Karl Marx rejected Judeo-Christian theology, replacing it with dialectical materialism, but Marxism nevertheless copies the biblical conception of time and history. Instead of Eden, we have primitive communism; instead of God's intervention in human history, we have the dialectic; and instead of the eventual Kingdom of God on earth, we have the classless society. Similarly, Hemingway rejected the civic values of Oak Park, the Midwest, and his family in favor of cosmopolitanism, atheism (or, at most, some vague deism), and Hispanic culture. But he retained to the end the ethos in which he was raised, one based on discipline, professionalism, competence, Rooseveltian rugged in-dividualism, sacrifice, and a Progressive concern for social justice (Lamb, "Ernest Hemingway" 488–89).

There are indeed mystical experiences in even Joyce's secularized epiph-anies, and William James's analysis remains pertinent. But rather than seeing these moments as a sudden emergence of the sacred from the pro-fane—which is how a historian of religion such as Mircea Eliade would view them—perhaps we can also say that in an epiphany the artist sud-denly feels an object with such precision and finds a language exact enough to convey that feeling to the reader, so that what we end up with, whether sacred or not, is a perfect communication of a perfect perception. The epiphany derives from such a combination, the perception *and* the com-munication, and this, as Ellmann observes, would become "a common-place of modern fiction. Arrogant yet humble too, it claims importance by claiming nothing; it seeks a presentation so sharp that comment by the au-thor would be an interference. It . . . makes the reader feel uneasy and cul-pable if he misses the intended but always unstated meaning . . . The artist abandons himself and his reader to the material" (84).

In this sense only, Hemingway's aesthetics do embrace the Joycean epiphany—by seeing objects with such complete clarity and describing them so precisely that the reader sees them too, with no need for autho-rial comment. This was the method of Joyce, and it was Chekhov's as well. In his method of conveying an "intended but always unstated meaning," Hemingway is surely working in that tradition.

8

The New Art of Constructive Dialogue

FROM JAMES TO HEMINGWAY

[Hemingway's] is an obscuring and at the same time a revealing way to write dialogue, and only great skill can manage it—and make us aware at the same time that communication of a limited kind is now going on as best it can.
—Eudora Welty, *The Eye of the Story*

As a writer I was astonished by Hemingway's skill . . . I have never understood, to this day, how Hemingway achieved his powerful dialogue . . . What Hemingway offered . . . was not dialogue overheard, but a concentrate of it, often made up of superficially insignificant elements—mere fragments of everyday phrases, which always managed to convey what was most important.
—Ilya Ehrenburg, "The World Weighs a Writer's Influence"

There is not a living writer in England who has been unaffected by the laconic speed of his dialogue, the subtle revelation of character that lies behind a spoken phrase.
—Alan Pryce-Jones, "The World Weighs a Writer's Influence

Hemingway's most original and influential contribution to the art of fiction was his creation of an entirely new role for dialogue. Between the completion of his sixth story, "Indian Camp," in February 1924 (the first new story written for *In Our Time*) and his thirtieth story, "Hills Like White Elephants," in May 1927 (the last story written for *Men Without Women*), he so thoroughly revolutionized dialogue that, had he done nothing else, this accomplishment alone would have secured his reputation in literary history. But although critics have frequently commented on his distinctive dialogue, the exact nature of his achievement remains rudimentarily explored.[1] I can posit only two reasons why. First, since the academy is dismissive of scholarship on articulated technique in fiction studies—if not in poetry, music, or art criticism—an examination of the craft of dialogue is, unfortunately, of far greater interest to writers, the direct beneficiaries of Hemingway's achievement, than to critics. Second, as renowned novelist Anthony Powell observes, "Hemingway systematized a treatment of dialogue in a manner now scarcely possible to appreciate, so much has the Hemingway usage taken the place of what went before" (110).

How, then, did Hemingway forever change an entire element of fiction? Before the mid-nineteenth-century advent of realism, dialogue served a limited set of functions. For instance, in romances and sentimental fiction, it was confined to melodramatic speeches, the communication of information, commonplace exchanges, and displays of the author's erudition and verbal wit. It was rarely used for characterization, especially since, as Mark Twain's "Fenimore Cooper's Literary Offences" makes devastatingly clear, characters either tended to talk alike or else speak in a way, often ad nauseam, that was meant to be illustrative (180–81, 189–90). Frequently, there was little difference between their speech and that of the author or narrator, and even the speeches of the same character would vary widely throughout a text. Worse, with a few notable exceptions such as Jane Austen in her novels of manners or Nathaniel Hawthorne in his romances, dialogue lacked subtlety: characters said what they consciously thought, meaning lay on the surface, and their words were remarkably free from the sorts of inner conflicts and psychological complexities inherent in the speech of real people.

With the emergence of realism and its focus on character, the art of dialogue advanced. As characters became consistent, so too did their speech; different characters spoke differently, and many of the intricacies of real-life speech emerged in fiction. Additionally, due to a new interest in regional differences in America stimulated by the Civil War and a thriving postwar market for national magazines, the accurate depiction of dialect became a convention, not only in the works of such masters as Twain, William Dean Howells, Harriet Beecher Stowe (in her later works), Sarah Orne Jewett, Mary Wilkins Freeman, Charles W. Chesnutt, Stephen Crane, and Kate Chopin, but across the literary landscape (see Jones, *Strange Talk*). As dialogue moved from the overwrought speeches of Poe's characters, the high rhetoric of Melville's Shakespearean sailors, the commonplaces of the domestic novel, and the schizophrenic verbosity of Cooper's Natty Bumppo to the shrewdly calculating speeches of Twain's Jim, Huck, Hank Morgan, and Roxy, the idiosyncratically specific and characterizing speeches of Howells's Lapham family, and the brilliantly modulated registers in the verbal battlefields of James's and Wharton's novels of manners, dialogue benefited from Howells's realist mandates of fidelity to experience and probability of motive. In short, one of the consequences of the movement toward verisimilitude was that fictional characters began to sound as though they were actual human beings.

But even as the quality of dialogue improved immeasurably, its role in fiction changed very little. For James, whose theory of dialogue was exemplary in the late nineteenth century, dialogue was purely complementary; its proper and only function was to be "directly illustrative of something given us by another method" of presentation ("London" 1404). The idea that dialogue could crystallize situation or advance plot was, to James, ludicrous. Complaining that the "fashion of our day" is "an inordinate abuse of the colloquial resource" (too much quoted speech), he believed that "there is a *law*" governing the use of fictional dialogue, and that while "admirable for illustration, functional for illustration, dialogue has its function perverted, and therewith its life destroyed, when forced . . . into the constructive office" ("Balzac" 137). Any attempt to have dialogue play more than this limited illustrative role he termed "singularly suicidal" ("London" 1404). The notion of "really constructive dialogue, dialogue organic and dramatic, speaking for itself, representing and embodying substance and form" was an "abhorrent thing," appropriate to the theater, which "lives by a law so different," but never to fiction (*Awkward Age* 1127; "Balzac" 137). Moreover, James, for whom mimesis and a direct impression of life were the paramount goals of fiction, did not believe that direct speech was even capable of being mimetically reproduced, and so he called for writers to recognize "the impossibility of making people both talk 'all the time' and talk with the needful differences." To get characters to do that, he frankly admitted, "is simply too hard. There is always at the best the author's voice to be kept out. It can be kept out for occasions, it can not be kept out always. The solution therefore is to leave it its function, for it has the supreme one" ("London" 1404).

In truth, James wrote dialogue superbly and used it liberally. But he could not countenance allowing it out of its box. Take, for instance, this brief passage from *The Portrait of a Lady* (1881), in which young Ned Rosier comes to Gilbert Osmond's house in pursuit of Pansy, Osmond's daughter, unaware, as is the reader at this point, that Osmond already knows the purpose of the visit:

"I saw a jolly good piece of Capo di Monte to-day."

Osmond answered nothing at first; but presently, while he warmed his boot-sole, "I don't care a fig for Capo di Monte!" he returned.

"I hope you are not losing your interest?"

"In old pots and plates? Yes, I am losing my interest."

Rosier for a moment forgot the delicacy of his position.

"You are not thinking of parting with a—a piece or two?"

"No, I am not thinking of parting with anything at all, Mr. Rosier," said Osmond, with his eyes still on the eyes of his visitor.

"Ah, you want to keep, but not to add," Rosier remarked, brightly.

"Exactly. I have nothing that I wish to match."

Poor Rosier was aware that he had blushed, and he was distressed at his want of assurance. "Ah, well, I have!" was all that he could murmur; and he knew that his murmur was partly lost as he turned away. (569–70)

Here we see many of the distinguishing features of James's dialogue. Rosier and Osmond speak in character and, as do all James characters, they speak with skill. Rosier, torn between his predisposition to diffidence and his desire for Pansy, attempts to soften up his auditor by addressing a subject of which Osmond is fond but is caught short by his host's unforeseen rudeness. Perhaps consciously, perhaps not, he tips his hand by continuing to talk ostensibly about china when the real subject of the conversation is Pansy, and he is more seriously rebuffed when Osmond substitutes "anything" for "a piece or two." With his blushing indicating a dawning awareness, Rosier attempts a witty rejoinder, verbally pursuing his goal from a slightly different angle. But Osmond's use of the verb *match* in his final rebuff (to Rosier's cleverly implied notion of "adding" a son-in-law) makes it unambiguously clear to Rosier that both know what the conversation is really about and that Osmond has strong feelings on the subject. The suitor turns away, feebly protesting, with diffidence momentarily overcoming desire.

For an author who abhorred "the colloquial resource," James included a great deal of dialogue in *The Portrait of a Lady*. Nevertheless, none of it conflicts with James's theory. This brief, dramatic confrontation is embedded in paragraphs in which James's narrator probes the consciousnesses of the characters, and, for all its artful execution, the dialogue merely illustrates what is given us by that other, main method of presentation. In the paragraph preceding this passage, James prepares us for Rosier's performance by stating that Rosier "was not quickly resentful, and where politeness was concerned he had an inveterate wish to be in the right" (569).

Even in the passage itself, James tells us that Rosier "forgot the delicacy of his position" rather than allowing the dialogue to make that clear on its own, and Rosier's final remark only illustrates the distress that James's narrator describes instead of allowing Rosier's words to indicate that discomfiture.

Ezra Pound first directed Hemingway to the works of James, and Hemingway's first wife, Hadley, was a James enthusiast. Although Hemingway alternately ridiculed and praised James and was loath to acknowledge any influence (his usual response to any writer who had truly mattered to his development), and although the impact of James on his work would not reach full fruition until the late 1940s and 1950s when Hemingway was trying to write Jamesian novels, nevertheless, early in his career his predecessor's texts had shown him, as Michael Reynolds has insightfully noted, that the significance of "dialogue appears frequently in the white space between the lines" and that "it is what the characters do not say that is highlighted by their conversation" (*Paris* 30). In this manner, James's dialogue served as a powerful model for Hemingway in its indirection, ambiguity, and portrayal of communication as veiled, partial, and difficult. As Sheldon Norman Grebstein observes, both authors "employed a technique of brief exchanges which tended to refer obliquely to the subject under discussion rather than to name it outright" (96). Carlos Baker terms this technique "the hovering subject":

> Another remarkable similarity in the conduct of dialogue by James and Hemingway is what may be called the hovering subject. James often establishes the subject of a conversation by hint and allusion rather than overt statement. At other times he introduces the subject briefly (often it is a single word at the end of a sentence), and then conducts the dialogue by reference to it, while it hovers, helicopter-like, over the surface of the conversation. In either instance the neuter pronoun *it,* or its unuttered equivalent, is the index to what is being talked about. *It* is the apex of a pyramid whose base is the dialogue, and the real subject is the star at which the apex points. (*Writer* 185, n. 32)

In addition, both authors share a technique that Grebstein calls "incremental repetition" or a "type of stichomythia": "In this rhetorical scheme each speaker will pick up a word or phrase from the other's speech and utilize it as the basis for his own remarks, but adding, subtracting, or changing, so that the dialogue continuously rehearses itself yet evolves as it proceeds" (96). Note for example, in the James passage, the repetitions of "Capo di Monte," "losing . . . interest," "not thinking of parting," and "I have," and also such substitutions as: "I don't care a fig" for "I saw a jolly good piece"; "old pots and plates" for "Capo di Monte"; "anything" for "a piece or two"; "nothing that I wish to match" for "want to keep, but not to add"; and "I have [something that I wish to match]" for "I have nothing that I wish to match."

It sometimes seems as though the main difference in their dialogue—aside from James's pervasive use of access to his characters' consciousnesses—consists of Hemingway's complete abandonment of James's stage directions. Hemingway's favorite identification tag is the simple "he said" or "she said," and even these he often eliminates. But in James, as Baker observes, "the phrases range from 'I gaily confessed' through 'she rather inscrutably added' and on to 'I attempted the grimace of suggesting.' Like his use of italicized words [in dialogue], these phrases are meant to mark the tone and emphasis, the special ring, of a particular speech. James is in effect gesturing silently from the prompt-box." Baker concludes by demonstrating how, if we remove the prompts from a James passage, "the dialogue proceeds in a manner scarcely distinguishable from Hemingway's" (*Writer* 183). Here, though, I must demur, for however much Hemingway learned about dialogue from James, his decision to let it play the constructive role that James considered inappropriate—to remove the author's voice and allow dialogue to speak solely for itself—was revolutionary.

James's theories of fiction—despite his movement toward increased dramatization, foreshortening, and the effacement of the narrator—derived from his work in the nineteenth-century novel of manners. The sine qua non of that genre was the dense depiction of social texture and the representation of temporality. James asserted that the novelist's most difficult, and therefore most dignified, effort "consists in giving the sense of duration, of the lapse and accumulation of time." In dialogue, narrative time slows down and begins to approximate real time. Such a "multiplication of quoted remarks" is an "expedient" that "works exactly to the opposite end, absolutely minimising, in regard to time, our impression of lapse and passage" ("London" 1403–4; also see "Balzac" 136). In addition, dialogue silences the author's "supreme" voice that, in its judiciousness, probity, and richness, is essential to the genre's discursive texture. Even when James admired another author's dialogue—as he did in the case of his friend William Dean Howells—he believed it needed to be "distributed, interspaced with narrative and pictorial matter. [Howells] forgets sometimes to paint, to evoke the conditions and appearances, to build in the subject . . . I cannot help thinking that the divinest thing in a valid novel is the compendious, descriptive, pictorial touch, *à la Daudet*" ("Howells" 505–6).

Hemingway's prosaics, however, derived from a different genre, the emerging modern short story, which, as did his earlier journalism, placed a premium on discrete events and delimited moments in time. That genre's demands for radical compression, which led to the need for a high degree of suggestiveness and implication, eliminated the thick portrayal of social texture and sense of duration that lay at the heart of the novel of manners. These generic demands enabled Hemingway, perhaps compelled him, to rely on and further compress dialogue, allowing it to assume a hitherto unknown role in fictional composition, even to the point of removing almost completely the narrative commentary and authorial voice without which, James had felt, fiction would cease to be fiction and would cross over into drama. James, of course, could not have anticipated the new genre's heavy reliance on direct speech, and even some of Hemingway's most illustrious contemporaries found his dialogue-laden stories unseemly. Virginia Woolf, for one, criticized him in Jamesian terms in her 1927 review of *Men Without Women:*

> A writer will always be chary of dialogue because dialogue puts the most violent pressure upon the reader's attention. He has to hear, to see, to supply the right tone, and to fill in the background from what the characters say without any help from the author. Therefore, when fictitious people are allowed to speak it must be because they have something so important to say that it stimulates the reader to do rather more than his share of the work of creation. But, although Mr. Hemingway keeps us under the fire of dialogue constantly, his people, half the time, are saying what the author could say much more economically for them. (8)

But Dorothy Parker, herself a gifted story writer, in reviewing that same volume understood that Hemingway's style was "far more effective" in "the short story than in the novel" (93) and that the modern story genre demanded radically different techniques of construction and representation that empowered readers precisely by giving them a larger role in what Woolf termed "the work of creation."

The clash between Woolf and Parker over the function of dialogue reveals a difference between the views of authors who were primarily novelists, for instance James and Woolf, and those, such as Hemingway, Parker, Elizabeth Bowen, and Eudora Welty, who were completely at home in the modern short story and willing, in their stories, to dispense with the author's "supreme" presence. One traditional notion at odds with the new genre was that dialogue should be limited to illustration. Bowen observes: "Each piece of dialogue *must* be 'something happening.' Dialogue *may* justify its presence by being 'illustrative'—but this secondary use of it must be watched closely, challenged. Illustrativeness can be stretched too far. Like straight description, it then becomes static, a dead weight—halting the movement of the plot" ("Notes" 256). Although Bowen greatly admired James, she felt that his stories, for all their virtuosity, represented a "dead end" in the genre's development that could neither be imitated nor advanced upon (*Faber* 39).

James's dialogue, and that of Edith Wharton—easily the most talented American writers of dialogue before Hemingway—depended on characters who were highly intelligent, refined, and sensitive to the slightest nuances of words and gestures. Granting both authors this *donnée,* it is nevertheless true that, until Hemingway, no writer was able to write dialogue that demonstrated the rich complexities of the speech of characters who were not particularly bright, cultured, or sensitive. Twain, of course, did vernacular characters justice, especially in first-person narration. The richest, most complex dialogue he ever wrote was for Jim in *Huck Finn,* and this he did with such subtlety that a century of criticism mistook that character's shrewdly manipulative minstrel performance for mere minstrel caricature (see Lamb, "America" 480–83). But although Jim and Huck may not be refined, they are assuredly intelligent and sensitive. As for the dialogue of such later writers as Frank Norris, Gertrude Stein, and Sinclair Lewis, it continued to play a limited role and, with regard to the speeches of common characters, was often condescending.

The Jamesian novel of manners was written for a pre-Freudian audience and treated the romantic egoist within a fully developed social world. Consequently, it focused on the consciousnesses of characters capable of rich perception, feeling, and self-awareness. Dialogue was akin to a game of chess, played by sophisticated characters highly skilled and inordinately clever. Although a great deal of miscommunication occurred, much communication took place too. The Hemingway short story, on the other hand, portrays transient modern individuals cut loose from their social moorings. His characters, no less capable of feeling, are much less articulate, sophisticated, versed in the strategies of speech, and consciously self-aware. But their conversations are every bit as rich as those of James's characters because, however limited their consciousnesses may be, they possess the same complex unconscious motivations as any human characters.

It *should* go without saying that one need not be a highly developed, self-aware, social creature to be worthy of consideration, either in literature or in life. Yet, from the start—with Lee Wilson Dodd's comments on Hemingway's "narrow" attention to "certain sorts of people" with "oddly limited minds, interests, and patterns of behavior" (323); Wyndham Lewis's vicious characterization in *Men Without Art* of Hemingway as a "dumb ox" whose characters are dull-witted and bovine; and D. S. Savage's nearly obscene assessment of Hemingway's art as representing "the *proletarianization* of literature; the adaptation of the technical artistic conscience to the sub-average human consciousness" (14–15)—Hemingway's detractors have invariably based their attacks on his *donnée*: his semiarticulate characters and their class-bound cultural limitations. Such sentiments are, of course, deplorable, and one would expect today's multicultural and putatively class-sensitive critics to denounce them as, at the very least, elitist. But literary criticism has always had an ambivalent attitude toward the uneducated classes, defending them in principle but finding itself viscerally repelled by fiction that features such characters not as a type of "noble savage" or "untutored folk democrat" but from the inside in all of their awkwardness and crudity. Hemingway—cosmopolitan, quadralingual, bookish, and intellectual though he was—did not turn from such characters. In finding ways to allow them to speak, the writer who once half-jokingly referred to himself as "the Henry James of the People" (*SL* 556), fashioned new techniques that brought their voices fully into the pages of fiction.[2]

What, then, were Hemingway's technical accomplishments in the writing of dialogue? They can be summed up in three phrases: minimum speech with maximum meaning, the elevation of banality into art, and the blurring of distinctions between the genres of drama and fiction. To achieve these goals, he removed or subtilized the controlling presence of the author's voice and incorporated into dialogue the techniques of his nondialogue prose: indirection, juxtaposition as a means of having meaning derive from proximity, irony, omission, repetition, the objective correlative, and referential ambiguity. In doing so, he met the challenge of writing modern dialogue: representing the dynamics of real-life speech. After Hemingway, writers would have the option of making dialogue illustrative or constructive and of having their characters show themselves in ways hitherto only revealed by other methods.

In a valuable series of observations about craft, published in 1945 in the aftermath of modernist fiction's heyday, Elizabeth Bowen cut to the crux of why writing modern dialogue is so difficult. Staking a position diametrically opposite to that of James, she observes that dialogue must imitate certain "realistic qualities": "Spontaneity. Artless or hit-or-miss arrival at words used. Ambiguity (speaker not sure, himself, what he means). Effect of choking (as in engine): more to be said than can come through. Irrelevance. Allusiveness. Erraticness: unpredictable course. Repercussion." But behind the "mask of these faked realistic qualities," it must be "pointed, intentional, relevant. It must crystallize situation. It must express character. It must advance plot." It must, in other words, be truly verisimilar—*seemingly* real but not an actual transcription of reality itself. "Speech," Bowen goes on to say, "is what the characters *do to each other*"; aside from a few extreme physical acts, it is "the most vigorous and visible inter-action of which characters . . . are capable." Consequently, speech "crystallizes relationships. It *should,* ideally, so be effective as to make analysis or explanation of the relationships between the characters unnecessary" ("Notes" 255). Although dialogue is generally ineffective for purposes of exposition, for conveying necessary information (what invariably occurs at the beginning of a play, which it takes all of the considerable artifice of the theater subsequently to overcome), it can express present relationships and, by implication, their past as well. But this requires great talent; dialogue must imply subtly, suggestively, and never through direct statement. Usually, the *way* characters say something is more important than *what* they say.

Bowen further observes that each sentence spoken by a character must display either "calculation" or "involuntary self-revelation." Great dialogue, I would add, displays both, for in fiction, as in life, it is virtually impossible not to be, to some degree, self-revelatory when speaking. Generally, she states, characters should "be under rather than over articulate," and what they "*intend* to say should be more evident, more striking (because of its greater inner importance to the plot) than what they arrive at *saying*" ("Notes" 256). Robie Macauley and George Lanning agree, noting that "speech, as a way of characterization, moves forward by means of partial concealment, partial exposure" because what characters say may be the result of inner conflictedness, or they may be saying what they think the other person wishes to hear (78). In speech, they may become aware of their own confusion, or something the other person does might make them modify their original intention. They may become even more confused and end up saying the opposite of what they wished to say. In short, all of the myriad complexities that inhere in real-life dialogue inhere as well in fictional dialogue, the one great difference being that in fiction there is an author who exercises some control over what is being expressed (or incompletely expressed). Dialogue therefore demonstrates not only communication but also its limits.

In Hemingway's earliest mature stories we see him still in thrall to, but starting to pull away from, the premodern practice of dialogue. In "Out of Season," written in April 1923, a foreign couple's fishing guide tries to persuade them to purchase some wine as they leave the village:

> Peduzzi stopped in front of a store with the window full of bottles and brought his empty grappa bottle from an inside pocket of his old military coat. "A little to drink, some marsala for the Signora, something, something to drink." He gestured with the bottle. It was a wonderful day. "Marsala, you like marsala, Signorina? A little marsala?"
>
> The wife stood sullenly. "You'll have to play up to this," she said. "I can't understand a word he says. He's drunk, isn't he?"
>
> The young gentleman appeared not to hear Peduzzi. He was thinking, what in hell makes him say marsala? That's what Max Beerbohm drinks.
>
> "Geld," Peduzzi said finally, taking hold of the young gentleman's sleeve. "Lire." He smiled, reluctant to press the subject but needing to bring the young gentleman into action. (SS 174)

This dialogue is quite effective, but in a Jamesian manner. Peduzzi and the wife are well characterized by their speeches; he pathetically attempts to ingratiate himself in order to obtain all that he can in return for his services, and she is contemptuous, classist, impatient, and possibly xenophobic. Peduzzi's importunity, nicely captured by his repetition of *marsala,* begins with him feigning concern for the wife's enjoyment and quickly degenerates into a frantic plea for money in whatever language will communicate this successfully to the husband. But Hemingway does not yet trust the dialogue to be constructive on its own. As James would have done, he uses an adverb to characterize the wife's attitude and subsequent speech ("sullenly"); instead of allowing the husband's silence to speak, he takes the opportunity to delve into that character's consciousness; and he didactically explains Peduzzi's strategy after the final appeal.

For nine months after completing Out of Season," Hemingway was beset by family responsibilities and had little time to write except for the *in our time* vignettes and his newspaper dispatches, but he continued making mental notes for future stories. Returning to Paris in January 1924, he embarked upon a remarkable period of creativity that would lead, in the next three years, to the publication of two of the finest story collections in literature and his first major novel. In the first of these stories, "Indian Camp," completed in February, he left behind the poorly written speech of the deleted opening (NAS 13–15; see Lamb, "Dialogue" 455–56) and unveiled his new art of constructive dialogue.

After successfully performing an emergency Caesarean with fishing equipment on an Indian woman who delivers a boy, Nick Adams' father discovers that her husband, confined to the upper bunk with a foot injury, has cut his throat. Preoccupied before the operation, in which he thoughtlessly had Nick assist, and exhilarated in its aftermath, he is sobered upon realizing that his child has witnessed the dead man. He leaves his brother George in the shanty and removes Nick. In the story's final dialogue, spoken as Nick and his father return to the rowboat, the author disappears completely, even eliminating identification tags, as pure dialogue advances the plot to its conclusion:

> It was just beginning to be daylight when they walked along the logging road back toward the lake.
> "I'm terribly sorry I brought you along, Nickie," said his father, all his post-operative exhilaration gone. "It was an awful mess to put you through."
> [Q1] "Do ladies always have such a hard time having babies?" Nick asked.
> [A1] "No, that was very, very exceptional."
> [Q2] "Why did he kill himself, Daddy?"
> [A2] "I don't know, Nick. He couldn't stand things, I guess."
> [Q3] "Do many men kill themselves, Daddy?"
> [A3] "Not very many, Nick."
> [Q4] "Do many women?"
> [A4] "Hardly ever."

[Q5] "Don't they ever?"

[A5] "Oh, yes. They do sometimes."

[Q6] "Daddy?"

[A6] "Yes."

[Q7] "Where did Uncle George go?"

[A7] "He'll turn up all right."

[Q8] "Is dying hard, Daddy?"

[A8] "No, I think it's pretty easy, Nick. It all depends." (SS 94–95)

The opening sentence efficiently locates the action following a narra-tive ellipsis. The word *daylight* is a literal descriptor that also resonates as a figurative comment on Dr. Adams, who is just beginning to see the light. The suicide has deflated his earlier illusion of power, forcing him to accept things beyond his control. Now aware of his son's needs and his parental responsibilities, in his first speech the doctor admits his mistake. His use of the diminutive *Nickie* suggests that he is concerned with Nick's anxiet-ies (he used the same diminutive in the deleted opening after his fright-ened child summoned him), but he also betrays his own feelings of guilt. His apology is not for Nick's having seen the dead Indian (which could not have been anticipated) nor for his thoughtlessness in having Nick attend the horrific operation (his most irresponsible act). Instead, he apologizes for having brought Nick to the Indian camp rather than leaving him alone in the woods (a necessary decision), which undercuts the apology by pass-ing over his truly unconscionable act. What he had previously termed a "little affair" (the operation), he now calls an "awful mess"—an understate-ment that covers everything Nick has witnessed (including his father's pa-ternal inadequacies) and, by its euphemistic nature, continues to diminish the apology. The phrase about his "post-operative exhilaration" being gone is superfluous and inappropriate in this story internally focalized through Nick, and should have been deleted. The last phrase of his statement shows Dr. Adams looking at these events from Nick's perspective ("to put you through") in order to console him, but his shame is manifest in his use of an inert construction; a more direct admission of culpability would have been: "I put you through an awful mess." By his need to assuage his own guilt, then, the doctor's apology is involuntarily self-revelatory; he is still absorbed in his own needs, not his child's.

If the doctor's initial speech is revealing, the ensuing eight questions and answers are a marvel of indirection, miscommunication, suggestiveness, and compression. Nick has conflated all the events he has witnessed and therefore asks about the operation, but by the end of the passage it is clear that what he really wants to know about is the probability of death (either his father's or his own). His father, however, is obsessed with the suicide and so, for all his newfound sensitivity toward his son and Nick's careful attention to his father, the two characters miscommunicate throughout the conversation.

Nick's first question ("Do ladies always have such a hard time having babies?") elicits a somewhat detached response from his father, whose thoughts are elsewhere. Dr. Adams can draw upon his medical knowledge to answer the question; the repetition of *very* and the understated *exceptional* give the impression of a considered, dispassionate reply. Nick's second question, however, directly presents the mystery at the heart of the story: "Why did he kill himself, Daddy?" The use of *Daddy*, which Nick said earlier when frightened by the woman's screams, suggests the anxiety beneath his outwardly calm demeanor. (In the story's opening scene, when Nick was calm, he called him *Dad*.) His father does not notice Nick's anxiety, and he cannot, in any case, satisfactorily answer the question. His profession has equipped him for medical queries, not psychological ones. He answers honestly—he does not know. But he also senses that this is not enough to satisfy his son, so he follows with a strategically vague explanation ("He couldn't stand things, I guess."). This reply is evasive yet suggestively self-revelatory. He consciously means to say that the Indian was emotionally unable to go on living, but he employs an idiom with the word *stand,* reminding the reader of the Indian's injured foot, which prevented him from joining the other Indian men outside the shanty and forced him to be a silent witness to his wife's ordeal. The Indian father's injury led to his humiliation and helplessness, and unconsciously functions in Dr. Adams's speech as a self-reflexive indication of the helplessness the story's other father now feels.

When Nick asks about the suicide, the dialogue takes a notable turn. The Indian's suicide revealed that Nick's father was not omnipotent. Now, he must confess that neither is he omniscient. The words "I don't know," coming from so proud a man, who has just performed so expertly under extreme conditions, resonate with the doctor's deep sense of confusion, guilt, and deflation. From this point on, Nick focuses on death and suicide, asking questions that cannot be answered or that his father does not wish to address. Dr. Adams's inability to answer these questions and the shock he feels over what has happened force him back into the self-absorption he displayed in the shanty. But although his answers are brief and perfunctory, they have an oddly calming effect on Nick, relieving his anxiety. The characters miscommunicate but, ironically, this failure produces a successful result.

With a child's curiosity and unerring ability to ask precisely the questions that an adult wishes to avoid, Nick pursues his interrogation. When he catches his father in an inattentive reply ("Hardly ever."), he immediately issues a follow-up question ("Don't they ever?") that reveals his dissatisfaction. Other times, he jumps from one question to another, catching his distracted father off guard. His father's preoccupation can be glimpsed in the laconic, vague nature of his replies. He answers Nick's questions, but just barely, making no effort to address the obvious anxieties lying beneath them. The sixth reply is particularly revealing. Nick says "Daddy?" just to get his attention, and Dr. Adams replies "Yes." The absence of a question mark indicates that his father's inflection is declarative rather than interrogative; he acknowledges Nick's speech but remains lost in his own thoughts. When Nick then asks about Uncle George, a subject his father is especially not interested in, the reply is again unspecific ("He'll turn up all right."). The phrase "all right" resonates with the two times the expression was previously used: Nick's response to his father's postoperative inquiry about how Nick liked being an intern and a sarcastic remark George made after the operation about Dr. Adams being a "great man, all right" (*SS* 93, 94). Nick's "all right" was intended to satisfy his father but revealed his lack of enthusiasm. George's use both intended and revealed his resentment of his brother. Here, Dr. Adams wishes to satisfy his son, but he unconsciously reveals his own lack of enthusiasm for answering any more questions and his resentment toward George, whose earlier sarcasm anticipated the doctor's present feelings of inadequacy.

Nick is too young to comprehend death and can only feel it as absence. His first glimpse of death was the Indian father's withdrawal from life. Therefore, the anxieties he expresses in this passage concern absent fathers. The four questions he asks ending with "Daddy?" (2, 3, 6, and 8) make manifest the subject of these anxieties (including his sixth question, which is intended to bring his mentally absent father back into the conversation). In his second question, he asks why the Indian baby's father killed himself and receives an uncomforting but honest reply. What he really wants to know, however, is whether he is safe from suffering the same fate as the Indian baby; that is, will his father kill himself too? He continues his inquiry circuitously. His next two questions, about the frequency of male and female suicide, are unconsciously self-referential—he wants to know about his own father and mother—and the responses are comforting. But the real point of the last three questions is revealed only in their juxtaposition. The sixth question is about Nick's sense of his own father's mental absence; the seventh question is about Uncle George's physical absence, foreshadowed by his brief disappearance during the first boat trip across the lake and here serving as a displacement of Nick's anxiety over his own father's mortality; and the eighth question ("Is dying hard, Daddy?"), read in the above context, is about the *probability* of Nick's father's death. Ironically, his father solipsistically assumes the question to be, in light of his own concerns, about whether the act of dying is difficult to face, and his answer is unintentionally chilling: "it's pretty easy." Even more ironically, however, the words that confirm Nick's anxieties about his father's mortality do not matter, for, as the doctor says, it all "depends."

The story concludes with an objective correlative that further illuminates this dialogue. What mortality "depends" on is revealed in the final two paragraphs:

> [1] They were seated in the boat, Nick in the stern, his father rowing. [2] The sun was coming up over the hills. [3] A bass jumped, making a circle in the water. [4] Nick trailed his hand in the water. [5] It felt warm in the sharp chill of the morning.
>
> [1a] In the early morning on the lake sitting in the stern of the boat with his father rowing, [1b] he felt quite sure that he would never die. (*SS* 95)

During the opening boat trip, Nick sat in the stern with his father's arm around him while an Indian rowed. Here Nick again sits in the stern, but his father is rowing and in control. His father's physical presence is strong enough for Hemingway to omit it and know that the reader will feel it: the sight of him pulling the oars, the sound (and perhaps smoke) of his breath as he rows, the steady surges of the boat along the water (as in the description of the first boat trip). That pervasive presence counteracts Nick's experiential sense of absence and his father's words about dying being easy; consequently, Nick no longer countenances the idea that his father could ever cease to be. In this way, his father's tangible physical actions are far more comforting than his vague words. These implied but omitted actions enable Nick to dismiss considerations of death and suicide, and resume his state of youthful innocence.

The other sensory impressions of the paragraph, abundantly suggestive and not omitted, are also comforting, unlike those of the initial trip. The scene is vibrant with life. The sun is just coming up, signaling the start of a new day and marking the end of the previous night's horrors. Nature is animated and, in a positive metaphor of birth, a bass emerges from the water; life appears from nowhere. The word *hand,* by now, has developed a good deal of symbolic significance. Earlier, his father's hands had been carefully scrubbed, but during the operation they were covered in blood and later his hand came away from the upper bunk "wet" with the Indian father's blood. The lake water cleans Nick's hand and also links him to the impressions of life going on around him. The water feels warm in the sharp morning chill, suggesting that this scene feels warm in the sharp chill of what has gone before. In the midst of all this palpable being, it is impossible for Nick to imagine nonbeing.

The form of the paragraph underscores its meaning, with five short sentences that slow down the reader's pace as he or she takes in the living sensations that impress themselves upon Nick. The paragraph scans as iambic and anapestic, mimicking the motion of the boat as it crosses the lake. The only double stresses, either spondees or else iambs followed by trochees or dactyls, are: "boat, Nick"; "up over"; "bass jumped"; "Nick trailed"; "felt warm"; and "sharp chill." The first double stress is mitigated by the comma; the second underscores the appearance of the sun and new day; the third contributes to the surprise of the fish's sudden appearance and links it to the emergence of the sun; the fourth prosodically links Nick to the thematics established by the "new" sun and the "newly emerged" fish; and the final two double stresses juxtapose the contrasting sensations of warmth and cold, heightening the effect of the former in a wonderfully tactile image of life.

In the first part of the final paragraph, Hemingway employs what I've termed *recapitulation with variation* as he gathers up the scattered impressions from the preceding paragraph and restates them in a continuous manner to convey their literal simultaneity and their processing, in retrospect, in Nick's and the reader's consciousness. As the images from the previous impressionistically presented paragraph are processed or integrated within the mind, they are repeated as variations (e.g., "the sun coming up" above the "water" becomes "the early morning on the lake"). The phrase "his father rowing" is repeated exactly, emphasizing Nick's focus on his father's hands, which are the engines of the action sequences throughout the story, and further linking the final two paragraphs.

Five years after composing "Indian Camp," Hemingway wrote fellow writer Owen Wister: "I know . . . how damned much I try always to do the thing by three cushion shots rather than by words or direct statement. But maybe we must have the direct statement too" (*SL* 301). So far, these two paragraphs have been three-cushion shots, impressionistically conveying Nick's state of mind. But they also prepare us for the direct statement comprising the second part of the final sentence. This statement functions not as an explanation but as an articulation and further confirmation of what has already been implied. It expresses Nick's feeling that the Indian camp is not his world. His is the world depicted in this scene in which his father is in control and Nick is free from responsibility, where the sun comes up and fish jump and the water feels warm in the morning chill. This bountiful natural world denies the reality of the dark and bloody Indian camp with its silent Indians, dying fathers, and screaming mothers. Immersed in this world, it is altogether believable that Nick would have "félt quíte súre" (the three consecutively stressed syllables emphasizing the certainty of his feeling) "thăt hé woŭld néver diĕ" (the iambic float-off ending).

The sentence is more than an affirmation, however. The first part, an objective correlative of Nick's sense of immortality, placed in juxtaposition with the earlier speech in which Uncle George's absence served as a signifier of death ("Where did Uncle George go?"), does indeed triumph over it, yet ambiguities and ironies compound. If the antecedent to the final "he" is Nick's father, a possibility that Hemingway purposely leaves open, then all the miscommunication between the two and his father's disquieting responses have inadvertently comforted Nick. On the other hand, if the antecedent is Nick, the much more likely possibility, then another irony is created by the disjunction between Nick's sense of his own immortality and the reader's knowledge that it is otherwise (Susan Beegel's fourth category of omission, discussed at the end of our second chapter). Moreover, it is the final turn of the screw of the previous dialogue's indirection, for it means that what Nick was really asking about all along concerned his anxieties about *his own* finitude, not his father's. Therefore, the entire conversation was really about Nick's first encounter with what I term *ontological shock,* the numbing realization of one's own mortality. Indeed, this is what Hemingway omitted from "Indian Camp" when he discarded the original opening—which addressed Nick's fear of death directly—only to treat it at the end of the final version by, characteristically, having Nick deny it. If the visible part of the iceberg is Nick's denial of his own mortality, then the seven-eighths lying beneath the surface of the dialogue is that he must have, at some point during this story, experienced, however fleetingly and inchoately, a recognition of his eventual nonbeing. Even in his "direct statement," Hemingway operated by three-cushion shots, and all of these matters are compressed into just a few "simple" sentences of enormously suggestive dialogue in which two characters thoroughly miscommunicate in such subtle ways that many critics of the passage, for the past eight decades, have assumed they were communicating clearly.

Hemingway's new dialogue would play a major role in six of his next seven stories, written in March and April of 1924. In the first of these, "Cat in the Rain," an American couple is confined by rain to their second-floor hotel room. From their window, the wife observes a cat crouched under a café table, "trying to make herself so compact that she would not be dripped on." The first dialogue ensues:

> [W1] "I'm going down and get that kitty," the American wife said.
> [H1] "I'll do it," her husband offered from the bed.
> [W2] "No, I'll get it. The poor kitty out trying to keep dry under a table."
> [DS] The husband went on reading, lying propped up with the two pillows at the foot of the bed.
> [H2] "Don't get wet," he said. (*SS* 167–68)

When critics talk about Hemingway's dialogue, they usually point to such stories as "The Killers" or "Hills Like White Elephants" in which its significance (if not its craft) is unmistakable. But this brief passage seems rather banal, merely a way of getting the story into gear. How is it different from James or from the dialogue in "Out of Season?" Why do I insist on viewing it as innovative?

The passage consists entirely of direct speech with some neutrally depicted actions. Not only is the focalization external, but the author's "supreme voice" is absent. The wife's first speech is subtly revealing. It appears intended to let the husband know why she is leaving the room, but, given his passivity throughout the story in which he never leaves the bed, it suggests much more. The rain has confined them to their room, and he has occupied himself with a book while she looks out the window with nothing to do. The resolve indicated in the words "going down" and "get that kitty" implies the wife's desire for self-assertion and/or a desire to get a reaction from her husband. The husband's reply seems responsive but is unconsciously revealing. First, by changing the specifics of her speech— "going down" and "get that kitty" to "I'll do it"—he exposes his actual indifference by making the act abstract, in effect saying "I'll do the thing you want done." The speech is thoughtless in its intention to pacify her (he has probably sensed her restlessness) rather than engage her expressed concern about the cat (or her implied concern about herself). It also ignores that she feels the need to do something herself in order to assert her agency, a need implicit in the specific wording of her original speech. Second, "offered from the bed" further undercuts the sincerity of his reply; he says the words of a caring husband but makes no move to give them substance.

That she senses his disinterest is clear in her reply. "No" appears intended to stop him from usurping her mission, but his actions seem to pose no threat of that happening; since he has not budged, her "no" is either sarcastic or else indicates her alarm at the possibility that he may, however grudgingly, arise. "I'll get it" suggests a great deal. Is it, too, a speech of self-assertion—in its insistence on her own ability to act and in the way she replaces his vague verb *do* with her original specific verb *get*— or is she self-conscious about disturbing his reading and seeming a burden, or both (her need for his attention conflicting with her desire not to irritate him and cause him to retreat even further into his self-absorption)? Whichever holds true, her intentions, which I think are unconscious, are clearly revealed in the second part of her speech. Although the "poor kitty" will, by the end of the story, come to symbolize the things, such as a baby, that she wants but cannot have, here she projects onto it her sense of her own situation. The cat and the wife are both confined by forces outside of their control (the rain for the cat, the rain and her marriage for the wife); both are frustrated by the limitations imposed upon them, and both want to assert their agency.

If her second sentence is, however unconsciously, some sort of plea for her husband's attention, he is, to put it in a Hemingwayesque manner, a disappointing audience. The juxtaposition of his reading with her plea makes us sense the poignancy of her marriage. In addition, the entire descriptive sentence [DS] is a wonderful example of Hemingway's technique of sequence displacement, which we saw in our analyses of the "drunk intertext" (at the end of our first chapter) and the suicide discovery in "Indian Camp" (in our fourth chapter). "Propped up" and "reading" is the position he was in during his first speech when he offered to "do it" (which makes that "offer" seem, if possible, even less genuine), and the beautifully subtle "went on reading" indicates that he never looked up from his book when he made that offer, a fact underscored later when he is described as putting the book down (to rest his eyes), reading it again (while she is pouring out her heart to him), looking up at her (when her back is turned and she is expressing concerns about her physical attractiveness), and finally telling her to shut up (after she tells him the things she wants out of life), going back to his book, and ceasing even to listen to her anymore. If the cat and the wife are restless in their confinements, the husband has turned his confinement into repose. His final speech ("Don't get wet") is highly revealing. He again feigns concern for his wife's welfare, he unconsciously acknowledges her identification with the cat (who is the only one trying not to "get wet"), and he demonstrates conclusively that his original offer was half-hearted (his eyes are still on his book). He even issues, again unconsciously, a subtle warning that if she is going to try asserting herself—instead of resting content to be his patient wife—then such assertion carries some risk.

As we saw in our fourth chapter, the shift in focalization from the wife to the husband just before the open ending of this story creates the text's ambiguity—we never know whether she receives the specific cat she wanted. But that aesthetically ingenious moment, upon which so much of the richness of the story depends, was set up from the start in this tiny unobtrusive passage of dialogue. Although Hemingway would write many dialogue passages more developed and complex, this sort of passage can be found throughout his stories. In just the stories he wrote in March and April 1924, examples would include the conversations between Nick and Marjorie and between Nick and Bill in "The End of Something," in which calculation and involuntary self-revelation can be found in virtually every speech, and the long conversations between Nick and Bill in "The Three-Day Blow" and between Nick and George in "Cross-Country Snow," in which Hemingway employs lengthy passages of indirection to show how characters discuss something by *not* addressing it. Even when they finally do address what's really on their minds, they do so with such phrases as "I guess so" and "I don't know" and "Sure" and "No" and, of course, just plain silence ("Nick said nothing"), in which more meaning is conveyed about what that character is thinking than could be depicted in hundreds of words of speech.

With the completion of "The Battler" in March 1925, Hemingway had written the final story for *In Our Time* and two stories that would go into *Men Without Women*. Between "An Alpine Idyll" in April 1926 and "Hills Like White Elephants" in May 1927, he wrote eleven stories for the new book. He continued to employ the innovative dialogue techniques of *In Our Time,* which he had also used extensively in *The Sun Also Rises.* Dialogue crystallized situation, expressed character, and advanced plot; verisimilitude was achieved by indirection, banality, simplicity of diction, and pervasive miscommunication; and speeches were marked by conscious calculation and involuntary self-revelation.

Repetition, already a significant part of his prose, began to enter his dialogue in four stories completed between April and September 1926. Extending repetition to dialogue mimicked the way people repeat themselves in conversations, which contributes to verisimilitude though it does not advance the plot. An example occurs in "An Alpine Idyll" when the characters refer to their skiing: "'You oughtn't to ever do anything too long.' / 'No. We were up there too long.' / 'Too damn long,' John said. 'It's no good doing a thing too long'" (SS 345). This repetition is mimetic but must be restricted to a brief exchange or else it would interfere with advancing the plot (even though the idea of "doing a thing too long" is relevant to the story's theme). An even more purely mimetic example is in "Today Is Friday," a brief story in the form of a play:

> *2d Soldier*—Why didn't he come down off the cross?
> *Ist Soldier*—He didn't want to come down off the cross. That's not his play.
> *2d Soldier*—Show me a guy that doesn't want to come down off the cross.
> *Ist Soldier*—Aw, hell, you don't know anything about it. Ask George there. Did he want to come down off the cross, George? (SS 357)

These sorts of banal repetitions also run throughout "The Killers," especially in the conversations between the two Chicago gunmen who wait in the diner to kill Ole Andreson. When George, the counterman, asks what they want to eat, the response is: "'I don't know,' one of the men said. 'What do you want to eat, Al?' / 'I don't know,' said Al. 'I don't know what

I want to eat'" (*SS* 279). Here, however, the repetitions also serve to characterize the two men as unimaginative and barely distinguishable from each other; all either can do is parrot the same phrases the other comes up with. After being introduced to Nick, Al's response is: "'Another bright boy,' Al said. 'Ain't he a bright boy, Max?' / 'The town's full of bright boys,' Max said" (*SS* 280). This is characteristic of conversations between people who spend much time together but have little to say to each other and is not significantly different from the exchanges in "Today Is Friday."

But the repetitions function more complexly when these characters come into conflict with characters whom they do not know. Informed that dinner is not served for another forty minutes, Max orders a chicken dinner and is told by George, "That's the dinner." Max replies: "Everything we want's the dinner, eh? That's the way you work it" (*SS* 280). Here, the differences between the two characters change the meaning of the repeated word. For George, "dinner" means an order has been placed from the wrong menu. To Max, "dinner" represents something he wants and is being refused; moreover, this refusal becomes a signifier of regulations he resents, making him see George's unwillingness to serve him dinner as a contest of power. George begins to repeat the list of available items—"I can give you ham and eggs, bacon and eggs, liver"—but is interrupted by Al, who says, "I'll take ham and eggs," indicating his desire not to get caught up in this trivial conflict when they have business at hand. Al's decision causes Max to repeat another item from George's list—"Give me bacon and eggs"— parroting Al's words but with the slight individuation of changing "I'll take" to "Give me" and "ham" to "bacon." Hemingway then expands on what he's already conveyed through the gunmen's dialogue: "[Max] was about the same size as Al. Their faces were different, but they were dressed like twins." He follows with another repetition in which a word's meaning changes according to the difference between the speaker's intention and the auditor's understanding: "'Got anything to drink?' Al asked. / 'Silver beer, bevo, ginger-ale,' George said. / 'I mean you got anything to *drink*?'" (*SS* 280). To George, "drink" means a beverage; to Al it means alcohol.

Most people repeat themselves endlessly when they speak, anxious that their auditors catch every detail and all intended meaning. For Max and Al, this sort of repetition is less the product of their desire to be understood or to have others see them as they wish to be seen than it is a form of insistence that they be obeyed. After George serves Max his meal, the gangster starts harassing him again:

"What are *you* looking at?" Max looked at George.

"Nothing."

"The hell you were. You were looking at me."

"Maybe the boy meant it for a joke, Max," Al said.

George laughed.

"*You* don't have to laugh," Max said to him. "*You* don't have to laugh at all, see?"

"All right," said George.

"So he thinks it's all right." Max turned to Al. "He thinks it's all right. That's a good one."

"Oh, he's a thinker," Al said. (*SS* 281)

The repetition of the command "*You* don't have to laugh" is an order, whereas the repetition of "he thinks it's all right" is a coded witticism that only Al grasps.

The closer people are, the more they speak to each other in a shorthand that makes their conversation incomprehensible to an outsider (or reader). Edith Wharton observes, "All that is understood between [people] is left out of their talk" in real life. Thus, if characters in fiction "have to tell each other many things that each already knows the other knows," then the only way "to avoid the resulting shock of improbability" would be to water down the dialogue with so many irrelevant commonplaces that the reader would grow bored (*Writing* 74). Wharton's own Jamesian solution was to resort to summary treatment or to interlace her dialogue with narrative, which enabled her to control dialogue through access to the consciousnesses of her characters. Hemingway, however, found a way out of the dilemma that allowed him to rely heavily on dialogue. By repeating phrases, words, sounds, and even cadences, he made his dialogue seem repetitive while the different contexts of these repetitions changed their meanings and enabled the dialogue to advance the story. In Bowen's terms, he created dialogue that *seems* irrelevant while, in fact, remaining perfectly relevant.

For instance, after Al comes up with the witty idea of calling George "bright boy," the two gunmen use this term to refer to George and Nick twenty-eight times over the next five pages. With each repetition, the potential danger to George and the other diner occupants becomes more alarming. They also mock their captives by repeating the boys' phrases back at them. After George asks, "What's it all about?" Max twice asks

George what he thinks it's all about, and George replies, "I don't know" and "I wouldn't say." To which, Max responds, "Hey, Al, bright boy says he wouldn't say what he thinks it's all about" (*SS* 282–83). Before they leave, in response to Al's implied question of whether they should allow their captives to live, Max says, "They're all right" (*SS* 285). Here, the context changes the meaning of George's previous use of the expression "all right" from "I'll do what you say and not laugh" to Max's "They won't tell anyone about us after we leave." In this manner, Hemingway mimics the repetitiveness of real-life speech while still using it for characterization and to keep the plot moving.

The dialogue repetitions of "The Killers" are foregrounded, but in the last of the four stories written during that six-month span in 1926, Hemingway raised his art to new heights in one of the finest, most complex passages of dialogue he would ever write. In "A Canary for One," completed in September, an American couple returning to Paris from southern France shares a train compartment with an older, xenophobic, obnoxious American lady who is bringing a caged canary to her daughter, whose romance she broke up. Although it is not revealed until the end of the story, the couple is about to separate. The passage commences with the narrator becoming aware of his "breakfast-less" state and then hearing the American lady speak the words *American* and *husband*. Because these words have relevance for him, his full attention is engaged, and he reports the entire dialogue:

"Americans make the best husbands," the American lady said to my wife. I was getting down the bags. "American men are the only men in the world to marry."

"How long ago did you leave Vevey?" asked my wife.

"Two years ago this fall. It's her, you know, that I'm taking the canary to."

"Was the man your daughter was in love with a Swiss?"

"Yes," said the American lady. "He was from a very good family in Vevey. He was going to be an engineer. They met there in Vevey. They used to go on long walks together."

"I know Vevey," said my wife. "We were there on our honeymoon."

"Were you really? That must have been lovely. I had no idea, of course, that she'd fall in love with him."

"It was a very lovely place," said my wife.

"Yes," said the American lady. "Isn't it lovely? Where did you stop there?"

"We stayed at the Trois Couronnes," said my wife.

"It's such a fine old hotel," said the American lady.

"Yes," said my wife. "We had a very fine room and in the fall the country was lovely."

"Were you there in the fall?"

"Yes," said my wife.

We were passing three cars that had been in a wreck. They were splintered open and the roofs sagged in.

"Look," I said. "There's been a wreck."

The American lady looked and saw the last car. (*SS* 340–41)

On the surface, the conversation seems superficial and repetitious—what one might expect from strangers on a train. It's also a model for using indirection in dialogue. First, the conversation appears to be about Vevey and the American lady's daughter, but it's really about the conflicted emotions experienced by the separating couple. Second, the passage observes Joseph Conrad and Ford Madox Ford's "unalterable rule" regarding the rendering of "genuine conversations": "no speech of one character should ever answer the speech that goes before it." As Ford explains, such "is almost invariably the case in real life where few people listen, because they are always preparing their own next speeches" (*Conrad* 200–201). This is what produces incremental repetition or stichomythia. But beneath the verisimilar surface there is conscious calculation and unconscious revelation, character is expressed, and plot is advanced (the passage provides the emotional climax to any rereading of the story). The repetition here is not merely verisimilar; even more than in "The Killers," by repeating words in different contexts Hemingway changes their referents. These semic qualities accrue to the repeated words, gathering force each time the word reappears.

The narrator and his wife face forward: he looks out the window toward Paris and the future, his wife looks at the American lady, and the American lady faces the rear of the train and the past. The American lady comments on the exclusive virtue of American husbands in conjunction with the narrator's apparently quotidian act of getting the bags, an act that seems to correspond to her views on the superiority of American husbands but that is given ironic relevance in juxtaposition with what must be the narrator's sense of his action as a step toward the separation of the couple's possessions. When the American lady repeats her observation about American husbands, the wife asks about Vevey, partly to change the painful course of the conversation. Yet, by choosing to divert it with talk of Vevey, she unconsciously betrays her desire to talk about the once happy past. The narcissistic American lady predictably takes the question about Vevey as a cue to talk about her daughter, and the wife goes along. Instead of conversing about the canary that the American lady has just mentioned, however, she is irresistibly drawn to asking about the nature of the broken love affair that resonates, for her, as symbolic of her own impending separation. When the American lady then tells of the Swiss with whom her daughter fell in love, she twice mentions Vevey, causing the narrator's wife, in a moment of weakness and out of a desire to turn from the symbol of her imminent unhappy future to the memory of her happy past, to utter the enormously understated "I know Vevey," revealing that it was the site of her honeymoon. From that moment on, the narrator's wife will try to hold onto Vevey and the past. At the same time, the narrator experiences her attempts, by dwelling on Vevey, to ward off the painful emotions caused by their ever-nearing separation. He, in turn, tries unconsciously to hold onto their married status by using, in his wife's remaining five speeches, the identification tag "said my wife" although these are obviously unnecessary for the purpose of identifying the speaker.

The American lady, who could not care less about the couple's honeymoon, predictably shifts the conversation back to her daughter's love affair and inadvertently reveals that she feels somewhat defensive, perhaps even guilty, about what she has done. As in a previous dialogue, she uses the phrase "of course" to justify her actions. But the narrator's wife drops even the amenity of talking about the unhappy daughter and continues her spoken reverie on Vevey. Here an extraordinary event occurs. The American lady, who throughout the story has been oblivious to all around her, *realizes* that the narrator's wife wants to talk about Vevey. For the rest of the conversation, she actually focuses on what the wife wants to talk about, asking questions about the honeymoon and responding to the wife's speeches.

Part of the emotional impact of the conversation derives from the fact that if the narrator's wife makes an impression strong enough to pierce the self-absorption and alter the discourse of the American lady, then it must be a strong impression indeed. The wife also emerges from her near anonymity in the story to become the center of the scene, a transformation heightened by the drum roll of "said my wife" tags supplied by the narrator. And when the wife's speeches are stitched together, they are emotionally compelling in and of themselves: "I know Vevey. We were there on our honeymoon. It was a very lovely place. We stayed at the Trois Couronnes. Yes. We had a very fine room and in the fall the country was lovely. Yes." It's almost as though Hemingway has taken a piece of Molly Bloom's soliloquy from *Ulysses* and broken it up into half of this dialogue.

When the American lady starts responding to the narrator's wife, she slips into the present tense: "Isn't it lovely?" But in asking about the honeymoon, she returns to the past tense: "Where did you stop there?" The wife unconsciously changes the verb to "stayed" (avoiding the primary meaning of "stopped") and gives the name of the hotel. Hemingway deliberately chooses Trois Couronnes for its literary allusiveness; it is the same hotel in which Henry James's "Daisy Miller" takes place. Both stories present American travelers who are robbed of their innocent illusions (although in "Canary" we are presented with the aftermath of the characters' initiation). Trois Couronnes means "three crowns," but both James and Hemingway, with their excellent command of French, probably knew that it also means "three fool's caps." If the narrator, so closely modeled on Hemingway himself, also knows the double meaning of Trois Couronnes, then perhaps he is aware of how the name ironically reflects on the three inhabitants of the compartment.

The conversation is manifestly repetitious, investing it with verisimilitude as the women repeat, in various contexts, each other's phrases. The American lady, who seems incapable of meaningful conversation, can only parrot what the narrator's wife says. And the wife, lost in her memories, latches onto phrases used by the American lady that she herself, in the grip of these memories, finds meaningful. As noted, however, the repetition serves a dual purpose, without which the entire passage, however mimetic, would be inert, as beneath the banal surface the repeated words and phrases expand in meaning because of the changing contexts in which they appear.

For instance, the words *fall, Vevey,* and *lovely* appear four times and the word *fine* twice. The American lady tells the narrator's wife that she and her daughter left Vevey two years ago "this *fall.*" Moments later, responding to the information that the couple had honeymooned in Vevey, she says, "That must have been *lovely*" but follows by saying that she did not know that her daughter would "*fall* in *love* with" the Swiss, changing the original meaning of "fall." The wife agrees that "it was a very *lovely* place," slightly changing the referent of "lovely" from honeymooning in Vevey to Vevey itself. A second implied meaning accrues to Vevey here: it was a place where one could "fall in love." The American lady then agrees with the wife who has just agreed with her but puts her statement in the present tense—"Isn't it *lovely*?"—changing the referent from Vevey past to Vevey present and calls the Trois Couronnes "a *fine* old hotel." The wife then utters her own recapitulation with variation, gathering the repeated words and phrases to sum up her sense of the conversation: "We had a very *fine* room and in the *fall* the country was *lovely*." In her sentence, the meaning of *fine* changes from "prestigious" (revealing the American lady's values) to "nice" or "lovely" (indicating the wife's values); *fall* once more refers to a season (although it still echoes with the previous sense of "to fall in love"); and *lovely* describes Vevey in the past tense (conflating lovely, fine, falling in love, the room, the countryside, and Vevey—but locating it all in the past). When the American lady then asks if the couple was "there in the *fall*" and the wife replies, "Yes," the conversation that began with the wife asking when the American lady left Vevey is brought full circle. Its focus has, by subtle increments, shifted from the American lady and her daughter in the present ("this fall") to the American couple in Vevey in the past. (All emphases in quotations mine.)

The narrator listens carefully, the bags at his feet. Perhaps he, too, is being lured into the past by the circular, mesmerizing conversation (which lacks discordant elements because of the repetitive phrases and the manner in which each speech seems to agree with and flow from the one that precedes it). But then he sees the wrecked train. When the American lady asks if they *were* in Vevey in the fall, his wife says yes, but now they *are* passing three wrecked cars. The narrator, in his second and final speech in the story, calls their attention to the present—"Look"—and announces, "There's been a wreck." Just as in an earlier speech when he used the term *braces* instead of *suspenders* (SS 339), his statement seems commonplace but actually reveals a half-calculated rudeness and resentment: toward the American lady, the dissolution of his marriage, and the painful reliving of the happy past. His statement works a comparable change in focus and tone as Jake's reply to Brett in the final line of *The Sun Also Rises*.

When the narrator points out the wreck—in five syllables totaling a mere twenty letters—his statement serves six functions (a remarkable example of dialogue compression) that bring together several strands of the story in a multilayered objective correlative. First, he indicates the literal wreck that has occurred. Second, the wreck is the physical realization of the fears about a train crash that the American lady has expressed throughout the story. Third, the couple's marriage, which the narrator's wife has been reliving, is a wreck. Fourth, the three people, similar to the three cars they are passing, are wrecks. (Significantly, the narcissistic American lady sees only the "last car," just as she "sees" only herself.) Fifth, the narrator, by his statement, wrecks the women's conversation. Sixth, since that conversation has been a reenactment, of sorts, of their previously happily married state, he has perhaps repeated in the present (especially since the story is based upon the real-life first marriage that Hemingway wrecked) what he had done in the past. Certainly, his speech seems to, in Bowen's words, "crystallize relationships." What he has said is pretty much the equivalent of "Shut the hell up!"

With the writing of "A Canary for One," Hemingway's innovations in constructive dialogue were complete. But the question of how far he could push his new art—to what extent dialogue could carry a whole story—remained. The answer came in May 1927 with "Hills Like White Elephants," a story almost entirely in dialogue. A couple sits outside a bar at a station in Spain waiting for the train to Madrid—and they talk. As opposed to the American lady and the narrator's wife in "A Canary for One," these characters know each other well and thus speak in the sort of shorthand that Wharton observed would make a conversation unintelligible to an outsider. Therefore, the premise of the story forced Hemingway to construct relevance for the reader from what should seem nonsense. He made his task even more difficult by omitting the actual subject of their conversation (she is pregnant and he wants her to have an abortion); as countless critics have noted, abortion, pregnancy, and babies are never once mentioned. As if to increase the challenge, he employed external focalization, eschewing access to any character's consciousness; the nondialogue is completely neutral and, with the exception of two objective correlatives, contributes nothing toward the reader's making sense of the dialogue.

Following a brief description of the setting, we get their first exchange:

> "What should we drink?" the girl asked. She had taken off her hat and put it on the table.

"It's pretty hot," the man said.

"Let's drink beer." (SS 273)

The woman's first speech gives us a glimpse of a character who lacks a sense of autonomy and looks to her partner to make the decisions. His reply is even more revealing. Although she is perfectly willing to let him make the decisions, whether about drinks or abortions, he needs to believe that she is taking part in the decision-making process even as he prevents her from doing so. Here, he gets her to request the beers he obviously wants merely by making a statement about the weather. Such successful manipulation conveys the dynamics of their relationship in the present and, we may assume, in the past. This first exchange, so easy to overlook, tells us what we need to know about these people; it crystallizes their relationship, expresses their characters, and encapsulates the ensuing plot. It also amply demonstrates Bowen's other main points about dialogue—it is what characters *do to each other,* and it contains calculation and involuntary self-revelation—all beneath a seemingly banal, spontaneous, and artless surface.

The remainder of the story leading up to their climactic exchange plays out the couple's problems as they discuss, in a veiled and shorthand manner, her pregnancy and their relationship. Much of the conversation is so obscure that it can be comprehended only in light of the entire story. For instance, early on when it's clear that they are having a conflict but not what that conflict is about, she says her *Anis del Toro* "tastes like licorice," and he seems to respond innocuously, "That's the way with everything." She agrees, but adds, "Everything tastes of licorice. Especially all the things you've waited so long for, like absinthe." He is caught short by her statement and can only weakly reply, "Oh, cut it out" (SS 274). To anyone but them, the conversation is about alcohol that tastes like licorice, whereas it's really about her desire to have a baby.

Or is it? Later on, she seems amenable to having the "simple operation," as he terms it, if that will make everything all right between them, by which she means if he will respond to her when she makes such statements as the hills "look like white elephants." Such a response, however, is beyond him—it requires a capacity to see the world through her eyes and not just his own—so he tries to distract her by saying that if she has the operation they will be "fine afterward." At the same time, he undercuts his promises even as he protests his love for her:

"And if I do it you'll be happy and things will be like they were and you'll love me?"

"*I love you now.* You know I love you."

"I know. But if I do it, then it will be nice again if I say things are like white elephants, and you'll like it?"

"I'll love it. *I love it now* but I just can't think about it. You know how I get when I worry." (SS 275; emphasis mine)

Although he ostensibly says what she wants to hear, the way he says it reveals more than what he says. Not only does he avoid answering her questions, the juxtaposition of "I love you" and "I love it" speaks volumes about his true feelings.

Throughout the story, he cloaks his desires in a "logic" that assaults her language of metaphorically expressed desire. Since he cannot understand her language, she resorts to mimicking his words and phrases ("things will be like they were"), or responding with passive-aggressive self-abnegation ("Then I'll do it. Because I don't care about me"), or merely negating his statements ("We can have everything." / "No, we can't." / "We can have the whole world." / "No, we can't." / "We can go everywhere." / "No, we can't. It isn't ours any more." / "It's ours." / "No, it isn't") (SS 275–76). Finally, she requests silence to avoid further verbal battering—"Can't we maybe stop talking?" (SS 276). But he won't shut up.

If she wants respect and understanding even more than she wants the baby, it is equally clear that what he wants is not just for her to have the abortion but to acknowledge that she *wants* to have it, that is, to feign volition, thus absolving him from responsibility for the actions he demands. His motive is revealed in an utterance made halfway through the story which he repeats, in various forms, six more times—"'Well,' the man said, 'if you don't want to you don't have to. I wouldn't have you do it if you didn't want to'" (SS 275). Her responses to these attempts at verbal manipulation range from asking him if *he* wants her to have the operation (making him assume responsibility), to asking whether he'll love her if she does (forcing a concession for agreeing to the abortion), to saying that she'll do it because she doesn't "care about" herself (a passive-aggressive counterattack), to requesting that they stop talking about it (avoidance). The only action she will not perform is to allow him to coerce her into pretending that the abortion is her own decision.

The following passage, which begins with the penultimate variation of his trademark utterance (here introduced with particular insistence), takes place after her weary plea that they "maybe stop talking" and is the emotional climax of the story:

[P1] "You've got to realize," he said, "that I don't want you to do it [#1] if you don't want to. I'm perfectly willing to go through with it [#2] if it [#3] means anything to you."

[P2] "Doesn't it [#4] mean anything to you? We could get along."

[P3] "Of course it [#5] does. But I don't want anybody but you. I don't want any one else. And I know it's [#6] perfectly simple."

[P4] "Yes, you know it's [#7] perfectly simple."

[P5] "It's [#8] all right for you to say that, but I do know it [#9]."

[P6] "Would you do something for me now?"

[P7] "I'd do anything for you."

[P8] "Would you please please please please please please stop talking?"

[P9] He did not say anything but looked at the bags against the wall of the station. There were labels on them from all the hotels where they had spent nights.

[P10] "But I don't want you to," he said, "I don't care anything about it [#10]."

[P11] "I'll scream," the girl said. (SS 277)

The techniques employed in the above passage, so representative of Hemingway's art of dialogue, should, by now, be manifest. The gender-based miscommunication in which the man's assertive declarative statements are parried by the woman's mimicking of him (paragraphs 2 and 4), by her questions (2, 6, 8), and by her urgent request that he stop talking at her (8) that terminates in frustration (11) are typical of their entire conversation. Equally typical is how he makes a general statement, the content of which is intended to pacify her ("I'd do anything for you."), that is revealed as a lie when she subsequently asks for "something" specific (8) and he puts her off (10). Moreover, he again reveals his hypocrisy through juxtaposition when he initially employs *perfectly* to modify his willingness to have the baby (1) and in his next speech uses it to modify the supposed simplicity of having an abortion (3). That juxtaposition does not go unnoticed, as her mimicry indicates (4).

The most remarkable aspect of the passage, however, is Hemingway's full-blown employment of repetition. The repetition of key words such as *want* and *perfectly* and polysyllabic words that have syllables in common (*anything, anybody, any one, something*) creates a powerful verisimilitude, but the changing contexts of these words keep advancing the plot. More extraordinary are the various uses of the referentially ambiguous pronoun *it* in achieving these dual purposes of dialogue. *It* (an example of Carlos Baker's "hovering subject") is used ten times but the antecedent/referent continually changes. The first *it* refers to having the abortion, the second to having the baby, and the third through fifth either to having the baby or to the baby itself. The sixth *it* again refers to having the abortion; the seventh *it* refers to having the abortion or, perhaps, to her sense of their entire situation; the eighth *it* is an expletive with no antecedent; and the ninth *it* refers to the "knowledge" that having an abortion is simple. These uses of *it* not only mirror the shorthand manner by which people refer to matters they both understand (or think they understand), "it" also creates the ironic ambiguity that makes for relevance. By subsuming such incompatible antecedents within one pronoun, Hemingway demonstrates how, in dialogue, communication can become impossible.

After the woman's emotional request for the man to stop talking (paragraph 8), Hemingway allows himself two brief sentences of nondialogue that aptly sum up the man's real attitude toward his mate. But he does not access the man's consciousness through a direct statement; instead, he employs an objective correlative with the man providing the camera angle. Looking at the bags with the hotel labels, which function as a symbol of his desire to make the woman into a purely sexual object, leaving him unencumbered by the responsibilities of love and family (and mutual respect), the man tries one last time his verbally violent sentence (in a truncated form) in order to coerce her into "choosing" the abortion of her own "free will" (paragraph 10). In the sentence he uses the word *care,* which he had previously used in insisting that he "cared" about her. Here, he says that he doesn't care about "it," which in its tenth and final incarnation conflates the abortion, the baby, the entire conversation, and (in juxtaposition with her as a mere sexual object in the objective correlative of paragraph 9) the unsubjugated, nonsexual part of the woman's self. Her reply, and ours? "I'll scream." Then, we have one final irony—"'I'd better take the bags over to the other side of the station,' the man said" (*SS* 277). Yes, by now, a very good place for that particular objective correlative! There is also one final moment of possible triumph as she smiles at him in the knowledge that she has not relinquished her last small shred of autonomy. With her con-cluding speech—"'I feel fine,' she said. 'There's nothing wrong with me. I feel fine'" (SS 278)—Hemingway leaves his talking couple to an ambiguous fate, all the more uncertain because we do not know, in this seeded closed ending, whether to attribute any significance to his taking the bags to the "other side" of the station. Thus Hemingway brings his dialogue experi-ment to a close.[3]

9

Plot, Characterization, and Setting

In the 3rd volume [of the *USA* trilogy] don't let yourself slip and get any perfect characters in—no Stephen Daedeluses—remember it was Bloom and Mrs. Bloom saved Joyce . . . If you get a noble communist remember the bastard probably masturbates and is jallous as a cat. Keep them people, people, people, and don't let them get to be symbols.

—Hemingway to John Dos Passos (1932),
Ernest Hemingway: Selected Letters

Remember Charlie in the first war all I did mostly was hear guys talk; especially in hospital and convalescing. Their experiences get to be more vivid than your own. You invent from your own and from all of theirs . . .

Then some son of a bitch will come along and prove you were not at that particular fight. Fine. Dr. Tolstoi was at Sevastopol. But not at Borodino. He wasn't in business in those days. But he could invent from knowledge we were all at some damned Sevastopol.

—Hemingway to Charles Poore (1953),
Ernest Hemingway: Selected Letters

Hemingway's habit of eliding words in his correspondence sometimes leaves his meaning open to multiple interpretations. A case in point is the above excerpt from a letter to Charles Poore, a longtime admirer of Hemingway in the pages of the *New York Times* Sunday *Book Review* and who was then editing *The Hemingway Reader* for Scribner's. Is Hemingway saying that because Tolstoy, who served at the battle of Sevastopol (1855) during the Crimean War, could invent from his own firsthand experience, therefore readers could now experience that battle through his fiction? The full wording of the last sentence would then be: "But [because] he could invent from [the] knowledge [of personal experience] we [readers] were all at some damned Sevastopol." Or is he implying that because Tolstoy could invent from knowledge, however acquired, including his own war experiences, he was thus able to depict the battle of Borodino (1812) in the Napoleonic wars, at which he was not present?[1] Or, to suggest a third possibility, is he saying that Tolstoy could invent the battle of Borodino by drawing on his readers' experience of war, conflict, and tragedy—"But he could invent from knowledge [because] we were all at some damned Sevastopol"? Hemingway believed each of these propositions: that writers invent from their own experiences; that they invent by drawing upon similar experiences they've had or have heard about; and that readers fill out the fiction they read from their own experiences, which is something that writers, especially impressionists, depend upon. The reader's role in making fiction come to life is what this final chapter addresses. Again we explore the critical role of suggestiveness, this time in story characterization. Before we do, however, I must dispense with what might seem an important element of short stories but really isn't—plot.

In 1949 Eudora Welty explained why this book has little to say about plot, situation, or incident (three roughly synonymous terms):

> Clearly, the fact that stories have plots in common is of no more account than that many people have blue eyes. Plots are, indeed, what the story writer sees with, and so do we as we read. The plot is the Why. Why? is asked and replied to at various depths; the fishes in the sea are bigger the deeper we go. To learn that character is a more awe-inspiring fish and (in a short story, though not, I think, in a novel) one some degrees deeper down than situation, we have only to read Chekhov. What constitutes the reality of his characters is what they reveal to us. And the possibility that they may indeed reveal everything is what makes fictional characters differ so greatly from us in real life; yet isn't it strange that they don't really *seem* to differ? This is one clue to the extraordinary magnitude of character in fiction. Characters in the plot connect us with the vastness of our secret life, which is endlessly explorable. This is their role. (90)

I sometimes think, although obviously hyperbolically, that there are about half a dozen narrative plots. Take, for instance, the revenge plot, which is the plot of *Hamlet, Moby-Dick* and "The Cask of Amontillado"— as well as that of the movie *Death Wish* and its four dreadful sequels. Then there's the love triangle plot, which we see in *Le Morte Darthur, The Scarlet Letter,* and Katherine Mansfield's "Bliss"—and also in the latest pulp novel or television soap opera. One version of the love triangle is the old Hollywood staple of "boy meets girl, boy loses girl, boy gets girl back," to which Fitzgerald gave his own special twist in *The Great Gatsby* by adding "boy gets killed." Philip Fisher has credited "the decisive contribution of Natu-

ralism to the small stock of curves for human action: the plot of decline"
(171). That is the plot of much of Zola, Stephen Crane's *Maggie,* Frank Norris's *McTeague,* and Hurstwood's story in Theodore Dreiser's *Sister Carrie,*
and it too is a film favorite. Indeed, many people do have blue eyes.

Whenever we read a narrative—novel, story, comic book—we are soon
aware of what plot we're in—e.g., coming of age, initiation in war, solv-
ing a crime, quest, etc.—and, although this guides how we read, what we
search for is something deeper. What will this author do with this plot?
Which means, what will these particular characters do within it? Ultimately, whether a story writer emphasizes plot, as do Jack London or Isaac
Babel, or deemphasizes it nearly to the vanishing point, in the manner of
Chekhov or Mansfield, everything that is plot is inevitably about character.
On this topic, as on so many others, Henry James has had the last word:
"What is character but the determination of incident? What is incident but
the illustration of character? What is either a picture or a novel that is *not*
of character? What else do we seek in it and find in it? It is an incident for a
woman to stand up with her hand resting on a table and look out at you in
a certain way; or if it be not an incident I think it will be hard to say what
it is. At the same time it is an expression of character . . . It sounds almost
puerile to say that some incidents are intrinsically much more important
than others" ("Art" 55). So much, then, for plot.

But what about characters? They have the capability of revealing, and
often do, elements of themselves that no real-life person would ever reveal.
Through them, we may see aspects of ourselves, what Welty calls "our secret life," which we hide even from self-scrutiny. Edith Wharton says of
Lily Bart, "Her personal fastidiousness had a moral equivalent, and when
she made a tour of inspection in her own mind there were certain closed
doors she did not open" (*House* 125). In real life, those doors would remain
shut, but by the end of *The House of Mirth* the reader has had a good look
into those hidden chambers of Lily's mind, as has Lily, for she—like all fictional characters and, indeed, like all readers—is "endlessly explorable."
Enduring fiction—whatever its value to cultural studies—is always about
character, about the human condition, which hasn't changed much over
millennia. We *were* all at some damned Sevastopol.

Although character is the heart of the matter in fiction, nevertheless,
the lack of space limits the extent of characterization in the short story.
Simply put, the less time we spend with characters—the less we hear them
speak, the less we hear them spoken of, the fewer situations we see them act

in—the less, it would seem, we can know of them. Furthermore, the story writer must resist the temptation to help with summary explanation, since a story leaves little room in which to overcome the consequences of an intrusive psychologizing narrator. On this point, even Chekhov and Maupassant agreed. "In the sphere of psychology," the Russian master told his brother, "details are also the thing." The writer must avoid, above all, explaining a character's "state of mind" (*LSS* 71). Explanations of moonlit nights hurt a story; direct statements about characters' motives, thoughts, and feelings destroy it. These kinds of explanations remind readers of the omnipresent, omniscient, omni-obnoxious author; they are boring; they prevent readers from playing their role in bringing a character to life; they reduce interesting characters to neat psychiatric profiles (often, in similarly psychiatric language); and they puncture the fictional dream. As Maupassant put it, the writer must "carefully avoid all complicated explanations, all disquisitions on motive, and confine [himself] to letting persons and events pass before our eyes." All "psychology should be concealed in [fiction], as it is in reality, under the facts of existence" (672).

The short story, Wharton observes, is a "direct descendent of the old epic or ballad" in which "action was the chief affair." In those earlier forms, characters usually remained "puppets" and rarely graduated past "types." The latter, Wharton notes, "may be set forth in a few strokes, but the progression, the unfolding of personality, of which the reader instinctively feels the need if the actors in the tale are to retain their individuality for him through a succession of changing circumstances—this slow but continuous growth requires space, and therefore belongs by definition to a larger, a symphonic plan" (*Writing* 47–48). A full exploration of character is simply beyond the means of a short story. As Henry James concludes, there are "particular effects that insist on space, and the thing, above all, that the short story has to renounce is the actual *pursuit* of a character." James emphasizes the word *pursuit* for good reason. He says that "temperaments and mixtures, the development of a nature, are shown us" in a story every bit as much as they "are shown us in life"—through "illustration." Even in a limited episode, characters bring their complete being to that situation. Therefore, what makes character different in the short story is not its depth or fullness, but the extent to which that depth and fullness can be developed in action throughout the plot (James's "actual *pursuit* of a character"). For James, whose artistic raison d'être was the full fictional rendering of character, the story was inhospitable because "when the tale is short the figure, before we have had time to catch up with it, gets beyond and away, dips below the horizon made by the little square of space that we have accepted" ("Story-Teller" 286). Even such a supreme story writer as Welty was forced to admit "that characters in a short story have not the size and importance and capacity for development they have in a novel, but are subservient altogether to the story as a whole" (112).

What, then, can we make of story characters, Welty's "awe-inspiring fish" whose function is no less than to "connect us with the vastness of our secret life" (90)? How can story writers create characters, as John Gardner insists they must, who "stand before us" with "such continuous clarity that nothing they do strikes us as improbable behavior," characters about whom we "must understand . . . more than we *know*" so that we may feel "confident of the character's behavior when the character acts freely" (45)? How can story writers avoid populating their tales entirely with what E. M. Forster calls "flat characters," who are "constructed round a single idea or quality" and never "capable of surprising in a convincing way" (67, 78)? How can a writer portray fully rounded characters without the space necessary to develop them, knowing that without such characters there is no story, only, at best, an anecdote or an allegory? How, in short, can a story writer avoid the view that characterization in a short story is simply impossible, begrudgingly acquiescing to Jorge Luis Borges' minority assessment that what "is most important in a short story is the plot or situation" and not the characters (46)?

Sean O'Faolain offers one answer. For him, story characterization is an illusion, made possible by the genre's conventions, which comprise an implicit contract between writers and readers, without which the modern short story could not exist. Stories and their characters are "an immense confidence-trick, an immense illusion, as immense a technical achievement as the performance of an adept magician. But there is no deception, or rather, the illusion here depends on our always knowing how it is done" (169). For O'Faolain, characterization is yet another element of the short story made possible by suggestiveness, the main method by which the genre makes "a very tiny part do for the whole" (163).

Characterisation is something that can be no more than assumed in a short-story. If one looks for a detailed characterisation one finds only puppets; one does not therefore look for it—another tacit agreement between author and reader. Instead we are given further hieroglyphics. We may, for example, be given situation, which always exposes some temperament or character; or conversation, which, if bright enough, reveals it; or gestures which express it, by which I do not mean that people make gestures—they are gestures, that and no more. (164–65)

Although acknowledging that James's story characters give us "a sufficient illusion of depth and roundness," O'Faolain nevertheless concludes that they remain "just as flat and as puppet-like as any of Dickens' flattest characters" (168).

Here, however, O'Faolain goes too far. To paraphrase Jessica Rabbit, characters are not really gestures, they're just drawn that way. That is, a story's characters are every bit as round as those in a novel—they certainly *must* be in the mind of the writer—but they are *represented* by gestures. The writer, who pictures fully rounded characters in his or her mind while writing, gives the ever-alert story reader "hieroglyphics" (a reaction to a situation, a conversation, a facial expression, an article of clothing, a gesture), and from these hieroglyphics readers must infer, or conjure up, the full character. There is a world of difference between a flat character and a round character evoked through a minimum of carefully chosen detail. To see that difference, one need only compare any story by O. Henry with any by Chekhov. The nature of story characterization is also nicely explained by Hemingway's theory of omission (and Kipling's and Cather's and Mansfield's)—the character is the figurative iceberg, one-eighth above water, and we feel something more than we understand about that character if he or she is effectively represented. To return to Welty, characters in a story are "awe-inspiring" because they depend more upon the reader's inner life to come alive than do the novel's fully delineated characters.

Often, as Rust Hills observes, the story writer presents hieroglyphics suggesting a "type," then gives other clues that individualize from that type, thus circumventing the impossibility of "characterization from the ground up" (58). For example, in Hemingway's "A Pursuit Race," Mr. Turner, the manager of a traveling burlesque show, discovers William Campbell, his advance man, strung out in a Kansas City hotel room (Turner assumes from drink but, it turns out, from drugs). We read of Turner, "He was a middle-aged man with a large stomach and a bald head and he had many things to do" (SS 351). These hieroglyphics conjure up a certain unflattering type. But Hemingway immediately begins to individualize Turner, who really does have lots to do and tries desperately to offer help, despite Campbell's incoherence, loutishness, and repeated insults. When Turner returns to the room later, an act that also reveals character, Campbell is asleep, and the story ends, "as Mr. Turner was a man who knew what things in life were very valuable he did not wake him" (SS 355). These hieroglyphics—or rather the inferences drawn from them by a good reader—suggest a complex character. That final sentence refers both to Turner's realization that the addicted Campbell needs to sleep *and* to the fact that he, Turner, must get back to work. These are the two conflicting obligations—to a person in need and to his job—that confront him in the story. We do not get much about Turner, but we feel the presence of an interesting character—ordinary, harried, physically unappealing, stuck in a rotten job, with a "horror of drugs" while "living in daily association with people who used drugs" (SS 353), trying to deal with his show having caught up to its putative "advance man"—and yet, against this, genuinely caring, thoroughly decent, and realistic. He wonderfully illustrates how suggestiveness works to create character in a Hemingway story.

Let us examine the Italian major of "In Another Country." We first encounter him in a hospital receiving treatment for his wounded hand, seated beside the young narrator who has been wounded in the leg. After the doctor tells the narrator his standard lie about the effectiveness of the machines—"You will play football again like a champion"—the major winks at the boy and asks, "And will I too play football, captain-doctor?" This is the lead-in to the old vaudeville joke in which the patient asks, "Will I be able to play the piano after surgery?" When the doctor replies in the affirmative, the patient says, "That's funny, I couldn't play it before." The doctor refuses to let this routine play out and presents a photograph of a hand that the narrator describes as "withered almost as small as the major's, before it had taken a machine course, and after it was a little larger." The major comments, "very interesting," but when the doctor asks if he has confidence, he replies "no." The narrator also reports that before the war the major had been "the greatest fencer in Italy" (SS 268).

So far, in only a few lines of text, we have the "type" of an Italian officer in World War I. That he was a great fencer—information that, given his modesty in the text, probably did not come from him—and is an officer suggests he is a member of the upper class and, perhaps, a professional military man. From these hieroglyphics we might ascribe to him a particular set of manners, a certain bearing, a degree of dignity and gravitas. Yet we also see that he is playful and possessed of an ironic sense of humor. He is kindly and sympathetic; he makes his joke for the narrator's benefit, establishing a bond with the frightened foreign youth. He makes a joke, but he is not one—his final reply to the doctor is curt, realistic, and serious.

After this scene come two summary pages in which the narrator reflects on bravery, his nighttime fears of death, and how he will be when he returns to the front. In contrast to the young convalescent Italian soldiers who accompany him around Milan, the narrator has received his medals not for a specific brave act but because he is an American wounded while fighting for Italy, and he is consequently beset by self-doubts. Perhaps the major senses this, for the narrator reports, "The major, who had been the great fencer, did not believe in bravery, and spent much time while we sat in the machines correcting my grammar." He compliments the boy on his Italian, but when his pupil boasts that it's an easy language to learn, he sarcastically replies, "Why, then, do you not take up the use of grammar?" He proceeds to instruct him in that grammar, and the narrator confesses that he "was afraid to talk to him until I had the grammar straight in my mind" (SS 270). These hieroglyphics suggest other aspects of the major's character and the narrator's relationship with him. Individualizing from the type "upper-class Italian military officer," these clues show the major taking the boy under his wing in the manner of a father or older brother. The narrator's admiration for the older man is seen in his unnecessary repetition about the major's fencing prowess, the sort of athleticism that an American teenager who plays football would be inclined to esteem. The major may actually not believe in bravery, but perhaps he senses the boy's fears and is assuaging them by this general statement, a statement that is also, in his own case, possibly an example of modesty. He has nothing to gain from his friendship with the narrator, so we must assume that he helps him out of kindness. A good mentor, he compliments his charge for his achievements but also chastises him when the boy gets cocky—the sarcasm about speaking grammatically is intended to instruct, not to humiliate, and it succeeds to the boy's benefit. The major's insistence on proper grammar further reveals character—this officer, fencer, and grammar teacher is a stickler, as is his author, for doing things the correct way.

Hemingway's characterization of the major is carefully woven into the story's fabric to set up the climax. After observing that the major comes to therapy every day, even though "he did not believe in the machines" (behavior that accords with the major's sense of duty and propriety), the narrator reports a sudden change of conduct. The major calls the machines "nonsense" and "idiotic"; he terms the narrator "a stupid impossible disgrace" for not having learned his grammar and himself "a fool to have bothered with" him. He initiates an argument with the boy for wanting to be married, and he snaps at the attendant and leaves the room (SS 271). These actions, seemingly out of character, are explained when he returns to apologize: "'I am so sorry,' he said, and patted me on the shoulder with his good hand. 'I would not be rude. My wife has just died. You must forgive me'" (SS 272). For the major, his breach of etiquette is inexcusable even under tragic circumstances. He struggles to regain his composure but cannot: "He looked straight past me and out through the window. Then he began to cry. 'I am utterly unable to resign myself,' he said and choked. And then crying, his head up looking at nothing, carrying himself straight and soldierly, with tears on both his cheeks and biting his lips, he walked past the machines and out the door" (SS 272). Three days later, he resumes therapy. The narrator observes, "The photographs did not make much difference to the major because he only looked out of the window" (SS 272).

In truth, we know little about the major, who occupies but a few pages in the story. He is physically small, a wounded officer, and once was a great fencer. He insists on proper grammar and proper behavior, and has an ironic sense of humor. He is kind to the narrator. His young wife has died unexpectedly from pneumonia. He is capable of emotion under dire circumstances, but tries not to be rude. These are not many "facts" to go by, and not once does the narrator offer summary commentary about the major's character. Yet, somehow we know this man who carries himself straight and soldierly with tears on his cheeks and biting his lips. We know him because Hemingway has presented the right clues for us to fill him in from our own experiences. It would take a callow reader not to know and care about this character.

Because story characterization relies so heavily on suggestiveness, even a minor character can be nicely depicted with the right hieroglyphic. At the conclusion of "The End of Something," after Marjorie leaves, Bill enters the story and asks, "Did she go all right?"—revealing to the reader that Nick's break-up with Marjorie was premeditated. He makes a couple of breezy inquiries—"Have a scene?"—that cause Nick to ask him to go away. The story concludes, "Bill selected a sandwich from the lunch basket and walked over to have a look at the [fishing] rods (SS 111)." This is all we get about Bill, but Hemingway manages to depict him as adolescently shallow and insensitive merely through the word "selected" and the expression "to have a look." Juxtaposed to his friend's heartbreak, Bill shows his lack of concern in the careful selection of a sandwich and a casual interest in how the fishing is going. The sentence underscores Nick's sudden loneliness, but it also characterizes Bill. Note how much less effective it would have been on both counts had he written: "Bill took a sandwich from the lunch basket and went to look at the fishing rods." But "selected" makes Bill seem a scavenger picking at the remains of the Nick-Marjorie relationship, while the emotional poverty of "have a look" contrasts with the intensity of feeling that Marjorie brought to fishing with Nick.

The characterization of Ole Andreson in "The Killers" lies somewhere between the Conradian split portrayal of the major and the use of Bill as a foil. When Nick enters Ole's room to warn him about the Chicago gunmen, the former fighter is lying on the bed fully clothed, too long for the bed, his head on two pillows. This odd combination of features seems to sum up his situation. As he later puts it, "I just can't make up my mind to go out" (SS 287). He knows he will be killed and has accepted his fate, yet he instinctively seeks the small comfort of the two pillows. He is then characterized in the following five ways in a mere page: (1) Twice Nick tells him that the gunmen are going to kill him and the responses are "Ole Andreson said nothing" and he "did not say anything." (2) Of Ole's twelve speeches, most made in response to Nick's attempts at helpful suggestions, seven are versions of "There isn't anything I can do about it." (3) Eight times we read either that Ole "did not look at Nick," that "he looked at the wall," or that "he rolled over to the wall." (4) After Nick's last attempt to help—"Couldn't you fix it up some way?"—Ole offers his only explanation of what happened in Chicago—"I got in wrong." (5) As Nick exits the rooming house, the woman caretaker tells him that Ole's "an awfully nice man" and that "except from the way his face is" you would never know he's been a fighter—he's "just as gentle" (SS 287–88). From these hieroglyphics a compelling portrait of a type emerges: a large gentle man caught up in the corrupt boxing world in which he's just a name on a fight card—"a big Swede," probably a boxer who didn't throw a fight he was supposed to (note the unintended irony in Nick's last question, "Couldn't you fix it up some way?"), a man whose life has been reduced to living in a rooming house and eating at the local diner every night at six o'clock, a man who faces his fate with stoic resignation and few words of explanation.

Nearly three decades later, Hemingway revealed the story's fabula to A. E. Hotchner: "In the gym all afternoon he had rehearsed taking a dive, but during the real fight he had instinctively thrown a punch that he didn't mean to and knocked his opponent out. That's why the boys were sent to kill him" (Hotchner 163). By omitting from the story Ole's reasons for not throwing the fight—in the imagined fabula it was due to instinct and accident—Hemingway brilliantly allows this to remain a mystery, which deepens the portrayal of Ole in a way that the clear depiction of Jack Brennan's motives for failing to take a dive in "Fifty Grand" does not. Although "Fifty Grand" is a much longer story, allowing Hemingway the luxury of delineating Brennan's character more comprehensively, Ole comes across as the deeper character.

It is a sixth detail of characterization, however, that truly individualizes Ole. Near the start of Nick's visit, he says, "Thanks for coming to tell me about it" (SS 287). This remark is offered almost as an attempt to dismiss Nick. But when Nick is about to leave, Ole, still facing the wall, says, "Thanks for coming around" (SS 288). This little detail adds great depth to the characterization as, on the verge of death, Ole demonstrates an instinctive thoughtfulness and gratitude toward the boy who has shown concern for him. In four words Ole reveals an element of his character that we might call decency, and that small glimpse of character is so powerful that, despite what I previously stated about normative centers being peculiar to the novel, one could almost call this exchange a normative center, against which we may judge the larger scene of the gunmen in the diner. It is the revelation of Ole's character, and not his situation, that so strongly affects the reader, affecting Nick as well, whose final speech back at the diner is: "I can't stand to think about him waiting in the room and knowing he's going to get it. It's too damned awful" (SS 289). "The Killers" may be a stunning example of Hemingway's dialogue techniques and use of external focalization, but the subtly implied character of Ole Andreson is what lies at the heart of the story.

"The Doctor and the Doctor's Wife," a four-page text, is a tour de force of story characterization, produced through variable internal focalization mixed with key moments of external focalization. Three Ojibwas come to the doctor's shorefront cottage to cut abandoned logs into firewood for him, Billy Tabeshaw carrying "two big cant-hooks," Eddy Boulton carrying a "long cross-cut saw," and his father Dick Boulton with "three axes under his arm." Through delayed exposition in the third paragraph, we learn that the logs drift off from log booms and will later be retrieved by the logging companies or else left to "rot on the beach." Using the doctor as the initial focalizer, Hemingway states the doctor "always assumed" the logs would be abandoned to rot (SS 99). Thus the reader understands that the doctor is not, in his own mind, stealing the logs.

For his initial characterization of Dick Boulton, Hemingway shifts the focalization to some anonymous farmers whose reliability is somewhat suspect: "Dick was a half-breed and many of the farmers around the lake believed he was really a white man. He was very lazy but a great worker once he was started" (SS 99–100). To highlight the unreliability of this characterization, he has Dick speak "in Ojibway" to Eddy and Billy. We now know how Dick is viewed by whites and also that we cannot know the real Dick, who is from another culture whose language we cannot even speak. The three men begin working, but Dick soon irritates the doctor by insinuating that the timber is stolen; after the doctor insists that it's driftwood, Dick washes it off to reveal the mark of the company that owns it. Again focalizing through the doctor, Hemingway reports that he "was very uncomfortable" and has him speak—"'You'd better not saw it up then, Dick,' he said, shortly." This reinforces our initial understanding of him as honest; he assumed the logs would be left to rot but, faced with these insinuations, he is ready to let them go after giving the matter some thought ("shortly"). But Dick's insinuations now turn into full-blown accusations and provocations: "'Don't get huffy, Doc,' said Dick. 'Don't get huffy. I don't care who you steal from.'" Two gestures/actions then indicate the moods of the two men without requiring access to the consciousness of either: the doctor's "face was red" and Dick "spat tobacco juice on the log" (SS 100). The doctor's embarrassment and Dick's defiance have reversed their usual class relations. The doctor is now, in effect, the "red man." All that remains is for Dick to light the fuse, after the doctor dismisses him, which he does by three more repetitions of the informal salutation "Doc." The doctor loses control and threatens Dick—"If you call me Doc once again, I'll knock your eye teeth down your throat." But Dick checkmates him—"Oh, no, you won't, Doc" (SS 101).

The doctor later comes up with a theory about why Dick instigated this argument when he tells his wife, "Dick owes me a lot of money for pulling his squaw through pneumonia and I guess he wanted a row so he wouldn't have to take it out in work" (SS 102). Perhaps this is a rationalization that enables him to avoid facing his own cowardice. Or perhaps it characterizes the doctor as a shrewd judge of human nature. But only within certain limits. When the doctor told Dick not to saw up the wood, Hemingway used the adverb *shortly*. The meaning of *shortly* seemed to be "not long after"; in other words, he spoke only after mulling things over. But *shortly* can also mean "abruptly," "curtly," or "sharply," indicating that the doctor's speech was delivered in an uncivil manner, an interpretation supported by Dick's subsequent reply when he tells the doctor, "Don't get huffy." Is Dick, then, provoking an argument to avoid paying off a debt, or is there more going on here?

Dick Boulton is a poor man of an impoverished people, dependent upon such well-to-do white men as the doctor not only to earn a living but to provide his family with medical care. To discharge his debt, he must perform menial labor in front of and alongside his son. When he calls the doctor "Doc," and when he refers to the logs as stolen, he is trying to reestablish relations along less hierarchical lines through an assumed familiarity and by implying that even financially secure, white men play fast and loose with the law. Perhaps this attempt at social leveling is what angers the doctor, rather than the accusation per se. Although Dick provokes the doctor into dismissing him, he twice tries to mollify him in speeches the doctor cuts off ("Now, Doc—" and "Listen, Doc."), but these are met with a threat of physical violence ("I'll knock your eye teeth down your throat."). Whether or not Dick saw this coming, the ground has now shifted; he is the doctor's superior in physical prowess, and Hemingway writes: "Dick Boulton looked at the doctor. Dick was a big man. He knew how big a man he was. He liked to get into fights. He was happy" (*SS* 101). It is impossible to determine the focalizer of these sentences; we don't know whether we are in Dick's consciousness, which would make these statements about Dick authoritative, or whether this is free indirect speech, that is, whether these statements convey the doctor's sense of Dick. If the former, it characterizes Dick as something of a bully. But if this is the doctor's sense of Dick, then it is an unflattering characterization of the doctor's bourgeois condescension toward the Ojibwa who stares him down. After watching the doctor stalk off angrily and enter his cottage, Dick says "something in Ojibway" and Eddy laughs, "but Billy Tabeshaw looked very serious." Although we cannot know what was said, clearly Dick has successfully asserted his manhood and Eddy is pleased with his father's triumph. But now we get a characterization of Billy that provides further context to the encounter. Billy, who "did not understand English," is in a sweat during the argument. After Dick purposely leaves the gate open upon departing, Billy "went back and fastened it" (*SS* 101). Hemingway characterizes Billy by these details as anxious not to provoke whites, and in doing so he further characterizes Dick, by contrast, as unwilling to accept being demeaned.

In the cottage, the doctor is "irritated" at the sight of "a pile of un-opened medical journals on the floor" of his room. His wife interrogates him from her room, where she is resting with the blinds drawn. When he informs her that he "had a row with Dick," she replies, "I hope you didn't lose your temper, Henry" (SS 101):

> "Remember, that he who ruleth his spirit is greater than he that taketh a city," said his wife. She was a Christian Scientist. Her Bible, her copy of *Science and Health* and her *Quarterly* were on a table beside her bed in the darkened room.
>
> Her husband did not answer. He was sitting on his bed now, cleaning a shotgun. (SS 101–102)

His wife calls him twice before he answers, then presses him to tell her what the row with Dick was about; when he presents his theory of why Dick provoked him, she twice replies, "I really don't think that any one would really do a thing like that." The doctor decides to "go for a walk," and his wife, who constantly refers to him as "Dear," asks him to tell their son that she wants to see him. When the screen door slams behind him, he hears her "catch her breath" and apologizes. "It's all right, dear," she replies. He finds Nick in the hemlock woods and informs the boy of his mother's request, but Nick says, "I want to go with you" (SS 102–3). The story ends with Nick leading his father to a place where there are black squirrels.

These two pages further characterize the doctor as simmering with anger and resentment. His irritation at the sight of the unopened medical journals is suggestive. Is he mad that he hasn't found time to open and read them? Does the sight of them cause him to feel that he's a better man than Dick and therefore shouldn't have to deal with such a person? Is the anger he represses so powerful that it makes him mad at everything? And is the affect disproportionate to the argument with Dick? This story is the second Hemingway wrote about Dr. Adams. In the first, "Indian Camp," which precedes it in *In Our Time,* the doctor says of the extraordinary Caesar-ean operation he has just performed, "That's one for the medical journal," but he is mocked by his brother and subsequently deflated upon discover-ing the suicide of his patient's husband (SS 94). Perhaps this is another rea-son why seeing the unopened journals angers him. Is he mad at Dick in the same way he's mad at the unopened journals and was earlier mad at Uncle George; that is to say, is there another, more central cause for his anger, one that leads him to be so easily provoked?

Upon entering the cottage, he was greeted with an accusatory question over whether he had lost his temper. Despite his denial, his wife smugly fed him a biblical quotation anyway, one that implied he is prone to losing it. His continued anger is suggested by his cleaning a shotgun in his room while she talks at him. The reader wonders whom he might be fantasizing using the gun on—Dick, his wife, or some other target of his suppressed rage. The wife is characterized as being in the dark, both literally and figuratively. Her knowledge of human motivation derives from Christian Science, its publications—unlike him, she has time to read her journals—and its particular biblical interpretations. Her take on Dick Boulton appears hopelessly inadequate, more so since the reader has already witnessed the actual conflict. Her husband leaves, seemingly to escape from her, yet he is so henpecked that she can demonstrate her control over him merely by catching her breath when the screen door slams and getting him to apologize. But she cannot yet exercise this control over Nick, who ignores her request and prefers to remain with his father.

Characterization and judgment abound in this brief story. Yet it all transpires *within* the dramatic action of the narrative, and Hemingway trusts the reader to see these characters as he does, by interpreting the hieroglyphics he presents to reveal them. The germ of the story—his own parents' relationship—could not be more personal to the author, and the reader senses Hemingway's feelings, but nowhere in this dispassionate presentation of character does the author reveal his hands and feet. Of course, a poor reader might not "get it," might see the doctor as a simple thief or his wife as a grand example of human piety, but that is a risk all story writers must take.

The main setting of the second half of "The Doctor and the Doctor's Wife" is unusual for Hemingway because it takes place in someone's home, albeit the family's summer cottage rather than their main dwelling. Only three other stories are set in homes ("Soldier's Home," "One Reader Writes," "Nobody Ever Dies"), in addition to three that have cottages or a shanty as locations ("The Three-Day Blow," "Ten Indians," "Indian Camp"). Furthermore, in none of these seven stories are homes or cottages the sole locations. A survey of the settings of the fifty-three stories we've been considering is highly revelatory. In the following list, I count all meaningful settings employed. Thus, for "Che Ti Dice la Patria?" I include foreign villages, a car, inside a bar, and on the road. What constitutes a meaningfully employed location is admittedly subjective, but the pattern is illuminating:

café/bar/saloon/inn/tavern (17), foreign city (11), hotel/rooming house (10), in transit / on the road (8), hospital/infirmary (7), foreign town/village (7), inside a house/cottage/shanty (7), a street / outside of a domestic space (5), restaurant / public dining space (4), fishing excursion (4), hunting excursion (4), aboard a train (3), train station (3), in a car (3), wilderness (3), outdoors in deserted space (3), battlefield (3), army barracks (2), evacuation during war (2), skiing (2), lake/sea (2), tent (1), boxing gym (1), boxing ring (1), boxing training camp (1), Indian camp/shanty (1), bedroom (1), bull ring (1), bullfight promoter's office (1), horse track (1), funeral procession (1)

In addition, the geographical locations of the stories are as follows (continents, nations, and, when possible, more specific locations):

Europe (27.5), United States (20.5), Italy (10), Spain (10), upper Michigan (9), Madrid (5), France (3.5), Switzerland (3), Milan (2), Africa (2), Kansas City (2), Arkansas/Mississippi (2), Paris (1.5), near Chicago (1), New York City area (1), Montana (1), Florida Keys (1), Wyoming (1), Oklahoma (1), Cuba (1), Mexico (1), Greece/Thrace (1), Padua (1), Spezia (1), Montreux (1), ancient Jerusalem (1), Roanoke, Virginia (1), Boston (.5)

In some cases—for example, in locating "Fathers and Sons" and "A Day's Wait" in the vicinity of Piggott, Arkansas, and Mississippi—I'm using extratextual evidence. In a story with two settings, such as Boston and Paris in "Mr. and Mrs. Elliot," I assign half a setting to each. Sometimes, as in "A Natural History of the Dead," it is impossible to determine the geographical setting—the hospital could be in several possible locations. Often, the setting is vital to the story and its characters. "A Canary for One" would be a very different story if it did not take place aboard a train, and in "Big Two-Hearted River" the natural landscape of upper Michigan is almost another character. At other times, especially in stories set in bars or train stations and rendered mostly in dialogue, the location makes little difference. But not always, as in the Spanish Civil War stories set in Chicote's Restaurant in Madrid.

In this overview we see many settings of "transience"—bars, restaurants, hotels, rooming houses, spaces outside dwellings, train stations, and moving trains or automobiles. We also see many sport settings (although I hesitate to term bullfighting a sport)—hunting, fishing, boxing, bullfighting, skiing, and horse racing. The third most frequent category revolves around war—battlefields, hospitals, barracks, and wartime evacuations. Almost half of the American settings are in upper Michigan and only three-and-a-half are in big cities. Most of the stories take place outside of the United States, with roughly two-thirds of these equally divided between Italy and Spain. In contrast to the American stories, half of the European stories take place in big cities. It would be difficult to find another story writer whose work has this diversity of geographical settings. Not only do individual locations speak to the matter of transience, the list as a whole is the product of an author whose life was, to say the least, peripatetic.

What sorts of characters inhabit stories in such transient settings? Unhappy couples play a central part in seventeen of the fifty-three stories and a lesser role in three others. In five of those twenty stories, a spouse dies. The unhappy couples span from young Nick and Prudie in "Ten Indians" to the adolescent Nick and Marjorie in "The End of Something" through Dr. Adams and his wife. But most of the couples are in their twenties and early thirties, not coincidentally the same age Hemingway was when he was writing the stories. Another frequent character is the traveler, alone or with a companion, who is either without a home (for example, Bugs and Ad in "The Battler"), in transit via car, train, or on foot (like Nick and Tom in "The Light of the World"); a tourist (the couples of "Out of Season" and "Cat in the Rain"); a visitor (the narrator and his wife in "Wine of Wyoming"); a foreign correspondent (the narrator of "The Denunciation" and "The Butterfly and the Tank"); a patient (Mr. Fraser in "The Gambler, the Nun, and the Radio"); or on an excursion (Francis Macomber). Such characters are featured in at least thirty-nine stories. Hemingway's travelers, whether heading somewhere in particular or else moving about for no discernible reason, are never motivated by an optimistic Whitmanesque "open road" philosophy. Their motivation is often to escape the complications of home or civilization. The road itself, except when part of the natural landscape, is a negative element in Hemingway. As Susan F. Beegel observes, "neither Nick Adams nor his creator is a Kerouac, a Steinbeck, a Least Heat Moon, an American poet of the open road. Highway, in Hemingway, is a wound on the land, destroyer of a way of life." The only good thing about a highway, for Hemingway, is that it carries one away from hideous human environments back into the restorative natural world ("Second" 76–77).

Unhappy couples are people who are together yet emotionally alone. Many Hemingway stories also contain solitary individuals, whether alienated from their surroundings (for example, Harold Krebs in "Soldier's Home"), aged and alone (the old man of "A Clean, Well-Lighted Place"), or a loner (the narrator of "After the Storm"). Solitary figures appear in at least eleven stories. Many have given up in despair, for instance, Bill Campbell of "A Pursuit Race," while others, such as the character in "Old Man at the Bridge," are without hope. Nothing signifies our ultimate solitude more than our mortality. As Hemingway observed, "all stories, if continued far enough, end in death, and he is no true-story teller who would keep that from you" (*DIA* 122). In eleven of the stories, a character is either physically wounded or else suffering from an injury. In seventeen stories a character dies (in eleven a character is killed and in six a character passes from other causes). In four additional stories, it is manifest that a character will shortly die or be killed, a number that might increase to six depending upon the eventual fates of Manuel in "The Undefeated" and the mutilated boy in "God Rest You Merry, Gentlemen."

Hemingway also observed that there is no lonelier person in death than the suicide (*DIA* 122). "Indian Camp" has a suicide, "A Clean, Well-Lighted Place" an earlier suicide attempt, and "Out of Season," according to Hemingway, an omitted future suicide. The already high figures for wounded characters do not include Nick Adams stories in which his wounding is not directly addressed or stories such as "A Way You'll Never Be," in which death and wounding are everywhere present but do not occur to a significant character during the story. Although sixteen of the stories take place in wartime or involve soldiers or former soldiers, the deaths, murders, and woundings in Hemingway stories also occur in peacetime.

Another major Hemingway character type is the "professional": an athlete, sportsman, or person competent in a specific profession. Just as Hemingway's unhappy couples, characters on the move, isolated individuals, and physically or emotionally wounded characters reflect aspects of his own experience, these professionals often represent his own sense of authorial competence, as well as his fears of failure. Some (for example, Wilson in "Macomber" and Zurito in "The Undefeated") are in their prime; others (Manuel of "The Undefeated" and Jack Brennan of "Fifty Grand") are barely holding on; still others (Ad of "The Battler" and Ole of "The Killers") are used up. One, the jockey father in "My Old Man," is corrupt and dies. The competent character is important in many other stories: Nick as a fisherman in "Big Two-Hearted River," Drs. Adams and Fischer in "Indian Camp" and "God Rest You Merry, Gentlemen," and Nick's father as a hunter in "Fathers and Sons."

Persons from the margins of society, although typically neither in transit nor featured characters, pervade Hemingway's stories, contributing to the settings: the Ojibwas of "Indian Camp," "The Doctor and the Doctor's Wife," and "Ten Indians"; the lumberjacks of northern Michigan; the prostitutes and villagers of "Ch Ti Dice la Patria?"; the Mexican migrant workers of "The Gambler, the Nun, and the Radio"; and an army of bartenders, innkeepers, padrones, gun bearers, guides, attendants, waiters, and drunks, as well as menial laborers from the worlds of boxing, bullfighting, and horse racing. "The Light of the World" features two young men on the road in a setting with a hostile bartender and "five whores waiting for the train to come in, and six white men [five lumbermen and an effeminate cook] and four Indians" (SS 385). One story, "After the Storm," is told in the first person by a character from the margin—a scavenger who ransacks sunken ships.

Children, too, are marginalized characters. Although Hemingway entered fatherhood at the start of his story-writing career, a child, always a young boy, is a significant character in only four stories. In "A Day's Wait," the boy is purely a figure of innocence. In "My Old Man" and "Indian Camp," an innocent boy's illusions are challenged. In "The Capital of the World," a boy dies before he can lose his illusions. In real life, Hemingway was extremely tender toward children and enjoyed being called "Papa." It would appear he had difficulty, in his fiction, facing what happens to children as they grow up and their innocence is shattered.

In modernist fiction—whether multiplaced and transient, as in Hemingway's works, or regionalist and decaying, as in Faulkner's—the world is fragmented and place itself is vulnerable, threatened by an increasingly global culture spreading beyond comprehension. The qualities of dominance and aggression so often attributed to Hemingway's fiction are, in reality, the product of a sense of insecurity, a permanent mode of flight represented in the fiction by transient settings and wounded or alienated characters. Neither a backdrop for sexism nor a stage for aggression, Hemingway's settings and characters present the modern world as a destabilizing force stronger than men and women, a force that instigates a full spectrum of responses between fight and flight.

Let us recall Sean O'Faolain's comment, from our first chapter, about the short story being an "emphatically personal exposition" (30), and Scott Fitzgerald's observation that story writers "tell our two or three stories—each time in a new disguise—maybe ten times, maybe a hundred, as long as people will listen." Fitzgerald then related the anecdote about the painter of boats, hired to paint a client's ancestors, who warned that they "would all turn out to look like boats" ("False" 132). Hemingway loved the things of this world—the landscapes, cityscapes, physical activities, and impressions he depicted with such startling clarity—but he was obsessed with human frailty and vulnerability. This obsession led to his writing about characters on the move, solitary, emotionally and physically wounded, growing old, facing death, and killed. For him, April truly was the cruelest month, reminding us that we are all betrayed in our finitude—"One generation passeth away, and another generation cometh; but the earth abideth forever" was the epigraph he chose for *The Sun Also Rises*. At the end of *A Farewell to Arms,* Frederic Henry muses: "That was what you did. You died. You did not know what it was about. You never had time to learn. They threw you in and told you the rules and the first time they caught you off base they killed you . . . they killed you in the end. You could count on that. Stay around and they would kill you" (*FTA* 327). Eleven years later, after Hemingway's career as a storywriter was over, near the conclusion of *For Whom the Bell Tolls,* a doomed Robert Jordan thinks, "The world is a fine place and worth the fighting for and I hate very much to leave it" (*FWBT* 467). Frederic and Robert voice sentiments that aptly articulate Hemingway's sensibility, as we see it in his life and in his art, sentiments that lie at the heart of his short stories. They are, as Fitzgerald would put it, his boats.

CODA

Hemingway's Legacy

INTERVIEWER [George Plimpton]: Who would you say are your literary forebears—those you have learned the most from?

ERNEST HEMINGWAY: Mark Twain, Flaubert, Stendhal, Bach, Turgenev, Tolstoi, Dostoevski, Chekhov, Andrew Marvell, John Donne, Maupassant, the good Kipling, Thoreau, Captain Marryat, Shakespeare, Mozart, Quevodo, Dante, Vergil, Tintoretto, Hieronymus Bosch, Brueghel, Patinir, Goya, Giotto, Cézanne, Van Gogh, Gauguin, San Juan de la Cruz, Góngora—it would take a day to remember everyone. Then it would sound as though I were claiming an erudition I did not possess instead of trying to remember all the people who have been an influence on my life and work. This isn't an old dull question. It is a very good but a solemn question and requires an examination of conscience. I put in painters, or started to, because I learn as much from painters about how to write as from writers. You ask how this is done? It would take another day of explaining. I should think what one learns from composers and from the study of harmony and counterpoint would be obvious.

—Hemingway, Interview by George Plimpton

Art is what makes the impossible look easy. And Hemingway was that artist; a name at the bottom of no man's list.

—John Ciardi, "The Language of an Age"

In 1904, two years before his death, Paul Cézanne was asked by a friend what he thought about the Masters. He replied: "They are good. I used to go to the Louvre every morning when I was in Paris; but in the end I attached greater importance to nature than to them. You have to create your own vision." Pressed further, he elaborated, "You have to create your own perspective, you must see nature as if no one had ever seen it before." But what did he mean by nature? Was art "a union of the world and the individual" or, restated in our terminology, what are the respective roles of the external world and the artist's perceiving mind in the creation of art? To this question Cézanne responded: "I understand it as a personal apperception. I locate this apperception in sensation and I ask of the intellect that it organize these sensations into works of art" (qtd. in Bernard 79–80;

translations mine).[1] Although his answers remain vague, nevertheless Cézanne here gathers up several of the topics we have been exploring in this book: what O'Faolain terms "literary personality" (personal apperception); impressionism and expressionism (perception and sensation); form, craft, and technique (organizing these perceptions and sensations into works of art); and what underlies innovations in technique (creating one's own perspective and seeing the world anew). Technique was not, to either Cézanne or Hemingway, culturally neutral; it's the method by which artists render their unique visions, their worldviews.

Hemingway learned lessons from many craftsmen—fiction writers, artists, musicians, journalists, poets, matadors, fishermen, hunters, soldiers—from anyone whose profession demands applied technique. In the end, he sided with what Cézanne termed "nature"; like the Frenchman, he broke it all down and rebuilt it according to his own vision, writing fictional prose different from any written before. Although his style has been more imitated than any author's of the last century, no one has ever successfully reproduced it. Whenever someone has tried, it's come out badly, producing unintentional versions of the entries in the now defunct annual "International Imitation Hemingway Competition," no different really than when Hemingway briefly emulated Jack London in his teens or Stein in his twenties.

When one truly understands Hemingway's art, one sees its traces everywhere, not just in those writers whose fiction most resembles his. One need not write in the manner of Hemingway in order to have learned from him, any more than one must be a late Impressionist to have felt the influence of Cézanne. In other words, except in the works of authors who've been dubbed, somewhat facilely, "hard-boiled" or "minimalist," Hemingway's immense legacy has not always been in plain sight. The many important writers whom he influenced eschewed imitation and learned to create their own styles. To take two examples, although Ralph Ellison called Hemingway his "ancestor" (140) and Gabriel García Márquez credited him as the premier influence on his own fictional craft ("Meets" 16), it is difficult to see clear connections between Hemingway's art and either *Invisible Man* or *One Hundred Years of Solitude*. Teasing out and tracing such connections—a study of Hemingway's influence—would carry us well beyond the bounds of this book; indeed, it would require a multivolume work of its own. But perhaps here, by way of conclusion, we might suggest some of the reasons, technical and other, why Hemingway has meant so much to such a vast array of authors over the past eight decades.

We ought to begin with his most innovative technical achievement. Hemingway liberated an entire element of fiction—dialogue—making it available for a range of purposes other than mere illustration. He demonstrated how dialogue could delineate character and advance plot, how it could simultaneously be verisimilar and constructive (two functions that had hitherto seemed mutually exclusive), and how what is *not* said can tell us as much about characters and their relationships, perhaps even more so, than what appears upon the page. Although such "silences" are not, technically speaking, forms of omission, they have much in common; both represent an absence that is felt by the reader as a powerful presence.

Omission itself, along with a radical use of concision, is another set of techniques that Hemingway bequeathed to fiction writers. As Dickinson had done in poetry, he showed how fewer, more carefully selected words can convey a wealth of meaning through suggestiveness, allowing the reader a greater role in making a story come alive. More than any author, before or since, Hemingway eliminated verbosity from fiction, which was especially crucial to the development of the modern short story with its limited amount of available space. Simply put, he showed writers how to do more with less, bringing to fruition Flaubert's notion of "le mot juste," the carefully selected, exactly right word. Henry James had complained about novels that were loose and baggy monsters; Hemingway dealt a death blow to the loose and baggy story. Each was a consummate craftsman in his own best genre, and if James is arguably atop any list for the title of "novelist's novelist," then the same can be said, if we perhaps exclude Chekhov, for Hemingway in the short story.

Hemingway also fulfilled the Flaubertian dictum that the author should be present as God at the creation—everywhere felt but nowhere seen—as successfully as did any writer of the twentieth century. Although he did not invent dispassionate presentation, impressionism, external focalization, or the objective correlative, he effaced the author as thoroughly as any writer ever has. No one has ever practiced impressionism in fiction, as we have defined it, as rigorously as Hemingway, and no author's work has been as constant a reminder to other writers "to see" exactly what they and their characters are looking at. This realist-inspired effacement of the author has been one of the two main modes of twentieth-century fictional presentation—along with the authorial playfulness brought to its fullest development by metafictionists and postmodernists—and although the latter remains the darling of academics, the former has predominated in the fiction of the past century. Once artifice has been completely paraded before us and parodied, what remains but to return to art?

Hemingway also greatly democratized fiction writing and fiction reading through his transmutation of vernacular discourse into high art. As Russell Banks observes, "If you want to write in American vernacular English—and most of us do—then you have to turn to Hemingway. It was his invention" (qtd. in Paul 116). Perhaps the best example of this lies in his uses of repetition, not only in his dialogue techniques but also in nondialogue. Before Hemingway, repetition in fiction was considered inelegant unless used selectively for poetic effects (as in the end of Joyce's "The Dead") or else for philosophical and/or linguistic experimentation (as in Stein). But Hemingway combined the casual repetitions of everyday discourse with the intricate patterns of art; as Robert Frost had done in poetry, he created a prose that was fluid and unobtrusive yet exceedingly complex in the evocation of its effects.[2]

A final point is that Hemingway's focalization techniques are almost a training course for other writers. He mastered every known type of focalization, except for the nonfocalized (omniscient) narrative he abhorred, and in his use of external narration, whether for whole stories or large stretches of stories, and even in first-person narratives, he perfected a mode of narration that has been particularly apt for the past century and our own. He did not invent external focalization, any more than he did omission, dispassionate presentation, or impressionism, but no author is more closely identified with these techniques.

Thematically, Hemingway's stories have engaged many of the most significant issues of the past hundred years: expatriation, cosmopolitanism, multiculturalism, war, transience, changes in gender codes, the failure of familial relationships, professionalism, the relations of humans to nature (what ecocritics refer to as the extrahuman world), and the search for meaning in an increasingly secularized, technological, and global culture. In addition, his recurrent but varied textualizations of the wound he suffered in the Great War, a type of wound that Frederick J. Hoffman has insightfully characterized as "unreasonable," locate his cultural and historical centrality to the past century in the same way as do Franz Kafka's textualizations of alienation in such works as *The Castle, The Metamorphosis,* and *The Trial.* As Hoffman observes:

Among other distinctions, Hemingway can claim that of having honestly attempted an explanation of a form of death to which the twentieth century is peculiarly heir—death that comes as a violent disruption of life. It is unreasonable (that is, it is not properly "motivated," cannot be understood in terms of any ordinary system of motivation). It puts traditional securities to shame, since they cannot satisfactorily keep pace with its indiscriminate destructiveness. It demands a new form of resourcefulness and courage, and—in Hemingway's case—a new type of moral improvisation. The sudden violent injury inflicted impersonally by efficient guns or planes too remote from the victim to "hold him any special grudge" is the symbol of this type of death and of the death-in-life which is its consequence. (97)

The ever-present threat of such an "unreasonable wound" is crucial to understanding how many hundreds of millions of people have experienced the twentieth and twenty-first centuries: from the two World Wars to such countless "local" wars as Korea, Vietnam, and now Iraq, to so many deliberate campaigns of ethnic cleansing and mechanized genocide, to 9/11, the massacres at Columbine and Virginia Tech, and the deadly Gulf of Mexico hurricanes of 2005 caused by an increasingly disastrous global warming that an incompetent American president willfully refused to acknowledge. Every bit as much as Kafka, Hemingway explored how history is felt on the personal level, the "social experience" of individuals in a world of large technology-bound nation-states and violent global politics. As Hoffman further notes, the unreasonable wound has persisted "in modern morality and literature. Hemingway described its circumstance and gave it its first and its most incisive literary statement and judgment" (97). In the half-century since Hoffman made this assessment, Hemingway's work has grown more, not less, relevant.

Last and far from least, Hemingway has served as an example—no, much more than that, as a hero—to other writers. In the academy today, such a sentence might be labeled a "fetishization" of the author (often by people who themselves fetishize their own favorite authors or theorists). But the incontrovertible fact is that other writers have been inspired by Hemingway, viewing him as a man of immense personal courage and as their beau ideal of what a writer should be and how he should approach his work. He was, to Gabriel García Márquez, the author "who was able to decipher, as few have done in human history, the practical mysteries of the most solitary occupation in the world" ("Our" 16). Let me repeat two of the quotations with which I introduced this study. Here is the judgment of no less than William Faulkner: "One of the bravest and best, the strictest in principles, the severest of craftsmen, undeviating in his dedication to his craft . . . To the few who knew him well he was almost as good a man as the books he wrote" (ACAW 6). And here is John Updike, speaking for his own generation of writers: "I suspect few readers younger than myself could believe . . . how we *did* love Hemingway and, after pity feels merely impudent, love him still" (489). What Faulkner, Updike, and García Márquez evince is awe, respect, and love. Hemingway earned that.

Writers, in common with the rest of us, have their literary heroes. Charles W. Chesnutt proudly displayed to visitors a bust of Mark Twain that he kept in his library, and Ralph Ellison wrote his fiction in front of a photograph of Twain on his desk. My dear friend, the novelist and story writer Patricia Henley, has a framed photograph of Hemingway on the wall above her computer. It matters to her to look up and see the face of the man whom she claims caused her to want to be a writer and who taught her so much about the craft. Although not myself a creative writer, merely a reader, I look up at photographs of Hemingway and Dickinson as I write this book. It matters to me, too.

I admire Hemingway the way I admire all artists of integrity faithfully devoted to their craft, and also the way I admire anyone who excels at what they do—whether that be a writer, a teacher, a parent, a firefighter, a musician, an athlete, or even (and this is much in the spirit of Hemingway) a legendary wolf, such as number 21M of the Druid Peak Pack in Yellowstone National Park. I admire Hemingway because, despite his flaws, he was a good man who struggled to rise above his imperfect humanity and produce something of value with the means he had at hand. I admire him because he fought bravely against his own inner demons and endured long enough to do his work until, emotionally and physically spent, he could fight no more. In the end, this proved a greater courage than the sort he wrote about in his fiction. I admire him enormously for that.

I say all of this knowing that it is not the proper way to end an academic study of craft, but what has motivated this study is far from academic to me. And somehow, for reasons I can only glimpse but not fully fathom, when it comes to Hemingway, it does not seem an entirely inappropriate note on which to conclude.

Acknowledgments

All academic careers begin with teachers, and I was a fortunate student. In the History of American Civilization Program at Harvard University, David Herbert Donald and Warner Berthoff were my mentors, role models, and guardian angels. In emulating them my grasp has fallen oceans short of my reach, but their example of how things should be done continues to inspire and guide me. They also provided me with the two best pieces of advice I've ever received about writing. Professor Donald told me that I should always write in such a way as to be accessible to the greatest number of intelligent general readers without losing the interest of specialists. Professor Berthoff never let me forget that imprecise prose is always a sign of imprecise thought. I am also deeply grateful to Daniel Aaron, whose magnanimous soul and intellectual curiosity are unexcelled, and the late Judith Shklar for their instruction and support. As an undergraduate in history and philosophy at the University of Hartford, I was ably mentored by Arthur Shippee, Larry Prusak, William Miller, and the late Eugene Sweeney. These wonderful teachers provided me with my initial eclectic assortment of academic passions—the history of religions, philosophy, European history, socialism, and American labor history—leading me to understand the interconnectedness of pretty much everything. Their encouragement and counsel changed my life, and I am profoundly grateful to them for it.

Because I've always been shy about foisting my work on others, I don't have the usual small army of fellow scholars who have read this manuscript and commented at length upon it. But several friends did read parts of my drafts and made valuable suggestions: John N. Duvall, Wendy Stallard Flory, G. R. (Dick) Thompson, and Marc Dolan. I am especially indebted to my former colleague S. K. (Kip) Robisch. While much of this book was being written, he took time off from working on his definitive *Wolves and the Wolf Myth in American Literature* to discuss my ideas with me and to offer sage advice on several of the chapters. I've never had a finer colleague, and I cherish the years we worked together. I am also grateful to the editors of the *Hemingway Review, Twentieth Century Literature, Mod-*

ern Fiction Studies, Studies in Short Fiction, and the *Midwest Quarterly* for giving me the opportunity to publish my initial efforts on Hemingway and the short story. A couple of snippets from these earlier pieces appear in this book, and an article on Hemingway's dialogue that appeared in *Twentieth Century Literature* has been much revised and extended here as the eighth chapter.

There are many others whose encouragement and advice have buoyed me before and during the writing of the book. Early in my career, I was shown much generosity by the late Michael S. Reynolds, the greatest of Hemingway scholars, and by Susan F. Beegel, the sterling editor of the *Hemingway Review.* Such kindness means the world to assistant professors, and I recall them fondly for it. I also wish to thank Mike Anesko, Ann Astell, Dorrie Armstrong, Jeff Baxter, Margie Berns, Jane Palatini Bowers, Mark Cirino, John Contreni, France Córdova, Deb Cunningham, Susan Curtis, Grace Farrell, David Flory, Lisa Karen Hartman, Julie Henderson, Doug Lamb, Stephanie LaTour, Clayton Lein, Laura McCammack, Lee Clark Mitchell, the late Charlie and Esther Mushaw, Len Neufeldt, Joe Palmer, Jill Quirk, Victor Raskin, Judy Raub, Janeen Clarke, Ryan Schneider, Tony Silva, Fara Stalker, John Stauffer, my late Uncle Jack and Aunt Adele Stotter, the late Bill Stuckey, Judy Ware, Big Syd and Jeane Weinstein, Bud Weiser, and alphabetically last but always the jewel in any crown, Patsy Yaeger. I'm also grateful to Dr. Padraic Burns, Dr. Joseph Fruland, Dr. Andrew Hart, Dr. Nancy Lyon Havlik, Dr. Robert Martin, and Dr. Richard McPherson.

Over the years, my students have come first, which is the way it should be in an institution of higher learning, and they have amply rewarded me for it. There is nothing that compares to the joy of seeing one's students grow and succeed, and the satisfaction of knowing you've played a part in that trajectory. I wish there were space to mention more of them, but I particularly wish to include, from my time in the history and literature program at Harvard, three students whose senior honors theses I was privileged to direct: Lois Leveen, Jack Kerkering, and the amazing Marilynn Richtarik. In my eighteen years at Purdue University, forty-six of my undergraduates have gone on to doctoral programs and twenty-six others to law and medical schools. Many are now professors themselves. They start out as teenagers, freshmen in an introductory literature course, who are a little awkward and unsure of themselves, and they end up as confident professionals: lawyers, physicians, scholars, and teachers influencing their own students. It is, as Hemingway would put it, a hell of a thing. And so a loving shout out to Kim Adank, Jill Anderson, Elizabeth Barnes, Matt Bastnagel, Brandi Bennett, Chris Comstock, Tyler Cybock, Brad Evans, Jodi Galla, Emily Hambidge, Tom Hertweck, Louis Hickman, Julie Jansen, Aimee Kappes, Corey Linkel, Adam Luckinbill, Rachel Mack, Wes Marion, Sarah Martini, Brian McCammack, Adrian McLure, Kristi Newhouse, Mark Norris, Aisha Peay, Emily Ponder, Alyssa Radcliffe, Bethany Robison, Cassandra Sanborn, Carla Scaglione, Emily Jo Scalzo, Le'Ann Scott, Kirk Smiley, Aimee Smith, Jeff Spanke, LeAnn Tolbert, Anton VanderZee, Jessica Weatherford, Stacy Weida, Maria Windell, Alli Witt, Jenny Wright, and Sara Young. I've also had the opportunity to work with many extremely talented graduate students in courses and seminars and while advising their dissertations or serving on their dissertation committees. Sixteen of those dissertations are now books, with more on the horizon, and I hope their authors know how very proud I am of them. I especially wish to acknowledge Fred Arroyo, Ellen Bayer, Steve Belluscio, Brent Blackwell, Philathia Bolton, Portia Boulware, Mark Bousquet, Anne Boyd, Tracy Bryson, Mike Cocchiarale, Rob Davidson, Laurence Davis, Kim Ellis, Chris Elzey, Scott Emmert, Steve Frye, Keith Hale, Launa Hall, Sarah Hagelin, Liz Hermans, Angela Hilton, John King, Mark Leahy, Eric Carl Link, Christine McDermott, Judith Musser, David (Mike) Owens, Tom Pendergast, Heather Penney, Duke Pesta, Bev Reed, Becky Reno, Kip Robisch, Derek Parker Royal, Karen Salt, Pam Sanders, Rebecca Saulsbury, Kevin Scott, Stephany Spaulding, Mark Staunton, Gwen Tarbox, Joe Walker, Shunzu Wang, and Brian Yothers.

My father, David, who passed from Alzheimer's in 1998, was a man of unbounded generosity who grew up in difficult circumstances, heard the pain in other people's voices, and could never ignore someone in need. A Polish-Jewish immigrant, he took great pride in the fact that his son was, in his words, "real good with the English," and although he would not have read this book, he most assuredly would have carried it with him everywhere and showed it to everyone he met. My mother, Lena, passed from ALS, Lou Gehrig's Disease, in 1978. The daughter of Jewish immigrants from the Ukraine, she also emerged from a childhood of privation, was possessed of a desire to help others, and was a born teacher. Mom would have read this book, over and over, and she would have discussed it with me while I was writing it, much to its benefit. She remains, to this day, the finest person I've ever known, and although she's been gone for thirty years, she is never really far away. I am grateful to my parents for their example of decency and kindness, and for an unconditional love that I hardly deserved. I also wish to mention my grandparents, Morris and Rose Siegel and Harold and Tillie Lamb, only one of whom, Morris, was alive when I was born. Because they worked so hard all their years—Morris sold fruit and vegetables from a sidewalk pushcart and Harold had a small butcher shop—I get to write a book on Hemingway. I feel humbled by their lives.

Having few living relatives, I've filled this void with a family of my own choosing, which has some obvious advantages. These are the people I lean on for support, whose successes I take joy in, and who love me for my own sake with all my failings, annoying habits, and eccentricities. I am grateful beyond words to my siblings: Dick ("The Raven") and Elizabeth Boyd ("The Big Cat") Thompson, Kip Robisch and Patricia (Trixie) Henley, Kevin and Mary Ann Scott. And my four children: Sarah Hagelin, who received her doctorate in American Studies at the University of Virginia and is now an assistant professor at New Mexico State University specializing in gender and film; Brian McCammack, who is earning his doctorate in the American Civilization Program at Harvard, and who has already published four excellent articles in journals, including *American Quarterly;* Maria Windell, who recently completed a groundbreaking dissertation on sentimentalism and transamerican literature at the University of Virginia, a chapter of which was published in *Nineteenth-Century Literature;* and Jenny Wright, who made law review, graduated *summa cum laude* at the top of her class at Syracuse Law School, and is now an associate at Ice Miller LLP in Indianapolis. We will all depend upon her to defend us in court should our transgressions come to light. I am also blessed with four perfect godchildren who keep everything in proper perspective: Connor Michael Scott, Margaret Ellen (Maisie) Scott, Robert Jerome LaTour Dolan, and Stephen James LaTour Dolan. Animals possess a purity that exceeds even that of children and they have much wisdom to teach us, if only we will cease our arrogance and listen. I am grateful to my late dogs, Nicky, Wendy, and Tiger, and my late cats, Percy, Emily, Toby, Big Syd, and Homer Wells Lamb for what they taught me, and I thank the inimitable Elizabeth Boyd Lamb and Simone Nicole Lamb for what they teach me every day.

Last, my heartfelt thanks to the wonderful staff at Louisiana State University Press, most especially my editor John Easterly, whose professionalism, kindness, and savvy common sense have made working with him one of my best experiences in academia. I also wish to thank Lee Sioles, who gracefully and expertly shepherded this manuscript and its often tardy author through the production process, and Barbara Outland, and Judy Collins. And a huge thank-you to Laura Gleason for her stunning design of the cover and book. I am particularly grateful to Julia Ridley Smith, whose thoughtful, insightful, and meticulous copyediting has done so much to improve the quality of my work. To an author, a good copyeditor is a stroke of luck, but a superb one like Julia is a blessing.

Marc Dolan has been my best friend for over a quarter of a century. His loyalty and generosity of spirit are infinite, his patience and selflessness nearly so—and no one is smarter, more ethical, or more honest. I dedicate this book to him in admiration of his genius and appreciation of his friendship.

We'll have that beer now, Sundance, that one and plenty more.

Appendix

Adopted from Paul Smith, *A Reader's Guide to the Short Stories of Ernest Hemingway*

When a story first appeared under a different title before it was collected, and also in the case of the two vignettes from *in our time* later elevated to the status of stories in *In Our Time*, the original title appears in parentheses in the first column under the final title. An asterisk next to the date in the "1st Published" column indicates that the story was initially published in a magazine, journal, or anthology before it was collected in the book listed in the "1st Collected" column. Hemingway sometimes significantly revised a story between its first appearance in a magazine and its subsequent publication in a collection. Lines separate stories by year of completion.

Three Stories and Ten Poems (TSTP)—1923
in our time (iot)—1924
In Our Time (IOT)—1925
Men Without Women (MWW)—1927
Winner Take Nothing (WTN)—1933
The Fifth Column and the First Forty-nine Stories (49)—1938
The Short Stories of Ernest Hemingway (SS)—1954
The Fifth Column and Four Stories of the Spanish Civil War (SCW)—
    1969
The Nick Adams Stories (NAS)—1972
The Complete Short Stories of Ernest Hemingway: The Finca Vigía Edition (CSS)—1987

Title	Dates of Composition	1st Published	1st Collected
1. "Up in Michigan"	Fall 1921, Feb. 1922	1923	*TSTP* (1923)
2. "My Old Man"	July–Sept. 1922	1923	TSTP (1923)
3. "Out of Season"	April 1923	1923	*TSTP* (1923)

Title	Dates of Composition	1st Published	1st Collected
4. "A Very Short Story" ("chapter 10")	June–July 1923	1924	*iot* (1924)
5. "The Revolutionist" ("chapter 11")	June–July 1923	1924	*iot* (1924)
6. "Indian Camp" ("Work in Progress")	Nov. 1923–Feb. 1924	1924*	*IOT* (1925)
7. "Cat in the Rain"	Feb. 1923–March 1924	1925	*IOT* (1925)
8. "The End of Something"	March 1924	1925	*IOT* (1925)
9. "The Three-Day Blow"	March 1924	1925	*IOT* (1925)
10. "The Doctor and the Doctor's Wife"	March–April 1924	1924*	*IOT* (1925)
11. "Soldier's Home"	April 1924	1925*	*IOT* (1925)
12. "Mr. and Mrs. Elliot"	April 1924	1924*	*IOT* (1925)
13. "Cross-Country Snow"	April 1924	1925*	*IOT* (1925)
14. "Big Two-Hearted River"	May–Nov. 1924	1925*	*IOT* (1925)
15. "The Undefeated"	Sept.–Nov. 1924	1925*	*MWW* (1927)
16. "Banal Story"	Jan.–Feb. 1925	1926*	*MWW* (1927)
17. "The Battler"	Dec. 1924–March 1925	1925	*IOT* (1925)
18. "Fifty Grand"	Jan.–Nov. 1925	1927*	MWW (1927)
19. "An Alpine Idyll"	April 1926	1927*	*MWW* (1927)
20. "The Killers"	Sept. 1925–May 1926	1927*	*MWW* (1927)
21. "Today Is Friday"	May 1926	1926*	*MWW* (1927)
22. "A Canary for One"	Aug.–Sept. 1926	1927*	*MWW* (1927)
23. "In Another Country"	Sept.–Nov. 1926	1927*	*MWW* (1927)
24. "Now I Lay Me"	Nov.–Dec. 1926	1927	MWW (1927)
25. "A Pursuit Race"	Nov. 1926–Feb. 1927	1927	*MWW* (1927)
26. "A Simple Enquiry"	Nov. 1926–Feb. 1927	1927	*MWW* (1927)
27. "On the Quai at Smyrna" ("Introduction by the Author")	winter 1926/27	1930	*IOT* (1930 ed.)
28. "Che Ti Dice la Patria?" ("Italy—1927")	April–May 1927	1927*	*MWW* (1927)
29. "Ten Indians"	Sept. 1925–May 1927	1927	*MWW* (1927)
30. "Hills Like White Elephants"	May 1927	1927*	MWW (1927)
31. "Wine of Wyoming"	Oct. 1928–May 1930	1930*	WTN (1933)
32. "The Sea Change"	Jan. 1930-June 1931	1931*	*WTN* (1933)

Title	Dates of Composition	1st Published	1st Collected
33. "A Natural History of the Dead"	Jan. 1929–Aug. 1931	1932*	WTN (1933)
34. "After the Storm"	April 1928–June 1932	1932*	WTN (1933)
35. "God Rest You Merry, Gentlemen"	Feb.–Dec. 1932	1933*	WTN (1933)
36. "Homage to Switzerland"	March–June 1932	1933*	WTN (1933)
37. "The Light of the World"	May–July 1932	1933	WTN (1933)
38. "The Mother of a Queen"	fall 1931–Aug. 1932	1933	WTN (1933)
39. "A Way You'll Never Be"	May–Nov. 1932	1933	WTN (1933)
40. "A Clean, Well-Lighted Place"	fall 1932	1933*	WTN (1933)
41. "The Gambler, the Nun, and the Radio" ("Give Us a Prescription, Doctor")	summer 1931–fall 1932	1933*	WTN (1933)
42. "One Reader Writes"	Feb. 1932–Feb. 1933	1933	WTN (1933)
43. "A Day's Wait"	March–July 1933	1933	WTN (1933)
44. "Fathers and Sons"	Nov. 1932–Aug. 1933	1933	WTN (1933)
45. "The Capital of the World" ("The Horns of the Bull")	Nov. 1935–Feb. 1936	1936*	49 (1938)
46. "The Short Happy Life of Francis Macomber"	Nov. 1934–April 1936	1936*	49 (1938)
47. "The Snows of Kilimanjaro"	Feb.–April 1936	1936*	49 (1938)
48. "Old Man at the Bridge" ("The . . .")	April 1938	1938*	49 (1938)
49. "The Denunciation"	May–Sept. 1938	938*	SCW (1969)
50. "The Butterfly and the Tank"	July–Sept. 1938	1938*	SCW (1969)
51. "Night Before Battle"	Sept.–Oct. 1938	1939*	SCW (1969)
52. "Nobody Ever Dies"	Oct.–Nov. 1938	1939*	CSS (1987)
53. "Under the Ridge"	Feb. 1939	1939*	SCW (1969)

Notes

INTRODUCTION

1. See Judith Fetterly, *The Resisting Reader,* chap. 2, which incredibly concludes that the message of *A Farewell to Arms* is that "the only good woman is a dead one" (71), versus such essays as Linda Wagner-Martin's "'Proud and Friendly,'" which sees him characterizing men as "adolescent, selfish, and misdirected" and notes "evidence of much sympathy on Hemingway's part" for "the women he portrays in [his] early fiction" (245); Nina Baym's "I Felt Sorry for the Lion," which observes that "stories like 'Cat in the Rain' and 'Hills Like White Elephants' present a woman's point of view and attribute her plight . . . to a combination of male self-involvement and self-aggrandizement, a combination of which the text is aware and to which it is not sympathetic" (112); and Wendy Martin, "Brett Ashley as New Woman," which sees in the figure of Brett Hemingway's refusal to consign women to the domestic sphere and his disengagement "from the tradition of the destruction of the female protagonist in American fiction from *Charlotte Temple* to *The House of Mirth* and *The Awakening*" (80). These different perspectives—between seeing Hemingway as a misogynist and realizing that his sympathies frequently lie with his female characters in fiction that is often self-critical of his own real-life romantic relationships—hinge on the critic's willingness to read the texts closely rather than reading them in the grip of preconceived assumptions. Addressing this question, David J. Ferrero makes this larger point: "When a male author interrogates the social institutions that obligate men to women, he is a misogynist. When a woman writes of women imposed upon by men and the same institutions, she is a feminist. In a sense, there is no contradiction here. The only difference is what the terminology foregrounds and erases (24). Put another way, if Kate Chopin had written "The End of Something," "Cat in the Rain," and "Hills Like White Elephants," these stories would be staples in anthologies of feminist fiction.

2. This brief list could be expanded to include such important scholarly articles as, for instance, two excellent ecocritical essays by Susan F. Beegel ("Second Growth" and "Eye and Heart") and a recent ecofeminist essay by Lisa Tyler ("How Beautiful the Virgin Forests Were").

3. Margaret D. Bauer observes that when students come to Hemingway's texts without the larger-than-life image of the author and his so-called misogyny in their minds, they tend to see the feminist elements in his work (124–37). I, too, have had this experience teaching Hemingway, who is even more popular with my female students than with my male students.

CHAPTER ONE

1. The question of historical genre is especially complex when discussing the short story. For instance, how does one classify a mid-nineteenth-century postmodern story such as Gogol's "The Nose"?

2. Hemingway made this comment—in a 1953 letter to Bernard Berenson, a genteel art critic—after first describing his own "gallow's humor" as "the violence of *our time*" (*SL* 808, my emphasis) and then going on for a paragraph to discuss his own drinking habits and "being drunk." Perhaps he was making some unconscious connection here to "chapter 2" of *in our time*.

CHAPTER TWO

1. One hears a strong echo of the *Star*'s distaste for extravagant words in the famous passage from *A Farewell to Arms* when Frederic Henry reflects on the emptiness of propagandistic wartime rhetoric: "Abstract words such as glory, honor, courage, or hallow were obscene beside the concrete names of villages, the numbers of the roads, the names of the rivers, the numbers of regiments and the dates" (185).

2. For more on Pound's influence, see Benson, "Story Writer," 303–10; Hurwitz; and Jacqueline Tavernier-Courbin. Even as late as the end of 1926, Pound was relentless in reminding Hemingway to focus on the exact image without using extraneous words, as in these comments on "An Alpine Idyll": "I wish you wd. keep your eye on the objek MORE, and be less licherary . . . ANYTHING put on top of the subject [i.e., the image] is BAD. Licherchure is mostly blanketing up a subject. Too much MAKINGS. The subject is always interesting enough without the blankets" (qtd. in Tavernier-Courbin 183).

3. In his recent book on craft, Robert Olen Butler observes: "All of the techniques that filmmakers employ, and which you understand intuitively as filmgoers, have direct analogies in fiction" (64). One of these techniques is montage, first developed by Sergei Eisenstein, in which two images are juxtaposed and the links between them are implied. Referring to the sentence in "Cat in the Rain" in which the cat is first sighted, Butler notes, "We have now cut to what she is seeing. You understand this same technique when you're watching a movie: in *Out of Africa,* you see Robert Redford's face on the screen. He looks. Cut. We now see a lion bounding toward the camera. We understand that this is what he is seeing because of that montage: Robert Redford's face, a lion coming this way; and the third thing emerges" (68).

CHAPTER THREE

1. Of course, within these historical genres there are always exceptions. For instance, William Carlos Williams was a modernist, but to him the world was not fragmented and made perfect sense. One had only to describe it accurately, and it would reveal its meaning.

2. My understanding of consciousness and mind derives from recent developments in neuroscience and cognitive psychology, especially from my reading of works by Gerald M.

Edelman, Giulio Tononi, Merlin Donald, Steven Pinker, Nicholas Humphrey, Daniel C. Dennett, and Antonio Damasio.

3. Ford singles out James, Crane, and Conrad as the "big three" of literary impressionism ("Techniques" 26–27), but Conrad had little respect for the term, and even disparaged Crane as *the only* impressionist and *only* an impressionist" (qtd. in Watt 173). Nevertheless, Conrad's embrace of impressionist techniques is unmistakable, as is his accelerated use of them after his close friendship with Crane commenced in autumn 1897.

4. Cather met Crane in 1894 and wrote about it in a newspaper piece published just after Crane's death ("When"). But the extent of their contact and the nature of their conversations are not entirely clear. See Sharon O'Brien (161–63).

5. Of Crane's concision, Ford observes: he "was possessed of a passion, almost as vivid as that of Conrad himself, for elisions—for cutting his phrases down to an almost infinite economy of words. He was never tired of exasperatedly declaring that it was his unattainable ambition to make every one damned word do the work of six" ("Techniques" 26).

6. In 1950, Hemingway would recall, "I learned how to make a landscape from Mr. Paul Cézanne by walking through the Luxembourg Museum a thousand times with an empty gut, and I am pretty sure that if Mr. Paul was around, he would like the way I make them and be happy that I learned it from him" (qtd. in Ross 36).

7. Ron Berman points out other Cézanne-like *routes tournantes* in "Indian Camp," "The Three-Day Blow," "The Battler," "In Another Country," and "An Alpine Idyll." To these stories, we can add "Che Ti Dice la Patria?" "Ten Indians," "A Way You'll Never Be," "Wine of Wyoming," "Fathers and Sons," and "The Snows of Kilimanjaro" (in addition to those found throughout the novels). Berman also explains that many of the phrases Hemingway uses in his landscape depictions deliberately allude to parts of the lengthy titles of Cézanne's late landscape paintings, a sort of homage to his French mentor (23–24).

8. There is an alternative way of viewing these small blank areas in Cézanne's later paintings and what Hemingway learned from them. Rather than spaces that outrange the artist's comprehension and thus epistemological roadblocks, Theodore L. Gaillard Jr. views them as a technique that causes "viewers to fill spaces with preconscious constructs of complementary line and color, subtly moving toward the substitution of impression and feeling for cognition" (67). From this perspective, Hemingway's sense of Cézanne's blank spaces can be linked to his own literary impressionism and technique of omission in which the artist knows what he's omitted but omits it in order to make the reader/viewer *feel* rather than understand it.

CHAPTER FOUR

1. The narrative theorist who has most influenced the way I look at the structure of fiction is Gérard Genette in *Narrative Discourse* and *Narrative Discourse Revisited*. My understanding is also much indebted to Roland Barthes's *S/Z* and "An Introduction to the Structural Analysis of Narrative," and I have greatly profited from works by Wayne Booth, Algirdas Greimas, Tzvetan Todorov, Seymour Chatman, Mieke Bal, Gerald Prince, Peter Brooks, Wallace Martin, and Dorrit Cohn.

2. I'm aware that most narrative theorists would say that when the narrator sights the

character who otherwise serves as the focalizer, rather than sighting *through* that character, then the narrator is the focalizer. Technically, this is true, but I do not want to have third-person limited point-of-view (which I shortly introduce as third-person fixed internal focalization) broken up into moments when the text is sighted through the focalizer and when the focalizer is sighted by the narrator (as opposed to being sighted by another character, who at that moment becomes the focalizer). Thus, I will maintain the notion of the internal focalizer, whether he or she is doing the sighting or being sighted by the disembodied narrator.

I should also note that Genette rejects the concept of a "focalizer," which he sees as a misreading by Mieke Bal of his ideas about focalization. He observes: "*focalized* can be applied only to the narrative itself, and if *focalizer* applied to anyone, it could only be the person who *focalizes the narrative*—that is, the narrator" (*NDR* 73). Genette is right, of course, but I still want to use the concept of focalizer as I have defined it above with this stipulation—I am using it *only* as a convenient shorthand for the character through whom the narrator/author is sighting the action and to whose consciousness he or she has access.

3. This schema is from Genette's revision of Tzvetan Todorov's formula. See Genette, *ND*, 189–94.

4. In the preface to *The Portrait of a Lady,* James writes: "Place the centre of the subject in the young woman's own consciousness" (1079). See also the prefaces to *Roderick Hudson* (1050) and *The American* (1067–68). Criticism has summed up his pronouncements with the term *central consciousness.*

5. These fifty-three stories exclude the vignettes of *in our time* (except for two that were promoted to the rank of "short story" in *In Our Time*), texts that were portions of the novel *To Have and Have Not,* stories he did not see fit to publish, unfinished stories, and the handful of stories written or published after 1939 when his story art was but a shadow of what it once had been. As Paul Smith observes, "Hemingway's art of the short story was born, flourished to greatness, and died within a brief life of some fifteen years, between 1923 and 1938" (*Reader's Guide* xx). I extend this assessment to February 1939 in order to include the final story of this period, "Under the Ridge."

6. Beginning with the 1930 edition of *IOT,* Hemingway changed Ag's name to Luz for fear that Ag was "libelous" (*SL* 469). Ag was a reference to Agnes von Kurowsky, the nurse he fell in love with during his wartime convalescence and who later ended the relationship.

7. I'm grateful to my own former stray kitties, Elizabeth Boyd Lamb, an intellectually gifted, emotionally intense tortoise-shell hellion, and her gentle, more philosophically reserved yet playfully mischievous seal-point Siamese sister, Simone Nicole Lamb, for cleverly leading me to this information.

8. Nick is the named first-person narrator of "Now I Lay Me." To this story, in *NAS,* Philip Young adds "The Light of the World," "An Alpine Idyll," and "In Another Country." Joseph M. Flora rightly also includes "A Day's Wait" and "Wine of Wyoming." I would extend the list by adding "A Canary for One," "On the Quai at Smyrna," and "Che Ti Dice la Patria?"

9. For those wishing to follow these focalization shifts, here are the page numbers where they occur in *SS:* Francis Macomber (5, 11, 14, 15–16, 18, 19, 20, 21, 22–23, 27–29, 31,

32, 35–36); Robert Wilson (5–11, 17, 18, 19, 21, 23–27, 30, 31, 32–33, 34, 36); Margot Macomber (4, 21, 22, 33, 34); the lion (15, 19); Kongoni the gun-bearer (19); and their social set and the columnist (22).

CHAPTER SIX

1. The terms *prologue-story* and *epilogue-story* are adopted from O'Faolain (196).

2. Sheldon Norman Grebstein refers to this sort of ending as the "zero ending," and suggests Hemingway may have learned it from Chekhov, whose endings are notoriously open. Grebstein observes, the "whole point of the zero ending is *irresolution*—to leave the reader suspended among the apparently unconnected lines of character and action, consequently forcing him back upon his own resources of insight and imagination" (2).

CHAPTER SEVEN

1. O'Faolain first called my attention to the Stevenson passage (198), but he, too, failed to notice the special application of this phenomenon to the short story.

2. I'm indebted to my friend, the ecocritic Kip Robisch, for showing me that I had unnecessarily limited my concept of the illustrative stamp by calling it a photographic image instead of a sensory moment. While Hemingway's illustrative stamps tend to emphasize sight, such is not true of every story writer, and I shouldn't limit a concept applicable to all stories, not just to his.

CHAPTER EIGHT

1. Even as late as 1996, when I published a less developed version of this chapter in *Twentieth Century Literature,* there existed only one sustained scholarly analysis of Hemingway's art of dialogue (a chapter in Sheldon Norman Grebstein's *Hemingway's Craft,* published in 1973). Critics had commented upon his dialogue endlessly, but no one had fully analyzed how it works, addressed all of the principles that lie behind it, or located it in the evolution of fictional dialogue or in the development of the modern short story.

2. The poet John Ciardi observes: "What counts . . . as I see it, is the way in which the GIs of World War II lived and died with Hemingway dialogue in their mouths . . . Their language was not out of Hemingway but out of themselves. Yet it justified his power as nothing else could. Hemingway had taken their emotions to war, and had expressed war and loss and the necessary reticence so truly that he evolved their language before they got to it" (32).

3. For an excellent complementary reading that explores how the characters' miscommunication derives from gender-based linguistic, ontological, and epistemological differences, see Pamela Smiley. For an insightful reading that locates the story in the context of Hemingway's courtship of Pauline Pfeiffer and concludes that the man gradually comes to understand and acquiesce in his lover's point of view, see Hilary K. Justice. Although I have a much more cynical view of the male character, Justice's biographical argument is extremely interesting.

CHAPTER NINE

1. In 1867, twelve years after serving at Sevastopol, Tolstoy visited the battlefield of Borodino to gather notes for the writing of *War and Peace*. He had read all the accounts in books, and now he studied maps, surveyed terrain, and interviewed peasants who had experienced the battle in 1812. Returning to Moscow, he exclaimed, "I shall describe the battle of Borodino as it has never been described before" (qtd. in Troyat 296).

CODA

1. The original Cézanne passages are: 1. "Ils sont bons. J'allais au Louvre tous les matins lorsque j'étais à Paris; mais j'ai fini par m'attacher à la nature plus qu'à eux. Il faut se faire une vision." 2. "Il faut se faire une optique, il faut voir la nature comme se personne ne l'avait vue avant nous." 3. "Je le conçois comme une apperception personelle. Je place cette apperception dans la sensation, et je demande à l'intelligence de organizer en oeuvre."

2. Consider these vernacular repetitions from Frost's "Mowing" (1913), especially the double "it": "What was it it whispered? I knew not well myself; / Perhaps it was something about the heat of the sun, / Something, perhaps, about the lack of sound— / And that was why it whispered and did not speak" (17).

Works Cited

Ammons, Elizabeth. "Stowe's Dream of the Mother-Savior: *Uncle Tom's Cabin* and American Women Writers before the 1920s." In Eric J. Sundquist, ed., *New Essays on* Uncle Tom's Cabin. Cambridge: Cambridge UP, 1986.

"Authors and Critics Appraise the Works." *New York Times,* 3 July 1961: 6.

Baker, Carlos. *Ernest Hemingway: A Life Story.* New York: Scribners, 1969.

———. *Hemingway: The Writer as Artist.* 1952. Rev. 4th ed. Princeton, NJ: Princeton UP, 1972.

Barthes, Roland. "Introduction to the Structural Analysis of Narratives." 1966. In *The Semiotic Challenge.* Trans. Richard Howard. New York: Hill and Wang, 1988. 95–135.

———. *S/Z.* Trans. Richard Miller. New York: Hill and Wang, 1974.

Bates, H. E. *The Modern Short Story: A Critical Survey.* Boston: The Writer, Inc., 1941.

Bauer, Margaret D. "Forget the Legend and Read the Work: Teaching Two Stories by Ernest Hemingway." *College Literature* 30.3 (2003): 124–37.

Baym, Nina. "Actually, I Felt Sorry for the Lion." In Benson, *New Critical Approaches to the Short Stories of Ernest Hemingway.* 112–20.

Beegel, Susan F. "Conclusion: The Critical Reputation of Ernest Hemingway." In Donaldson, *The Cambridge Companion to Ernest Hemingway.* 269–99.

———. "Eye and Heart: Hemingway's Education as a Naturalist." In Linda Wagner-Martin, ed., *A Historical Guide to Ernest Hemingway.* New York: Oxford UP, 2000. 53–92.

———. *Hemingway's Craft of Omission: Four Manuscript Examples.* Ann Arbor, MI: UMI Research Press, 1988.

———, ed. *Hemingway's Neglected Short Fiction: New Perspectives.* Ann Arbor, Michigan: UMI Research Press, 1989.

———. "Second Growth: The Ecology of Loss in 'Fathers and Sons.'" In Paul Smith, ed., *New Essays on Hemingway's Short Fiction.* 75–110.

Benson, Jackson J. "Ernest Hemingway as Short Story Writer." In Benson, *The Short Stories of Ernest Hemingway: Critical Essays.* 272–310.

———, ed. *New Critical Approaches to the Short Stories of Ernest Hemingway.* Durham, NC: Duke UP, 1990.

———, ed. *The Short Stories of Ernest Hemingway: Critical Essays.* Durham, NC: Duke UP, 1975.

Berman, Ron. "Recurrence in Hemingway and Cézanne." *Hemingway Review* 23.2 (2004): 21–36.

Bernard, Émile. *Souvenirs sur Paul Cézanne* and *Une Conversation avec Paul Cézanne*. Paris: R. G. Michel, 1926.

Borges, Jorges Luis. *Borges on Writing*. Ed. Norman Thomas di Giovanni, Daniel Halpern, and Frank McShane. New York: Dutton, 1973.

Bowen, Elizabeth. *Collected Impressions*. New York: Knopf, 1950.

———. "The Faber Book of Short Stories." 1936. In *Collected Impressions*. 38–46.

———. "Notes on Writing a Novel." 1945. In *Collected Impressions*. 249–63.

Brian, Denis, ed. *The True Gen: An Intimate Portrait of Ernest Hemingway by Those Who Knew Him*. New York: Grove, 1988.

Bridgman, Richard. *The Colloquial Style in America*. New York: Oxford UP, 1966.

Broer, Lawrence R., and Gloria Holland, eds. *Hemingway and Women: Female Critics and the Female Voice*. Tuscaloosa: U of Alabama P, 2002.

Brooks, Cleanth, and Robert Penn Warren. *Understanding Fiction*. 1943. 2nd ed. New York: Appleton-Century-Crofts, 1959.

Buell, Lawrence. "Literary History Without Sexism? Feminist Studies and Canonical Reconception." *American Literature* 59.1 (Mar. 1987): 102–14.

Bunin, Ivan. *Memories and Portraits*. Trans. Vera Traill and Robin Chancellor. Garden City, NY: Doubleday, 1951.

Burwell, Rose Marie. *Hemingway: The Postwar Years and the Posthumous Novels*. Cambridge: Cambridge UP, 1996.

Butler, Robert Olen. *From Where You Dream: The Process of Fiction Writing*. New York: Grove, 2005.

Capote, Truman. Interview by Pati Hill. 1958. In Malcolm Cowley, ed., *Writers at Work: The* Paris Review *Interviews*. 1st ser. New York: Penguin, 1977. 283–99.

Carpenter, Humphrey. *A Serious Character: The Life of Ezra Pound*. Boston: Houghton Mifflin, 1988.

Cather, Willa. "Introduction." *The Work of Stephen Crane*. Vol. 9. Ed. Wilson Follet. New York: Russell and Russell, 1926. ix–xiv.

———. *My Ántonia*. 1918. *Willa Cather: Early Novels and Stories*. Ed. Sharon O'Brien. New York: Library of America, 1987. 707–937.

———. "The Novel Démeublé." 1922. In *Willa Cather: Stories, Poems, and Other Writings*. 834–37.

———. "On the Art of Fiction." 1920. In *Willa Cather: Stories, Poems, and Other Writings*. 939–40.

———. "When I Knew Stephen Crane." 1900. In *Willa Cather: Stories, Poems, and Other Writings*. 132–38.

——. *Willa Cather: Stories, Poems, and Other Writings.* Ed. Sharon O'Brien. New York: Library of America, 1992.

Cézanne, Paul. *Paul Cézanne: Letters.* Trans. Seymour Hacker. Ed. John Rewald. New York: Hacker, 1984.

Chekhov, Anton. *Anton Chekhov's Short Stories.* Ed. Ralph E. Matlaw. Norton Critical Edition. New York: Norton, 1979.

——. *The Complete Plays: Anton Chekhov.* Trans. Laurence Senelick. New York: W. W. Norton, 2006.

——. *Letters on the Short Story, the Drama, and Other Literary Topics by Anton Chekhov.* Ed. Louis S. Friedland. New York: Minton, Balch and Company, 1924.

——. *Stories by Anton Chekhov.* Trans. Richard Pevear and Larissa Volokhonsky. New York: Bantam, 2000.

Ciardi, John. "The Language of an Age." *Saturday Review* 44 (29 July 1961): 32.

Cohen, Milton. "'There Was a Woman Having a Kid'—From *Her* Point of View: An Unpublished Draft of *In Our Time*'s Chapter II." *Hemingway Review* 22.1 (2002): 107–10.

Comley, Nancy R., and Robert Scholes. *Hemingway's Genders: Rereading the Hemingway Text.* New Haven, CT: Yale UP, 1994.

Conrad, Joseph. *Heart of Darkness.* 1899. Revised Norton Critical Edition. Ed. Robert Kimbrough. New York: Norton, 1963.

Crane, Stephen. "The Blue Hotel." 1898. In *Stephen Crane: Prose and Poetry.* 799–828.

——. "The Open Boat." 1897. In *Stephen Crane: Prose and Poetry.* 885–909.

——. *The Red Badge of Courage.* 1895. In *Stephen Crane: Prose and Poetry.* 79–212.

——. *Stephen Crane: Prose and Poetry.* Ed. J. C. Levenson. New York: Library of America, 1984.

Curnutt, Kirk. "'In the Temps de Gertrude': Hemingway, Stein, and the Scene of Instruction at 27, rue de Fleurus." In J. Gerald Kennedy and Jackson R. Bryer, eds. *French Connections: Hemingway and Fitzgerald Abroad.* New York: St. Martin's, 1998. 121–39.

Dickinson, Emily. *The Complete Poems of Emily Dickinson.* Ed. Thomas H. Johnson. Boston: Little, Brown, 1960.

Didion, Joan. Interview by Linda Kuehl. 1978. In George Plimpton, ed., *Writers at Work: The* Paris Review *Interviews.* 5th ser. New York: Viking, 1981. 339–57.

Dodd, Lee Wilson. "Simple Annals of the Callous." Review of *Men Without Women* by Ernest Hemingway. *Saturday Review of Literature* 4 (19 Nov. 1927): 322–23.

Donaldson, Scott, ed. *The Cambridge Companion to Ernest Hemingway.* Cambridge: Cambridge UP, 1996.

———. "Preparing for the End: Hemingway's Revisions of 'A Canary for One.'" *Studies in American Fiction* 6 (1978): 203–11.

Eby, Carl P. *Hemingway's Fetishism: Psychoanalysis and the Mirror of Manhood.* Albany: State U of New York P, 1999.

Ehrenburg, Ilya. "The World Weighs a Writer's Influence: USSR." *Saturday Review* 44 (29 July 1961): 20.

Eliot, T. S. "A Commentary." *Criterion* 12.48 (Apr. 1933): 468–73.

———. *The Complete Poems and Plays, 1909–1950.* New York: Harcourt Brace, 1962.

———. "Hamlet and His Problems." In *The Sacred Wood.* 87–94.

———. "Philip Massinger." In *The Sacred Wood.* 112–30.

———. *The Sacred Wood: Essays on Poetry and Criticism.* London: Methuen, 1920.

Ellison, Ralph. "A Rejoinder." 1964. In *Shadow and Act.* New York: Vintage, 1972. 120–43.

Ellmann, Richard. *James Joyce.* 1959. Rev. ed. Oxford: Oxford UP, 1982.

Faulkner, William. *Absalom, Absalom!* 1936. New York: Vintage International, 1990.

———. "Faulkner to Waugh to Hemingway." *Time* 56 (13 Nov. 1950): 6.

Fenton, Charles A. *The Apprenticeship of Ernest Hemingway: The Early Years.* New York: Viking, 1954.

Ferrero, David J. "Nikki Adams and the Limits of Gender Criticism." *Hemingway Review* 17.2 (1998): 18–30.

Fetterly, Judith. *The Resisting Reader: A Feminist Approach to American Fiction.* Bloomington: Indiana UP, 1978.

Fisher, Philip. *Hard Facts: Setting and Form in the American Novel.* New York: Oxford UP, 1985.

Fitzgerald, F. Scott. *Afternoon of an Author: A Selection of Uncollected Stories and Essays.* Ed. Arthur Mizener. New York: Scribner's, 1957.

———. "How to Waste Material: A Note on My Generation." 1926. In *Afternoon of an Author.* 117–22.

———. *The Letters of F. Scott Fitzgerald.* Ed. Andrew Turnbull. New York: Scribner's, 1963.

———. "One Hundred False Starts." 1933. In *Afternoon of an Author.* 127–36.

———. *Tender Is the Night.* 1934. New York: Scribner's, 1962.

Flaubert, Gustave. *The Letters of Gustave Flaubert, 1830–1857.* Ed. and trans. Francis Steegmuller. Cambridge, MA: Belknap / Harvard UP, 1980.

Fleming, Robert E., ed. *Hemingway and the Natural World.* Moscow: U of Idaho P, 1999.

Flora, Joseph M. *Hemingway's Nick Adams.* Baton Rouge: Louisiana State UP, 1982.

Fogle, Bruce. *The Complete Illustrated Guide to Cat Care and Behavior.* San Diego, CA: Thunder Bay Press, 1999.

Ford, Ford Madox. *Joseph Conrad: A Personal Remembrance.* Boston: Little, Brown, 1924.

———. "Techniques." *Southern Review* 1 (1935–36): 20–35.

Forster, E. M. *Aspects of the Novel.* 1927. New York: Harvest, 1955.

Frank, Joseph. *The Idea of Spatial Form.* New Brunswick, NJ: Rutgers UP, 1991.

Frost, Robert. *The Poetry of Robert Frost.* Ed. Edward Connery Lathem. New York: Holt, Rinehart, 1969.

Fry, Edward F. *Cubism.* 1966. New York: Oxford UP, 1978.

Gaillard, Theodore L., Jr. "Hemingway's Debt to Cézanne: New Perspectives." *Twentieth Century Literature* 45.1 (1999): 65–78.

Gajdusek, Robert E. *Hemingway in His Own Country.* Notre Dame, IN: U of Notre Dame P, 2002.

García Márquez, Gabriel. "Gabriel García Márquez Meets Ernest Hemingway." *New York Times Book Review.* 26 July 1981: 1, 16, 17.

———. "Hemingway—Our Own." Introduction to Norberto Fuentes, *Hemingway in Cuba.* Secaucus, NJ: Lyle Stuart, 1984. 7–16.

Gardner, John. *The Art of Fiction: Notes on Craft for Young Writers.* New York: Knopf, 1984.

Gasquet, Joachim. *Cézanne.* Paris: Les Éditions Bernheim-Jeune, 1921.

Gelpi, Albert. *A Coherent Splendor: The American Poetic Renaissance, 1910–1950.* Cambridge: Cambridge UP, 1987.

Genette, Gérard. *Narrative Discourse: An Essay in Method.* Trans. Jane E. Lewin. Ithaca, NY: Cornell UP, 1980.

———. *Narrative Discourse Revisited.* Trans. Jane E. Lewin. Ithaca, NY: Cornell UP, 1988.

Gogol, Nikolai. "The Overcoat." 1840. *The Complete Tales of Nikolai Gogol.* Trans. Constance Garnett. Rev. by Leonard J. Kent. Vol. 2. Chicago: U of Chicago P, 1985. 304–34.

Gordimer, Nadine. *Conversations with Nadine Gordimer.* Ed. Nancy Topping Bazin and Marilyn Dallman Seymour. Jackson: UP of Mississippi, 1990.

———. "Hemingway's Expatriates." *Transition* 80 (1998): 86–99.

Grebstein, Sheldon Norman. *Hemingway's Craft.* Carbondale: Southern Illinois UP, 1973.

Hagemann, E. R. "'Only Let the Story End as Soon as Possible': Time-and-History in Ernest Hemingway's *In Our Time.*" 1980. In Benson, *New Critical Approaches to the Short Stories of Ernest Hemingway.* 192–99.

Hawthorne, Nathaniel. *The Scarlet Letter.* 1850. New York: Penguin, 1986.

Hemingway, Ernest. "The Art of the Short Story" (written 1959). In Benson, *New Critical Approaches to the Short Stories of Ernest Hemingway.* 1–13.

———. *By-Line: Ernest Hemingway: Selected Articles and Dispatches of Four Decades.* Ed. William White. New York: Scribner's, 1967.

———. *Complete Poems.* Ed. Nicholas Gerogiannis. Rev ed. Lincoln: U of Nebraska P, 1983.

———. *The Complete Short Stories of Ernest Hemingway: The Finca Vigía Edition.* New York: Scribner's, 1987.

———. *Death in the Afternoon.* New York: Scribner's, 1932.

———. *Ernest Hemingway, Cub Reporter: Kansas City Star Stories.* Ed. Matthew J. Bruccoli. Pittsburgh: U of Pittsburgh P, 1970.

———. *Ernest Hemingway, Dateline: Toronto: The Complete* Toronto Star *Dispatches, 1920–1924.* Ed. William White. New York: Scribner's, 1985.

———. *Ernest Hemingway: Selected Letters, 1917–1961.* Ed. Carlos Baker. New York: Scribner's, 1981.

———. *A Farewell to Arms.* 1929. New York: Scribner's, 1969.

———. *For Whom the Bell Tolls.* New York: Scribner's, 1940.

———. *Green Hills of Africa.* 1935. New York: Scribner's, 1963.

———. *in our time.* Paris: Three Mountains Press, 1924.

———. *In Our Time.* 1925. New York: Scribner's, 1970.

———. Interview by George Plimpton. 1958. In George Plimpton, ed., *Writers at Work: The* Paris Review *Interviews.* 2nd ser. New York: Penguin, 1963. 217–39.

———. *A Moveable Feast.* New York: Scribner's, 1964.

———. *The Nick Adams Stories.* Ed. Philip Young. New York: Scribner's, 1972.

———. *The Only Thing That Counts: The Ernest Hemingway / Maxwell Perkins Correspondence, 1925–1947.* Ed. Matthew J. Bruccoli. Columbia: U of South Carolina P, 1996.

———. *The Short Stories of Ernest Hemingway.* New York: Scribner's, 1954.

———. *The Sun Also Rises.* 1926. New York: Scribner's, 1954.

Hemingway, Mary Welsh. *How It Was.* New York: Knopf, 1976.

Hermann, Thomas. "Formal Analogies in the Texts and Paintings of Ernest Hemingway and Paul Cézanne." In Kenneth Rosen, ed., *Hemingway Repossessed.* Westport, CT: Praeger, 1994. 29–33.

Hills, Rust. *Writing in General and the Short Story in Particular.* Rev. ed. Boston: Houghton Mifflin, 1987.

Hoffman, Frederick J. *The Twenties: American Writing in the Postwar Decade.* 1955. Rev. ed. New York: Free Press, 1965.

Hotchner, A. E. *Papa Hemingway: A Personal Memoir.* New York: Random House, 1966.

Humphrey, Nicholas. *A History of the Mind: Evolution and the Birth of Consciousness.* New York: Simon and Schuster, 1992.

Hurwitz, Harold M. "Hemingway's Tutor, Ezra Pound." *Modern Fiction Studies* 17.4 (1971–72): 469–82.

Isenberg, Arnold. "The Technical Factor in Art." 1946. *Aesthetics and the Theory of Criticism: Selected Essays of Arnold Isenberg*. Ed. William Callaghan et al. Chicago: UP of Chicago, 1973. 53–69.

James, Henry. "The Art of Fiction." 1884. In *Henry James: Literary Criticism: French Writers*. 44–65.

——. *The Complete Notebooks of Henry James*. Ed. Leon Edel and Lyall H. Powers. New York: Oxford UP, 1987.

——. *Henry James: Literary Criticism: Essays on Literature, American Writers, English Writers*. Ed. Leon Edel. New York: Library of America, 1984.

——. *Henry James: Literary Criticism: French Writers, Other European Writers, the Prefaces to the New York Edition*. Ed. Leon Edel. New York: Library of America, 1984.

——. "The Lesson of Balzac." 1905. In *Henry James: Literary Criticism: French Writers*. 115–39.

——. "London Notes." 1897. In *Henry James: Literary Criticism: Essays on Literature*. 1387–1413.

——. "The Middle Years." 1893. *Henry James: Complete Stories 1892–1898*. Ed. David Bromwich and John Hollander. New York: Library of America, 1996. 335–55.

——. *The Portrait of a Lady*. 1881. *Henry James: Novels 1881–1886*. Ed. William T. Stafford. New York: Library of America, 1985. 191–800.

——. Preface to *The American*. 1907. In *Henry James: Literary Criticism: French Writers*. 1053–69.

——. Preface to "The Author of Beltraffio." 1909. In *Henry James: Literary Criticism: French Writers*. 1238–45.

——. Preface to *The Awkward Age*. 1908. In *Henry James: Literary Criticism: French Writers*. 1120–37.

——. Preface to *The Portrait of a Lady*. 1908. In *Henry James: Literary Criticism: French Writers*. 1070–85.

——. Preface to *The Princess Casamassima*. 1908. In *Henry James: Literary Criticism: French Writers*. 1086–1102.

——. Preface to *Roderick Hudson*. 1907. In *Henry James: Literary Criticism: French Writers*. 1039–52.

——. "The Story-Teller at Large: Mr. Henry Harland." 1898. In *Henry James: Literary Criticism: Essays on Literature*. 282–88.

——. "William Dean Howells." 1886. In *Henry James: Literary Criticism: Essays on Literature*. 497–506.

James, William. *The Varieties of Religious Experience*. 1902. In *William James:*

Writings 1902–1910. Ed. Bruce Kuklick. New York: Library of America, 1987. 1–477.

Jones, Gavin. *Strange Talk: The Politics of Dialect Literature in Gilded Age America.* Berkeley and Los Angeles: U of California P, 1999.

Josephs, Allen. "Hemingway's Spanish Civil War Stories, or the Spanish Civil War as Reality." In Beegel, *Hemingway's Neglected Short Fiction.* 313–27.

———. "Hemingway's Spanish Sensibility." In Donaldson, *The Cambridge Companion to Ernest Hemingway.* 221–42.

Joyce, James. *Stephen Hero.* 1944. Complete edition. Ed. Theodore Spencer, John J. Slocum, and Hernbert Cahoon. New York: New Directions, 1963.

Justice, Hilary K. "'Well, Well, Well': Cross-Gendered Autobiography and the Manuscript of 'Hills Like White Elephants.'" *Hemingway Review* 18.1 (1998): 17–32.

Kennedy, J. Gerald. *Imagining Paris: Exile, Writing, and American Identity.* New Haven, CT: Yale UP, 1993.

Kinnamon, Keneth. "Hemingway, the *Corrida,* and Spain." In Linda Wagner-Martin, ed., *Ernest Hemingway: Five Decades of Criticism.* East Lansing: Michigan State UP, 1974. 57–74.

Kipling, Rudyard. *Something of Myself: For My Friends Known and Unknown.* Garden City, NY: Doubleday, Doran and Co., 1937.

Lamb, Robert Paul. "'America Can Break Your Heart': On the Significance of Mark Twain." In Robert Paul Lamb and G. R. Thompson, eds., *A Companion to American Fiction, 1865–1914.* Malden, MA: Blackwell, 2005. 468–98.

———. "Ernest Hemingway." In Andrew Cayton, Richard Sisson, and Christian Zacher, eds., *Encyclopedia of the Midwest.* Bloomington: Indiana UP, 2007. 488–89.

———. "Fishing for Stories: What 'Big Two-Hearted River' Is Really About." *Modern Fiction Studies* 37.2 (1991): 161–82.

———. "Hemingway and the Creation of Twentieth-Century Dialogue." *Twentieth Century Literature* 42.4 (1996): 453–80.

———. "Hemingway's Critique of Anti-Semitism: Semiotic Confusion in 'God Rest You Merry, Gentlemen.'" *Studies in Short Fiction* 33.1 (1996): 25–34.

———. "The Love Song of Harold Krebs: Form, Argument, and Meaning in Hemingway's 'Soldier's Home.'" *Hemingway Review* 14.2 (1995): 18–36.

———. "Prophet and Idolater: Walt Whitman in 1855 and 1860." *South Atlantic Quarterly* 84.4 (1985): 419–34.

Larguier, Léo. *Le Dimanche avec Paul Cézanne (Souvenirs).* Paris: L'Édition, 1925.

Levi, Carlo. "The World Weighs a Writer's Influence: Italy." *Saturday Review* 44 (29 July 1961): 19.

Levin, Harry. "Observations on the Style of Ernest Hemingway." 1957. In Weeks, *Hemingway.* 72–85.

Lewis, Wyndham. *Men Without Art.* London: Cassell, 1934.

Lodge, David. *Working with Structuralism: Essays and Reviews on Nineteenth- and Twentieth-Century Literature.* London: Routledge and Kegan Paul, 1981.

Love, Glen A. *Practical Ecocriticism: Literature, Biology, and the Environment.* Charlottesville: U of Virginia P, 2003.

Lynn, Kenneth S. *Hemingway.* New York: Simon and Schuster, 1987.

Macauley, Robie, and George Lanning. *Technique in Fiction.* 2nd ed. New York: St. Martin's, 1987.

MacLeish, Archibald. "His Mirror Was Danger." *Life* 51 (14 July 1961): 70–71.

Madariaga, Salvador de. "The World Weighs a Writer's Influence: Spain." *Saturday Review* 44 (29 July 1961): 18.

Mansfield, Katherine. *Journal of Katherine Mansfield.* 1927. Rev. ed. Ed. J. Middleton Murry. London: Constable, 1954.

Martin, Wallace. *Recent Theories of Narrative.* Ithaca, NY: Cornell UP, 1986.

Martin, Wendy. "Brett Ashley as New Woman in *The Sun Also Rises.*" In Linda Wagner-Martin, ed., *New Essays on* The Sun Also Rises. Cambridge: Cambridge UP, 1987. 65–82.

Marx, Leo. "The Vernacular Tradition in American Literature." 1958. In *The Pilot and the Passenger: Essays on Literature, Technology, and Culture.* Oxford: Oxford UP, 1988. 3–17.

Maupassant, Guy de. Preface to *Pierre et Jean.* 1887. Rpt. as "Essay on the Novel." *The Portable Maupassant.* Ed. Lewis Galantière. New York: Viking, 1947. 663–78.

McHenry, Eric. "BU Scholars Grace Hemingway Centennial." *Boston University Bridge,* 16 Apr. 1999.

Mellow, James R. *Hemingway: A Life Without Consequences.* Boston: Houghton Mifflin, 1992.

Melville, Herman. *The Confidence-Man: His Masquerade.* 1857. Indianapolis: Bobbs-Merrill, 1967.

———. *Moby-Dick or, The Whale.* 1851. New York: Penguin, 1992.

Messent, Peter. *Ernest Hemingway.* New York: St. Martin's, 1992.

Meyers, Jeffrey. *Hemingway: A Biography.* New York: Harper and Row, 1985.

Moddelmog, Debra A. *Reading Desire: In Pursuit of Ernest Hemingway.* Ithaca, NY: Cornell UP, 1999.

———. "The Unifying Consciousness of a Divided Conscience: Nick Adams as Author of *In Our Time. American Literature* 60.4 (1988): 591–610.

Morrison, Toni. *Playing in the Dark: Whiteness and the Literary Imagination.* Cambridge, MA: Harvard UP, 1992.

Nabokov, Vladimir. *Lectures on Literature.* Ed. Fredson Bowers. New York: Harcourt Brace, 1980.

Nagel, James, ed. *Ernest Hemingway: The Oak Park Legacy.* Tuscaloosa: U of Alabama P, 1996.

———, ed. *Ernest Hemingway: The Writer in Context.* Madison: U of Wisconsin P, 1984.

———. *Stephen Crane and Literary Impressionism.* University Park: Pennsylvania State UP, 1980.

O'Brien, Sharon. *Willa Cather: The Emerging Voice.* New York: Oxford UP, 1987.

O'Connor, Flannery. *Mystery and Manners: Occasional Prose.* Ed. Sally Fitzgerald and Robert Fitzgerald. New York: Farrar, Straus and Giroux, 1969.

O'Connor, Frank. "Guests of the Nation." *Guests of the Nation.* 1931. Dublin: Poolbeg Press, 1985. 5–18.

———. Interview by Anthony Whittier. 1958. In Malcolm Cowley, ed., *Writers at Work: The* Paris Review *Interviews.* 1st ser. New York: Penguin, 1977. 161–82.

———. *The Lonely Voice: A Study of the Short Story.* 1963. New York: Harper and Row, 1985.

O'Faolain, Sean. *The Short Story.* 1951. Old Greenwich, CT: Devin-Adair, 1974.

O'Meally, Robert G. "The Rules of Magic: Hemingway as Ellison's 'Ancestor.'" *Southern Review* 21.3 (July 1985): 751–69.

Parker, Dorothy. "A Book of Great Short Stories." Review of *Men Without Women* by Ernest Hemingway. *New Yorker* 3 (29 Oct. 1927): 92–94.

Paul, Steve. "On Hemingway and His Influence: Conversations with Writers." *Hemingway Review* 18.2 (1999): 115–32.

Plimpton, George, and John Crowther, eds. "John Steinbeck." In George Plimpton, ed., *Writers at Work: The* Paris Review *Interviews.* 4th ser. New York: Penguin, 1977. 179–207.

Poe, Edgar Allan. *Edgar Allan Poe: Essays and Reviews.* Ed. G. R. Thompson. New York: Library of America, 1984.

———. "The Philosophy of Composition." 1846. *Edgar Allan Poe: Essays and Reviews.* 13–25.

———. Review of *Night and Morning: A Novel* by Edward Lytton Bulwer. 1841. *Edgar Allan Poe: Essays and Reviews.* 146–60.

Pound, Ezra. *Make It New.* New Haven, CT: Yale UP, 1935.

———. "Small Magazines." *English Journal* 19.9 (Nov. 1930): 689–704.

Powell, Anthony. *Messengers of Day.* Vol. 2 of *To Keep the Ball Rolling: The Memoirs of Anthony Powell.* New York: Holt, Rinehart, 1978.

Praz, Mario. "Hemingway in Italy." *Partisan Review* 15.10 (Oct. 1948): 1086–1100.

Pryce-Jones, Alan. "The World Weighs a Writer's Influence: England." *Saturday Review* 44 (29 July 1961): 21.

Putnam, Thomas. "Hemingway on War and Its Aftermath." *Prologue* 38.1 (2006).

Reynolds, Michael S. *Hemingway: The American Homecoming.* Cambridge, MA: Blackwell, 1992.

———. *Hemingway: The 1930s.* New York: Norton, 1997.

———. *Hemingway: The Paris Years.* Oxford: Blackwell, 1989.

———, ed. *Hemingway's Reading, 1910–1940: An Inventory.* Princeton, NJ: Princeton UP, 1981.

———. "'Homage to Switzerland': Einstein's Train Stops at Hemingway's Station." In Beegel, *Hemingway's Neglected Short Fiction.* 255–62.

———. *The Young Hemingway.* Oxford: Blackwell, 1986.

Ross, Lillian. "How Do You Like It Now, Gentlemen?" *New Yorker,* 13 May 1950. Rpt. in Weeks, *Hemingway.* 17–39.

Roth, Philip. *The Ghost Writer.* 1979. *Zuckerman Bound.* New York: Farrar Straus Giroux, 1985. 1–180.

Ruddick, Lisa. *Reading Gertrude Stein: Body, Text, Gnosis.* Ithaca, NY: Cornell UP, 1990.

Savage, D. S. "Ernest Hemingway." In *Focus Two.* Ed. B. Rajan and Andrew Pearse. London: Dennis Dobson, 1946. 7–27.

Scholes, Robert. *Textual Power: Literary Theory and the Teaching of English.* New Haven, CT: Yale UP, 1985.

Scholes, Robert, and Robert Kellogg. *The Nature of Narrative.* London: Oxford UP, 1966.

Seidensticker, Edward. "The World Weighs a Writer's Influence: Japan." *Saturday Review* 44 (29 July 1961): 21–22.

Smiley, Pamela. "Gender-Linked Miscommunication in 'Hills Like White Elephants.'" *Hemingway Review* 8.1 (1988): 2–12.

Smith, Paul. "Hemingway's Early Manuscripts: The Theory and Practice of Omission." *Journal of Modern Literature* 10.2 (1983): 268–88.

———, ed. *New Essays on Hemingway's Short Fiction.* Cambridge: Cambridge UP, 1998.

———. "1924: Hemingway's Luggage and the Miraculous Year." In Donaldson, *The Cambridge Companion to Ernest Hemingway.* 36–54.

———. *A Reader's Guide to the Short Stories of Ernest Hemingway.* Boston: G. K. Hall, 1989.

Spilka, Mark. *Hemingway's Quarrel with Androgyny.* Lincoln: U of Nebraska P, 1995.

Stein, Gertrude. "Composition as Explanation." 1926. In *Selected Writings of Gertrude Stein.* Ed. Carl Van Vechten. New York: Vintage, 1972. 513–23.

———. *The Making of Americans*. 1925. New York: Something Else Press, 1966.

———. *Picasso*. 1938. New York: Dover, 1984.

———. "Portraits and Repetition." *Lectures in America*. 1935. Boston: Beacon, 1985.

———. *Three Lives*. 1909. New York: Vintage, 1936.

Stevens, Wallace. *The Collected Poems of Wallace Stevens*. New York: Knopf, 1978.

———. *Letters of Wallace Stevens*. Ed. Holly Stevens. New York: Knopf, 1966.

Stevenson, Robert Louis. *Learning to Write: Suggestions and Counsel from Robert Louis Stevenson*. New York: Scribner's, 1920.

———. *Memories and Portraits*. New York: Scribner's, 1887.

Stock, Noel. *The Life of Ezra Pound* (1970). Expanded ed. San Francisco: North Point Press, 1982.

Stoppard, Tom. "Reflections on Ernest Hemingway." In Nagel, *Ernest Hemingway: The Writer in Context*. 19–27.

Stowe, Harriet Beecher. *Uncle Tom's Cabin or, Life among the Lowly*. 1852. New York: Penguin, 1986.

Strychacz, Thomas. *Hemingway's Theaters of Masculinity*. Baton Rouge: Louisiana State UP, 2003.

Tavernier-Courbin, Jacqueline. "Ernest Hemingway and Ezra Pound." In Nagel, *Ernest Hemingway: The Writer in Context*. 179–200.

Thompson, G. R. "Literary Politics and the 'Legitimate Sphere': Poe, Hawthorne, and the 'Tale Proper.'" *Nineteenth-Century Literature* 49.3 (1994): 167–95.

Troyat, Henri. *Tolstoy*. Trans. Nancy Amphoux. Garden City, NY: Doubleday, 1967.

Twain, Mark. *Adventures of Huckleberry Finn*. 1884. Berkeley and Los Angeles: U of California P / Mark Twain Library, 2001.

———. "Fenimore Cooper's Literary Offences." 1895. *Mark Twain: Collected Tales, Sketches, Speeches, and Essays, 1891–1910*. Ed. Louis J. Budd. New York: Library of America, 1992. 180–92.

———. *Life on the Mississippi*. 1883. New York: Penguin Classics, 1984.

———. *Pudd'nhead Wilson* and *Those Extraordinary Twins*. 1894. 2nd Norton Critical Edition. Ed. Sidney E. Berger. New York: Norton, 2005.

Tyler, Lisa. "'How Beautiful the Virgin Forests Were Before the Loggers Came': An Ecofeminist Reading of Hemingway's 'The End of Something.'" *Hemingway Review* 27.2 (2008): 60–73.

Updike, John. "Papa's Sad Testament." *New Statesman* 80 (16 Oct. 1970): 489.

Van Gunsteren, Julia. *Katherine Mansfield and Literary Impressionism*. Amsterdam: Rodopi, 1990.

Wagner-Martin, Linda (Linda Welsheimer Wagner). *The Modern American Novel, 1914–1945: A Critical History*. Boston: Twayne, 1990.

———. "'Proud and Friendly and Gently': Women in Hemingway's Early Works." *College Literature*. 7.3 (1980): 239–47.

Watt, Ian. *Conrad in the Nineteenth Century*. Berkeley and Los Angeles: U of California P, 1979.

Watts, Emily Stipes. *Ernest Hemingway and the Arts*. Urbana: U of Illinois P, 1971.

Weeks, Robert P., ed. *Hemingway: A Collection of Critical Essays*. Englewood Cliffs, NJ: Prentice-Hall, 1962.

Weisstein, Ulrich, ed. *Expressionism as an International Literary Phenomenon*. Paris: Didier, 1973.

Welty, Eudora. *The Eye of the Story: Selected Essays and Reviews*. New York: Vintage, 1979.

Wharton, Edith. *The House of Mirth*. 1905. New York: Scribner's, 1995.

———. *The Writing of Fiction*. 1925. New York: Octagon, 1966.

Whitman, Walt. *Walt Whitman: Complete Poetry and Collected Prose*. Ed. Justin Kaplan. New York: Library of America, 1982.

Williams, Terry Tempest. "'Hemingway and the Natural World': Keynote Address, Seventh International Hemingway Conference." In Robert E. Fleming, ed., *Hemingway and the Natural World*. 7–17.

Wilson, Edmund. *Patriotic Gore: Studies in the Literature of the Civil War*. New York: Oxford UP, 1962.

Woolf, Virginia. "An Essay in Criticism." Review of *Men Without Women* by Ernest Hemingway. *New York Herald Tribune Books* 9 (9 Oct. 1927): 1, 8.

Young, Philip. "Big World Out There: The Nick Adams Stories" (1972). In Benson, *The Short Stories of Ernest Hemingway*. 29–45.

———. *Ernest Hemingway: A Reconsideration*. 1952. Rev. ed. University Park: Pennsylvania State UP, 1966.

Index

Ammons, Elizabeth, 156
Anderson, Sherwood, 14, 15, 83–84, 104
Auden, W. H., 1
Austen, Jane, 170
Auster, Paul, 15
Authorial judgment: "chapter 2" *iot,* 31–33; "chapter 8" *iot,* 30; "Chekhov on, 24, 27; H on, 27; H's characters reveal themselves, 27–28, 218; and normative centers, 154–57; and spatial form, 128; through structure in H, 30–33; through structure in Howells, Cahan, and Wharton, 31; through word choice in H, 29–30; in "The Undefeated," 29–30. *See also* Dispassionate presentation; Impressionism in H

Babel, Isaac, 6, 15, 23, 206
Baker, Carlos, 71–72, 173–74, 202
Bal, Mieke, 243n1, 244n2
Balzac, Honoré de, 58
Banks, Russell, 6, 65, 227
Barth, John, 15
Barthes, Roland, 117, 243n1
Bates, H. E., 48
Bauer, Margaret D., 241n3
Baym, Nina, 7, 241n1
Beattie, Ann, 6
Beauvoir, Simone de, 6
Beegel, Susan F., 7, 44–45, 47, 186, 220–21, 241n2
Bellow, Saul, 6
Benson, Jackson J., xii, 242n2
Benstock, Shari, 118
Berenson, Bernard, 242n2
Berman, Ron, 74–75, 243n7
Bierce, Ambrose, 162
Bloom, Harold, 45
Bogart, Humphrey, 9

Böll, Heinrich, 6
Booth, Wayne, 243n1
Borges, Jorge Luis, 15, 208
Bowen, Elizabeth, 15, 23–24, 176, 178, 192, 198, 199
Braques, Georges, 114
Bridgman, Richard, 37
Broer, Lawrence R., 8
Brooks, Cleanth, 81
Brooks, Peter, 243n1
Brooks, Van Wyck, 4, 7
Buell, Lawrence, 1–2, 10
Bukowski, Charles, 6
Bunin, Ivan, 14, 24, 136
Burwell, Rose Marie, 8
Butler, Robert Olen, xiv–xv, 6, 242n3

Cabrera Infante, Guillermo, 6
Cahan, Abraham, 31
Camus, Albert, 6
Capmany, Maria Aurèlia, 6
Capote, Truman, 4
Carver, Raymond, 6
Castillo-Puche, José Luis, 6
Cather, Willa, 42, 58–59, 63, 67, 68, 70, 209, 243n4; *My Ántonia*, 59; *My Mortal Enemy,* 104; *The Professor's House,* 18
Cela, Camilo José, 6
Cézanne, Paul, 72–73, 114, 118, 127, 134, 224, 225, 243n6, 243n7; aesthetics of, 1, 64–66, 73–75, 114, 122, 124, 224–25, 243n8, 246n1
Chandler, Raymond, 6
Characterization: Hills on, 209; limitations on, 206–208; O'Faolain on, 208–209; and omission, 209; Wharton and Henry James on impossibility of in short story, 207–208. *See also* Characters; Dialogue
—in Hemingway's stories: Bill in "The End

Implication omission, 143; in "An Alpine Idyll," 65; *defined*, 45–46

Impressionism: and Cézanne, 243n8; Conrad's ambivalence toward, 243n3; in Crane's *Red Badge*, 55–56, 57; delayed decoding, 57–58; Ford Madox Ford's definition, 52, 53, 243n3; foundations in French visual art, 54; German critics on, 54; and imagist poetry, 54; Nagel's definition, 52, 53; *redefined*, 52–53. *See also* Delayed decoding; Expressionism; Objective correlative

—in Hemingway, 205, 225, 226, 227; "An Alpine Idyll," 61–66; Banks on the "logic of the eye," 65; Bates on, 48; "Big Two-Hearted River," 73–75; "A Canary for One," 75–77; "chapter 3" *iot*, 99–100; "chapter 7" *iot*, 86–87, 88–90; "chapter 13" (*iot*), 61; "Che Ti Dice la Patria?," 66; and Eliot, 71; and external focalization, 81, 86–87, 89–90, 100, 102–103, 127–28, 226; Fitzgerald on, 68–69; H on, 48, 59–61; "Indian Camp," 91–92, 184–86; and Joycean epiphany, 165–66; in relation to other techniques, 127–28; Terry Tempest Williams on, 65; "A Way You'll Never Be," 66–68

James, Henry, xiii, 2, 12, 14, 15, 36, 38, 80, 106–107, 144, 171–80, 187, 192, 206, 207–208, 209, 226, 243n3, 244n4; "Daisy Miller," 196; *The Portrait of a Lady*, 44, 171–73, 174, 244n4; "The Middle Years," 36

James, William, 134, 163–64, 168

Jewett, Sarah Orne, 14, 170

Joselito (José Gómez y Ortega), 114

Josephs, Allen, 112, 166

Joyce, James, xii, 2, 4, 12, 14, 15, 21, 38, 88, 108, 121, 134, 150, 162–65, 167–68; "The Dead," 150, 164, 227; *Stephen Hero*, 162–63, 165, 167; *Ulysses*, 204

Justice, Hilary K., 245n3

Juxtaposition: in H's stories, 46, 122–23, 124, 184, 186, 188, 194–95, 200, 201, 202; "In Another Country," 124, 127; "Now I Lay Me," 134; and Pound's imagism, 127,

140–41; relation to other H techniques, 127–28; and spatial form, 128, 134; and Stein's "continuous present," 128. *See also* Repetition; Repetition in H; Spatial form

Kafka, Franz, 14–15, 54, 227–28

Kansas City Star, 37, 81–82, 120–21, 242n1

Kazin, Alfred, 4, 7

Kellogg, Robert, 107

Kennedy, J. Gerald, 8

Kerouac, Jack, 6, 220

Kipling, Rudyard, 14, 17, 42, 209, 224

Kurowsky, Agnes von, 137, 244n6

Lamb, Elizabeth Boyd, 244n7

Lamb, Simone Nicole, 244n7

Lancaster, Burt, 9

Lanning, George, 178

Lardner, Ring, 14

Laxness, Halldór, 6

Lawrence, D. H., 1, 14

Le Clézio, Jean-Marie Gustav, 6

Least Heat-Moon, William, 220

Leonard, Elmore, 6

Lermontov, Mikhail, 14

Leskov, Nikolai, 14

Levi, Carlo, 3

Lewis, Sinclair, 176

Lewis, Wyndham, 177

Lodge, David, 96

Loeb, Harold, 85

London, Jack, 14, 17, 206, 225

Love, Glen A., 8

Lu Hsun, 14–15, 161–62

Lynn, Kenneth S., 68

Macauley, Robie, 178–79

MacLeish, Archibald, 3, 110

Madariaga, Salvador de, 3

Maera, Manuel García, 90

Mailer, Norman, 6

Malamud, Bernard, 6

Malory, Sir Thomas, 205

Mansfield, Katherine, 14, 41–42, 161–62, 206, 209; "Bliss," 205

Marlowe, Christopher, 137

"The Light of the World," 35. *See also* Characterization; Characterization in H; Characters; Dialogue

Thomas Aquinas, Saint, 162–63
Thompson, G. R., 15
Thompson, Hunter, 6
Thurber, James, 2, 6
Todorov, Tzvetan, 243n1, 244n3
Tolstoy, Leo, 14, 108, 224; *War and Peace,* 204–205, 246n1
Tonal opening. *See under* Openings in H's stories
Tononi, Guilio, 243n2
Toomer, Jean, 14; *Cane,* 18
Toronto Star, 81–82, 99, 120
Tracy, Spencer, 9
Trilling, Lionel, 3–4, 7
Turgenev, Ivan, 14, 15, 17, 224
Twain, Mark (Samuel Langhorne Clemens), 9, 17, 37, 170, 224, 229; *Adventures of Huckleberry Finn,* 100–102, 156–57, 176; *Life on the Mississippi,* 49
Tyler, Lisa, 241fn2

Updike, John, 5, 6, 229

Van Gunsteren, Julia, 54
Vidal, Gore, 6
Villon, François, 38
Vittorini, Elio, 6
Voice, 79; "chapter 7" *iot,* 88–90; direct, free indirect, summarized, and immediate speech *defined,* 87–88; Dorman-Smith's voice in "chapter 4" and "chapter 5" *iot,* 198–99; Genette on, 87–88; of the fabula,

39; Henry James on the author's voice, 171; immediate speech in *For Whom the Bell Tolls,* 110; Wallace Martin on heteroglossia in "The Short Happy Life of Francis Macomber," 109. See also Dialogue; Dialogue in H

Wagner-Martin, Linda, 7, 38, 140–41, 241n1
Walcott, Derek, 1, 6
Warner, Susan, 22
Warren, Robert Penn, 81
Watt, Ian, 58
Watts, Emily Stipes, 73
Waugh, Evelyn, 2, 6
Weisstein, Ulrich, 54
Wellington, Pete, 37
Welty, Eudora, 6, 169, 176, 205, 206, 208, 209
Wharton, Edith, 19, 14, 107, 136, 170, 176, 192, 198, 207; *The House of Mirth,* 31, 157, 206
Whitman, Walt, 1, 163, 164, 166–67, 220
Williams, Tennessee, 2
Williams, Terry Tempest, 6, 65
Williams, William Carlos, 242n1
Wilson, Edmund, 37, 83
Wister, Owen, 186
Wolfe, Thomas, 70
Woolf, Virginia, 2, 70, 175–76
Wright, Richard, 4–5

Yeats, William Butler, 2, 167
Young, Philip, 67–68, 84, 134, 244n8

Zapata Olivella, Manuel, 6
Zola, Émile, 20, 206